D1245975

How to
Master Skills for the
TOEFL iBT

新托福考试专项进阶
——高级听力

Listening

Advanced

Gerald de la Salle | Jasmine C. Swaney | Monika N. Kushwaha | E2K

群言出版社
QUNYAN PRESS
·北京·

图书在版编目(CIP)数据

新托福考试专项进阶. 高级听力 /（美）萨伦（Salle,
G. D. L.），（美）斯沃尼（Swaney, J. C.），（美）库瓦
哈（Kushwaha, M. N.）编著. —北京：群言出版社，2009（2015.11重印）
　ISBN 978-7-80080-977-4

　Ⅰ.①新⋯　Ⅱ.①萨⋯ ②斯⋯ ③库⋯　Ⅲ.①英语—听说教学—
高等教育—自学参考资料　Ⅳ.①H310.41

中国版本图书馆CIP数据核字（2009）第027384号

版权登记：图字01—2014—6178号

How to Master Skills for the TOEFL iBT Listening Advanced + 1MP3
Copyright © 2007, Darakwon Press
Chinese language translation rights © 2009
by Qunyan Press
Chinese language translation rights arranged with Darakwon Press

责任编辑：张　茜
封面设计：大愚设计

出版发行：群言出版社
社　　址：北京市东城区东厂胡同北巷1号（100006）
网　　址：www.qypublish.com
自营网店：http://xdfdytushu.tmall.com（天猫旗舰店）
　　　　　http://qycbs.shop.kongfz.com（孔夫子旧书网）
　　　　　http://www.qypublish.com（群言出版社官网）
电子信箱：bj62605588@163.com　qunyancbs@126.com
联系电话：010-62418641 62605019 65267783 65263836
经　　销：全国新华书店
法律顾问：北京市君泰律师事务所

印　　刷：北京四季青印刷厂
版　　次：2009年9月第1版　2015年11月第14次印刷
开　　本：880mm×1230mm　1/16
印　　张：21.5
字　　数：307千字
书　　号：ISBN 978-7-80080-977-4
定　　价：45.00元

Contents

Contents(Answer Book)

Introduction

A. Information on the TOEFL® iBT

The Format of the TOEFL® iBT

Section	Number of Questions	Timing	Score

Reading	• **3~5 Passages**
	  – approximately 700 words each
	  – 12~14 questions per passage
		60~100 min.	30 points

Listening	• **2~3 Conversations**
	  – 12~25 exchanges each (3 min.)
	  – 5 questions per conversation
	• **4~6 Lectures**
	  – 500~800 words each (3~5 min.)
	  – 6 questions per lecture
		60~90 min.	30 points

BREAK		10 min.	

Speaking	• **2 Independent Tasks**
	(preparation: 15 sec. / response: 45 sec.)
	❶ 1 personal experience
	❷ 1 personal choice/opinion
	
	• **2 Integrated Tasks:** Read-Listen-Speak
	(preparation: 30 sec. / response: 60 sec.)
	❶ 1 campus situation topic
	  – reading: 75~100 words (45 sec.)
	  – conversation: 150~180 words (60~80 sec.)
	❷ 1 academic course topic
	  – reading: 75~100 words (45 sec.)
	  – lecture: 150~220 words (60~90 sec.)
	
	• **2 Integrated Tasks:** Listen-Speak
	(preparation: 20 sec. / response: 60 sec.)
	❶ 1 campus situation topic
	  – conversation: 180~220 words (60~90 sec.)
	❷ 1 academic course topic
	  – lecture: 230~280 words (90~120 sec.)
		20 min.	30 points

Writing	• **1 Integrated Task:** Read-Listen-Write (20 min.)
	  – reading: 230~300 words (3 min.)
	  – lecture: 230~300 words (2 min.)
	  – a summary of 150~225 words
	
	• **1 Independent Task** (30 min.)
	  – a minimum 300-word essay
		50 min.	30 points

B. Information on the Listening Section

The Listening section of the TOEFL® iBT measures test takers' ability to understand spoken English in English-speaking colleges and universities. This section has 2~3 conversations that are 12~25 exchanges (about 3 minutes) long and 4~6 lectures that are 500~800 words (3~5 minutes) long. Each conversation is followed by 5 questions and each lecture by 6 questions. Therefore, test takers have to answer 34~51 questions in total. The time allotted to the Listening section is 60~90 minutes, including the time spent listening to the conversations and lectures and answering the questions.

1. Types of Listening Passages

(1) Conversations
_ Between a student and a professor or a teaching assistant during office hours
_ Between a student with a person related to school services such as a librarian, housing director, bookstore employee, etc.

(2) Lectures
_ Monologue lectures delivered by a professor unilaterally
_ Interactive lectures with one or two students asking questions or making comments
* One lecture may be spoken with a British or Australian accent.

2. Types of Questions

Basic Comprehension Questions

(1) Listening for Main Ideas _ This type of question asks you to identify the overall topic or main idea of a lecture or conversation.
(2) Listening for Main Purpose _ This type of question asks you why the speakers are having a conversation or why a lecture is given.
(3) Listening for Major Details _ This type of question asks you to understand specific details or facts from a conversation or lecture.

Pragmatic Understanding Questions

(4) Understanding the Function of What Is Said
_ This type of question asks you why a speaker mentions some point in the conversation or lecture.
_ This involves replaying part of the listening passage.

(5) Understanding the Speaker's Attitude
_ This type of question asks you what a speaker's feelings, opinions, or degree of certainty is about some issue, idea, or person.
_ This may involve replaying part of the listening passage.

Connecting Information Questions

(6) Understanding Organization _ This type of question asks you how the listening passage is organized or how two portions of the listening passage are related to each other.
(7) Connecting Content _ This type of question asks you to classify or sequence information in a different way from the way it was presented in the listening passage.
(8) Making Inferences _ This type of question asks you to draw a conclusion based on information given in the listening passage.

How to Use This Book

How to Master Skills for the TOEFL® iBT Listening Advanced is designed to be used either as a textbook for a TOEFL® iBT listening preparation course or as a tool for individual learners who are preparing for the TOEFL® test on their own. With a total of 8 units, this book is organized to prepare you for the test with a comprehensive understanding of the test and thorough analysis of every question type. Each unit consists of 6 parts and provides a step-by-step program that provides question-solving strategies and the development of test-taking abilities. At the back of the book are two actual tests of the Listening section of the TOEFL® iBT.

❶ Overview

This part is designed to prepare you for the type of question the unit covers. You will be given a full description of the question type and its application in the passage. You also will be given some useful tips as well as an illustrated introduction and sample.

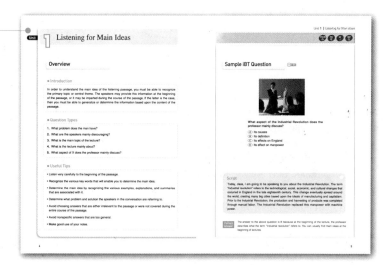

❷ Practice with Conversations

This part is one of the two practical exercise sections where you can actually practice and improve your ability to solve questions. With a total of 4 conversations, you will be able to confirm your understanding of the question types and master skills presented in each unit. Well-organized notes will be given to help you understand the material, and glossed vocabulary will also be given to help you solve the questions. Dictation practice material is downloadable at www.darakwon.co.kr.

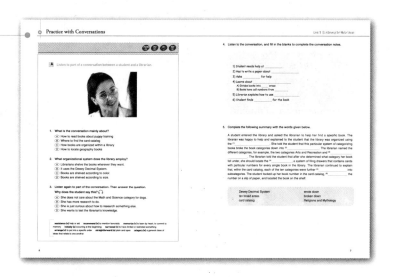

❸ Practice with Lectures

This part is the other practical exercise section where you can actually practice and improve your ability to solve questions. With a total of 4 lectures, you will be able to confirm your understanding of the question types and master skills presented in each unit. Glossed vocabulary and well-organized notes will be given to help you understand the material and answer the questions. Dictation practice material is downloadable at www.darakwon.co.kr.

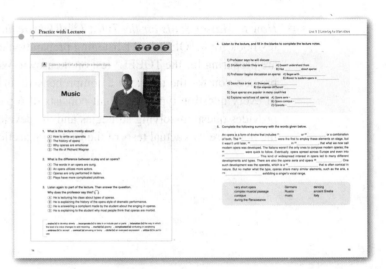

❹ Integrated Listening & Speaking

The TOEFL® iBT is different from previous tests in that it is more integrated than ever. So in this part, you are given the chance to experience the iBT style study by linking your listening skills with your speaking skills. Listen to the different versions of the previous lectures, and answer the questions. But remember! This time you have to say the answers. There is no writing.

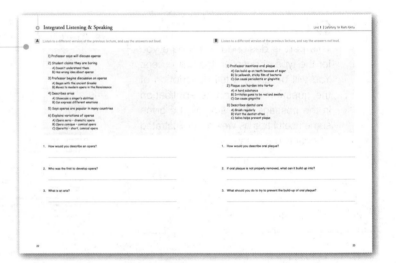

❺ TOEFL iBT Practice Test

This part will give you a chance to experience an actual TOEFL® iBT test. You will be given a conversation with 5 questions and a lecture with 6 questions. The topics are similar to those on the actual test, as are the questions.

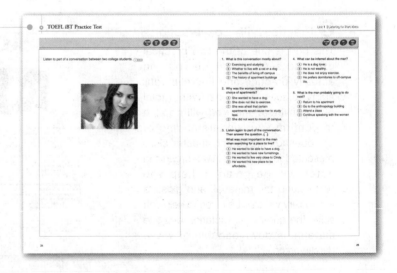

❻ Vocabulary Review

This part offers you a chance to review some of the words and phrases you need to remember after finishing each unit. Vocabulary words for each unit are also provided at the back of the book to help you prepare for each unit.

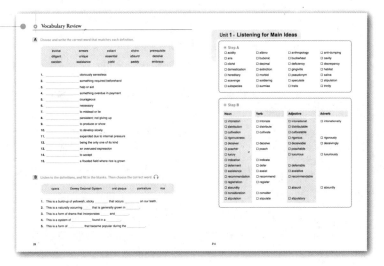

❼ Actual Test

This part offers two full practice tests that are modeled on the Listening section of the TOEFL® iBT. This will familiarize you with the actual test format of the TOEFL® iBT.

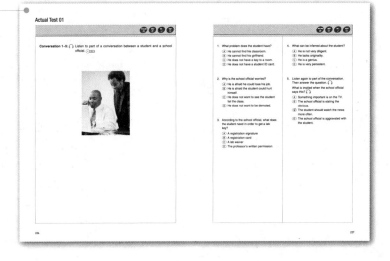

PART 1

Basic Comprehension

Basic comprehension of the listening passage is tested in three ways: listening for the main ideas, listening for the main purpose, and listening for the major details. Listening for the main ideas is to identify the overall topic of the contents. Listening for the main purpose is to search for the reason behind the contents. For questions about the major details, you must understand and remember explicit details or facts from a lecture or conversation.

- **Unit 1 Listening for Main Ideas**
  Music / Agriculture / Public Health / Literature

- **Unit 2 Listening for Main Purpose**
  Zoology / Geology / Astronomy / Climatology

- **Unit 3 Listening for Major Details**
  Dramatics / Literature / Language / Entomology

In order to understand a passage of the listening material, you must be able to recognize its primary topic or central theme. This is because they present the information from the whole of the passage, or it may be included during the course of the message. If the answer is not clear, then you must be able to generalize or determine the information based upon the passage.

Unit 1

Listening for Main Ideas

1 Listening for Main Ideas

Overview

■ Introduction

In order to understand the main idea of the listening passage, you must be able to recognize the primary topic or central theme. The speakers may provide this information at the beginning of the passage, or it may be imparted during the course of the passage. If the latter is the case, then you must be able to generalize or determine the information based upon the content of the passage.

■ Question Types

1. What problem does the man have?
2. What are the speakers mainly discussing?
3. What is the main topic of the lecture?
4. What is the lecture mainly about?
5. What aspect of X does the professor mainly discuss?

■ Useful Tips

- Listen very carefully to the beginning of the passage.

- Recognize the various key words that will enable you to determine the main idea.

- Determine the main idea by recognizing the various examples, explanations, and summaries that are associated with it.

- Determine what problem and solution the speakers in the conversation are referring to.

- Avoid choosing answers that are either irrelevant to the passage or not covered during the entire course of the passage.

- Avoid nonspecific answers that are too general.

- Make good use of your notes.

Sample iBT Question

What aspect of the Industrial Revolution does the professor mainly discuss?

(A) Its causes.
(B) Its definition.
(C) Its effects on England.
(D) Its effect on manpower.

Script

Today, class, I am going to be speaking to you about the Industrial Revolution. The term "industrial revolution" refers to the technological, social, economic, and cultural changes that occurred in England in the late eighteenth century. This change eventually spread around the world, creating many big cities based upon the ideals of manufacturing and capitalism. Prior to the Industrial Revolution, the production and harvesting of products was completed through manual labor. The Industrial Revolution replaced this manpower with machine power.

Correct Answer The answer to the above question is B because at the beginning of the lecture, the professor describes what the term "industrial revolution" refers to. You can usually find main ideas at the beginning of lectures.

Practice with Conversations

A Listen to part of a conversation between a student and a librarian. 1-02

1. What is the conversation mainly about?
   (A) How to read books about puppy training.
   (B) Where to find the card catalog.
   (C) How books are organized within a library.
   (D) How to locate geography books.

2. What organizational system does the library employ?
   (A) Librarians shelve the books wherever they want.
   (B) It uses the Dewey Decimal System.
   (C) Books are shelved according to color.
   (D) Books are shelved according to size.

3. Listen again to part of the conversation. Then answer the question.
   Why does the student say this?
   (A) She does not care about the Math and Science category for dogs.
   (B) She has more research to do.
   (C) She is just curious about how to research something else.
   (D) She wants to test the librarian's knowledge.

• **assistance (n)** help or aid • **recommend (v)** to mention favorably • **memorize (v)** to learn by heart; to commit to memory • **initially (ad)** occurring at the beginning • **narrow (v)** to have limited or restricted something • **arrange (v)** to put into a specific order • **straightforward (a)** plain and open • **category (n)** a general class of ideas that relate to one another

4. Listen to the conversation, and fill in the blanks to complete the conversation notes.

1) Student needs help at _____

2) Has to write a paper about _____

3) Asks _____ for help

4) Learns about _____
    A) Divides books into _____ areas
    B) Books have call numbers from _____

5) Librarian explains how to use _____

6) Student finds _____ for the book

5. Complete the following summary with the words given below.

A student entered the library and asked the librarian to help her find a specific book. The librarian was happy to help and explained to the student that the library was organized using the (1)_____. She told the student that this particular system of categorizing books broke the book categories down into (2)_____. The librarian named the different categories, for example, the two categories Arts and Recreation and (3)_____ _____. The librarian told the student that after she determined what category her book fell under, she should locate the (4)_____, a system of filing drawers that contains cards with particular numbers for every single book in the library. The librarian continued to explain that, within the card catalog, each of the ten categories were further (5)_____ into subcategories. The student looked up her book number in the card catalog, (6)_____ the number on a slip of paper, and located the book on the shelf.

Dewey Decimal System	wrote down
ten broad areas	broken down
card catalog	Religions and Mythology

7

B   Listen to part of a conversation between a student and a professor. ◉ 1-03

1.   **What is the conversation mainly about?**

   Ⓐ How to complete a calculus problem.
   Ⓑ What to do if one's boyfriend or girlfriend moves to a different city.
   Ⓒ A student seeking special treatment from her professor.
   Ⓓ Caring for sick children.

2.   **According to the student, why is she lagging behind in the class?**

   Ⓐ She sleeps too much.
   Ⓑ She broke up with her boyfriend.
   Ⓒ She does not understand the lectures.
   Ⓓ She has a part-time job.

3.   **What can be inferred from the conversation?**

   Ⓐ Asking for special treatment is unethical.
   Ⓑ Favoritism is okay outside of calculus classes.
   Ⓒ The professor did not like the student's boyfriend.
   Ⓓ There is never a time when schoolwork can be late.

- **lag (v)** to fail to maintain a desired pace • **consideration (n)** careful thought • **absurd (a)** obviously senseless
- **spreadsheet (n)** a piece of paper with rows and columns to record data • **cope (v)** to contend with difficulties
- **relationship (n)** a connection between two or more people • **improve (v)** to get better • **undertake (v)** to commit oneself to something • **flu (n)** a viral infection (also known as influenza)

4. Listen to the conversation, and fill in the blanks to complete the conversation notes.

1) Student meets professor to talk about _____
2) Professor looks up grade
   A) Student is not doing well on _____
   B) Student _____ many classes
3) Student discusses _____
4) Professor gives her advice
5) Student asks for _____
6) Professor refuses
   A) Tells her _____
   B) Discusses personal story
7) Student _____

5. Complete the following summary with the words given below.

A student approached her professor, informing him that she had a problem. The professor looked over her records and noticed that she'd been (1)_____ behind in her studies and that she'd missed (2)_____. He asked her what was wrong. The student told him that she was under a lot of (3)_____ because she'd recently (4)_____ _____ and was having a (5)_____ on her schoolwork. The student then proceeded to ask if she could be given (6)_____ and receive a good grade despite (7)_____ in class. The professor was not impressed with her question and told her that she was forcing him to consider making an (8)_____ decision. He told her that the only way she could go forward and learn from this experience was to take (9)_____ and to work harder in class.

not performing well	lagging
unethical	broken up with her boyfriend
stress	special consideration
quite a number of classes	hard time staying focused
responsibility for her actions	

C   Listen to part of a conversation between a student and a bookstore clerk. 🔘 1-04

1. **What is the conversation mainly about?**

   Ⓐ The price of a book.
   Ⓑ The bookstore clerk's newness to the job.
   Ⓒ The student's inability to purchase a book.
   Ⓓ The store's going-out-of business sale.

2. **What did the student actually pay for through the mail?**

   Ⓐ A dress.
   Ⓑ Pencils.
   Ⓒ Paper.
   Ⓓ A set of folders.

3. **Listen again to part of the conversation. Then answer the question.**

   What does the student mean when she says this? 🎧

   Ⓐ She still needs a textbook for her English class.
   Ⓑ She forgot that she was supposed to go to class in the morning.
   Ⓒ There is a test in her English class tomorrow, and she needs to study.
   Ⓓ She lost her purse with all her money in it.

• **indicate (v)** to point out or point to • **deferment (n)** a postponement • **dubious (a)** doubtful • **arrears (n)** something overdue in payment • **stipulation (n)** a condition or demand • **purchase (v)** to buy • **possession (n)** the state of owning something • **borrow (v)** to receive something on loan

4. Listen to the conversation, and fill in the blanks to complete the conversation notes.

> 1) Student wants to _____
>
> 2) Does not have _____
>
> 3) Clerk gets her _____
>
> 4) Student has not yet paid for two books
>   A) Can't buy new book
>   B) Must pay for _____
>
> 5) Student claims to have no money
>
> 6) Student remembers _____
>
> 7) _____ and offers to pay later

5. Complete the following summary with the words given below.

A student approached the bookstore clerk and told him that she (1) _____.
The clerk checked the student's record on the computer and told her that he was very sorry but he could not ring up her new book since she had not paid for two textbooks the previous week. The clerk told the student that she'd (2) _____ but they'd never received her money. The student was upset; she told the clerk that she was certain she'd made the payment for the textbooks and now she would not (3) _____ money for both the textbooks and the new book. The student insisted that the post office had lost her payment. The clerk said he was very sorry but the store (4) _____ for lost payments. The student was suddenly very apologetic since she (5) _____ that what she'd really paid for through the mail was a set of folders, not the two textbooks. She offered to put the book back in order to have (6) _____ for the previous two. The clerk said that would be fine.

> had forgotten   asked to make a deferred payment
> enough money to pay   was not responsible
> would like to purchase a book   have enough

D Listen to part of a conversation between a student and a professor. 1-05

1. **What is this conversation mostly about?**

   (A) How to become a good journalist.
   (B) Registering for courses and completing the necessary requirements for a major.
   (C) Securing a job at a university.
   (D) How to take proper notes during a lecture.

2. **Why is it better that the student take another science class?**

   (A) The student wants to be a science major.
   (B) The professor likes science.
   (C) The student does not have to take mass communication.
   (D) The student needs two science classes in order to meet the graduation requirement.

3. **What can be inferred from the conversation?**

   (A) It is a good idea to keep your end goal in mind when registering for classes.
   (B) Journalism is the best choice of majors in college.
   (C) Professors are not very good at advising students.
   (D) Science classes should always be taken first.

- **requirement (n)** a thing demanded or obligatory • **register (v)** to enter or record on an official list • **prerequisite (n)** something required beforehand • **appointment (n)** a scheduled meeting • **consideration (n)** a careful thought • **definitely (ad)** for certain • **suspect (v)** to surmise to be true; to imagine • **afford (v)** to manage

4. Listen to the conversation, and fill in the blanks to complete the conversation notes.

1) Student visits professor for _____
2) Wants to _____ next semester's classes
3) Professor asks about hours
   A) Wants to know _____
   B) Student wants to finish in _____
   C) Student wants to take _____
4) Both discuss classes
   A) Student has not taken a prerequisite mass communication class
   B) Student needs to _____

5. Complete the following summary with the words given below.

A student visited her professor to go over her choices for next semester's classes. The student wanted to make sure that she was taking the right classes for her journalism major. The professor agreed that a very important part of succeeding in college was (1)_____ _____ correctly, and she looked at the student's records. The professor asked the student if she wanted to (2)_____ in the usual four years. The student said that she wanted to graduate on time, as she (3)_____ to stay longer. The professor told the student that, considering the (4)_____, she should think about taking the mass communication class since it is a (5)_____ for other classes that she will need. The professor also inquired if there were any other science classes the student was interested in taking. The student indicated that she had an (6)_____.

could not afford	interest in geology	major she was choosing
graduate on time	scheduling classes	prerequisite

Practice with Lectures

A   Listen to part of a lecture in a music class. **1-06**

1. **What is this lecture mostly about?**

   Ⓐ How to write an operetta.
   Ⓑ The history of opera.
   Ⓒ Why operas are emotional.
   Ⓓ The life of Richard Wagner.

2. **What is the difference between a play and an opera?**

   Ⓐ The words in an opera are sung.
   Ⓑ An opera utilizes more actors.
   Ⓒ Operas are only performed in Italian.
   Ⓓ Plays have more complicated plotlines.

3. **Listen again to part of the lecture. Then answer the question.**

   Why does the professor say this?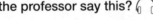

   Ⓐ He is lecturing his class about types of operas.
   Ⓑ He is explaining the history of the opera style of dramatic performance.
   Ⓒ He is answering a complaint made by the student about the singing in operas.
   Ⓓ He is explaining to the student why most people think that operas are morbid.

• **evolve (v)** to develop slowly • **incorporate (v)** to take in or include part or parts • **intonation (n)** the way in which the level of a voice changes to add meaning • **morbid (a)** gloomy • **complicated (a)** confusing or perplexing • **embrace (v)** to accept • **comical (a)** amusing or funny • **cliché (n)** an overused expression • **utilize (v)** to put to use

4. Listen to the lecture, and fill in the blanks to complete the lecture notes.

    1) Professor says he will discuss _____

    2) Student claims they are _____   A) Doesn't understand them
                                            B) Has _____ about operas

    3) Professor begins discussion on operas   A) Begins with _____
                                               B) Moves to modern opera in _____

    4) Describes arias   A) Showcase _____
                         B) Can express different _____

    5) Says operas are popular in many countries

    6) Explains variations of operas   A) *Opera seria* – _____
                                       B) *Opera comique* – _____
                                       C) *Operetta* – _____

5. Complete the following summary with the words given below.

    An opera is a form of drama that includes (1)_____ or (2)_____ or a combination of both. The (3)_____ were the first to employ these elements on stage, but it wasn't until later, (4)_____ in (5)_____, that what we now call modern opera was developed. The Italians weren't the only ones to compose modern operas; the (6)_____ were quick to follow. Eventually, opera spread across Europe and even into (7)_____. This kind of widespread interest in opera led to many different developments and types. There are also the *opera seria* and *opera* (8)_____. One such development was the operetta, which is a (9)_____ that is often comical in nature. But no matter what the type, operas share many similar elements, such as the aria, a (10)_____ exhibiting a singer's vocal range.

very short opera	Germans	dancing
complex musical passage	Russia	ancient Greeks
comique	music	Italy
during the Renaissance		

B Listen to part of a lecture in an agriculture class. 🔘 1-07

Agriculture

1. **What is the lecture mainly about?**

   (A) How to harvest rice.

   (B) The uses for domestic rice.

   (C) The origins of both wild and domestic rice.

   (D) How China became a great producer of rice.

2. **What is the main difference between wild and domestic rice?**

   (A) Wild rice has more flavor than domestic rice.

   (B) Wild rice occurs naturally, and domestic rice is planted according to desired traits.

   (C) Wild rice is only found in Australia.

   (D) Domestic rice has more flavor.

3. **What can be inferred from the lecture?**

   (A) Rice is the most nutritious grain.

   (B) The Chinese make the best rice.

   (C) Wild rice is better than domestic rice.

   (D) It is hard to identify the exact date and origin of rice.

• **cultivate (v)** to prepare and work on land in order to raise crops • **yield (v)** to produce or show • **distribution (n)** an arrangement • **origin (n)** the point at which something is born • **precise (a)** exact • **microscopic (a)** too small to be seen by the naked eye • **paddy (n)** a flooded field where rice is grown • **generation (n)** offspring that is at the same stage from a common ancestor • **sow (v)** to scatter seeds for growing

4. Listen to the lecture, and fill in the blanks to complete the lecture notes.

1) Professor discusses _____
2) Describes wild rice
   A) Occurs _____
   B) Existed _____ years
   C) Probably originated _____
3) Describes domestic rice
   A) Goes back to _____
   B) Carries certain desired _____
4) Discusses _____ about rice
   A) The Gift of _____

5. Complete the following summary with the words given below.

The origin of (1)_____ is a complicated question because it can potentially contain three parts: the origins of (2)_____ rice and domestic rice or the mythological stories surrounding rice. The exact origin of wild rice is (3)_____ to pinpoint, but evidence suggests that our early (4)_____ it as early as 16,000 years ago. The evidence also suggests that wild rice was spread over four continents: (5)_____, Asia, Africa, and North America. Domestic rice originated in (6)_____ in Hunan Province; evidence of ancient (7)_____ has been discovered there. The difference between wild rice and domestic rice is that wild rice (8)_____ while domestic rice seeds are selectively planted according to the potential (9)_____. And finally, another way that the origin of rice is explained is through the use of ancient myths. One such myth about the origin of rice is the story of Shuhwa, a girl who planted a seed she had found in a dog's fur during a flood and which later produced rice.

China	rice paddies	Australia
rice	ancestors were harvesting	to yield desired traits
wild	occurs naturally	nearly impossible

C Listen to part of a lecture in a public health class. 🎧 1-08

Public Health

1. What is the lecture mainly about?

   (A) How to diagnose a case of gingivitis.

   (B) A good technique to brush one's teeth.

   (C) The cause of oral plaque and how to prevent it.

   (D) How to schedule visits to the dentist.

2. What is one way that oral plaque can affect teeth?

   (A) It hardens and becomes tartar.

   (B) It makes teeth healthy.

   (C) It can cause teeth to fall out instantly.

   (D) It causes oral cancer of the tongue.

3. How does the professor organize this lecture?

   (A) As an informal question and answer session.

   (B) Chronologically based on the history of dentistry.

   (C) He begins with a guest speaker and then prompts the students to ask questions.

   (D) He tells the story of a person who does not take care of his teeth.

• **imperative (a)** necessary • **diligent (a)** persistent; not giving up • **incorporate (v)** to take in or include as part or parts • **rigorous (a)** very exact • **ingest (v)** to take food into the body via the mouth • **failure (n)** not having achieved the desired end • **defense (n)** a method of protecting something • **swollen (a)** expanded due to internal pressure • **neutralize (v)** to counterbalance • **penetrate (v)** to enter into something

4. Listen to the lecture, and fill in the blanks to complete the lecture notes.

    1) Professor mentions _____
       A) Can build up on teeth because of _____
       B) Is yellowish, sticky film of _____
       C) Can cause _____ or _____
    2) Plaque can harden into tartar
       A) A hard _____
       B) Irritates gums so that they are _____ and_____
       C) Can cause _____
    3) Describes dental care
       A) Brush _____
       B) Visit the dentist often
       C) _____ helps prevent plaque

5. Complete the following summary with the words given below.

    Oral plaque is a (1)_____ that forms naturally on our teeth. However, if not properly removed, oral plaque can form into a (2)_____ known as tartar. In turn, if tartar is not properly treated, then it can lead to much more serious diseases like (3)_____ or periodontis. The body does its best to combat the build-up of oral plaque into tartar; it even has its own (4)_____ – saliva. Our saliva helps break down the bacteria by (5)_____ the acidic environment. The best way to prevent plaque from building up in your mouth is to incorporate a rigorous daily routine of brushing and flossing your teeth with regular visits to your dentist so he can (6)_____ all the plaque from your teeth and gums.

hard substance	remove
natural defense	gingivitis
actively neutralizing	yellowish, sticky film of bacteria

D   Listen to part of a lecture in a zoology class. 1-09

Zoology

1.   **What is the lecture mainly about?**

   Ⓐ How to hunt large cats.
   Ⓑ How to tell the difference between an albino tiger and a Siberian tiger.
   Ⓒ The characteristics of tigers.
   Ⓓ Where to find large cats in Asia.

2.   **What is one way that human hunting can affect tigers?**

   Ⓐ It does not affect them.
   Ⓑ It causes the population to grow.
   Ⓒ It causes tiger cubs to be afraid of humans.
   Ⓓ It has made tigers an endangered species.

3.   **What can be inferred from the above lecture?**

   Ⓐ Tigers are a beautiful and unique animal worth saving from extinction.
   Ⓑ Hunting tigers should be allowed during certain times of the year.
   Ⓒ Tigers should be transported back to eastern Turkey.
   Ⓓ Albino tigers are superior to all other tigers.

• **deficiency (n)** the state of not having enough • **deceive (v)** to mislead or lie • **poacher (n)** a person who kills an animal illegally • **mention (v)** to refer to something • **unique (a)** being the only one of its kind • **hereditary (a)** transmitted from parent to offspring • **illusion (n)** a wrong perception of reality

4. Listen to the lecture, and fill in the blanks to complete the lecture notes.

1) Professor describes _____   A) A mammal
                                       B) Has _____ and _____ striped fur
                                       C) Has _____ in some places

2) Describes the albino tiger   A) Has a deficiency of _____
                                 B) Has no _____

3) Gives physical characteristics of tigers   A) Is the largest cat
                                               - Up to _____ feet long
                                               - Weighs _____ pounds

4) There are _____ subspecies of tigers

5) Describes current situation of tigers   A) About _____ tigers alive
                                            B) Some species are extinct
                                            C) Other species are endangered
                                            D) Live only in ____

5. Complete the following summary with the words given below.

A tiger is a (1)_____ that generally has orange fur and (2)_____ stripes with white markings on its face, (3)_____ and underside. Tigers are also the (4)_____ of all the cats. The largest of the tigers is the (5)_____. Tigers can range in length from four to (6)_____ feet and can weigh anywhere between (7)_____ and 700 pounds. They are broken down into (8)_____, three of which are (9)_____. The extinct subspecies are the Bali, the Caspian, and the (10)_____. The fact that there are extinct subspecies of tigers is also a reason why tigers are listed as (11)_____ _____. While tigers once roamed anywhere between eastern (12)_____ and Asia, what tigers remain are now only found in certain parts of Asia. Tigers are becoming extinct because they are being (13)_____ for their skins and because they sometimes kill cattle and other livestock.

Javan tigers	eight different subspecies	largest
Turkey	chest	mammal
200	Siberian tiger	endangered species
black	poached	thirteen
extinct		

Integrated Listening & Speaking

Listen to a different version of the previous lecture, and say the answers out loud. ⊙ 1-10

1) Professor says he will discuss operas

2) Student claims they are boring
   A) Doesn't understand them
   B) Has wrong ideas about operas

3) Professor begins discussion on operas
   A) Begins with the ancient Greeks
   B) Moves to modern opera in the Renaissance

4) Describes arias
   A) Showcase a singer's abilities
   B) Can express different emotions

5) Says operas are popular in many countries

6) Explains variations of operas
   A) *Opera seria* – dramatic opera
   B) *Opera comique* – comical opera
   C) *Operetta* – short, comical opera

1. How would you describe an opera?

   _____

2. Who was the first to develop opera?

   _____

3. What is an aria?

   _____

B Listen to a different version of the previous lecture, and say the answers out loud. 1-11

1) Professor mentions oral plaque

    A) Can build up on teeth because of sugar
    B) Is yellowish, sticky film of bacteria
    C) Can cause periodontis or gingivitis

2) Plaque can harden into tartar

    A) A hard substance
    B) Irritates gums so that they are red and swollen
    C) Can cause gingivitis

3) Describes dental care

    A) Brush regularly
    B) Visit the dentist often
    C) Saliva helps prevent plaque

1. How would you describe oral plaque?

    _____

2. If oral plaque is not properly removed, what can it build up into?

    _____

3. What should you do to try to prevent the build-up of oral plaque?

    _____

TOEFL iBT Practice Test

VOLUME · HELP · OK · NEXT

Listen to part of a conversation between two college students. 1-12

1. What is this conversation mostly about?

    A Exercising and studying.
    B Whether to live with a cat or a dog.
    C The benefits of living off campus.
    D The history of apartment buildings.

2. Why was the woman limited in her choice of apartments?

    A She wanted to have a dog.
    B She did not like to exercise.
    C She was afraid that certain apartments would cause her to study less.
    D She did not want to move off campus.

3. Listen again to part of the conversation. Then answer the question.

    What was most important to the man when searching for a place to live?

    A He wanted to be able to have a dog.
    B He wanted to have new furnishings.
    C He wanted to live very close to Cindy.
    D He wanted his new place to be affordable.

4. What can be inferred about the man?

    A He is a dog lover.
    B He is not wealthy.
    C He does not enjoy exercise.
    D He prefers dormitories to off-campus life.

5. What is the man probably going to do next?

    A Return to his apartment.
    B Go to the anthropology building.
    C Attend a class.
    D Continue speaking with the woman.

Listen to part of a lecture in a literature class. 1-13

Literature

1. What is the main idea of the lecture?

   Ⓐ How to write plays.
   Ⓑ The life of William Shakespeare.
   Ⓒ Life in Stratford-Upon-Avon in the late sixteenth century.
   Ⓓ The hardships of London theater life.

2. Why is there a discrepancy with some of the facts of William Shakespeare's life?

   Ⓐ No one liked William Shakespeare during his lifetime.
   Ⓑ Shakespeare wrote his plays under a pseudonym.
   Ⓒ Records, such as William's birth certificate, were either not kept or lost.
   Ⓓ The theater world is secretive and mysterious.

3. Listen again to part of the lecture. Then answer the question. 🎧

   Why do scholars speculate that William Shakespeare had a variety of jobs in between the years 1585–1592?

   Ⓐ He immediately moved to London.
   Ⓑ There is evidence in books that Shakespeare was a gardener.
   Ⓒ Shakespeare's plays feature an in-depth knowledge of a variety of jobs.
   Ⓓ In 1592, Shakespeare took up sailing.

4. Listen again to part of the lecture. Then answer the question.

   What does the professor mean when he says this? 🎧

   Ⓐ Nobody knows anything about Shakespeare.
   Ⓑ There are many mysterious things about Shakespeare.
   Ⓒ Shakespeare was better than any other writer.
   Ⓓ Most of Shakespeare's works are difficult to understand.

5. Why does the professor mention the bubonic plague?

   Ⓐ To explain why Shakespeare had enough time to write so many plays.
   Ⓑ To account for the subject matter of *The Comedy of Errors*.
   Ⓒ To give the reason as to why Shakespeare purchased New Place.
   Ⓓ To explain why Shakespeare wrote poetry during that time.

6. During which of the following time periods did Shakespeare write each of these plays?

	1589-1594	1599-1608
(A) *Troilus and Cressida*		
(B) *Hamlet*		
(C) *Titus Andronicus*		
(D) *King Lear*		

Vocabulary Review

A Choose and write the correct word that matches each definition.

evolve	arrears	valiant	cliché	prerequisite
diligent	unique	imperative	absurd	deceive
swollen	assistance	yield	paddy	embrace

1. _____ obviously senseless

2. _____ something required beforehand

3. _____ help or aid

4. _____ something overdue in payment

5. _____ courageous

6. _____ necessary

7. _____ to mislead or lie

8. _____ persistent; not giving up

9. _____ to produce or show

10. _____ to develop slowly

11. _____ expanded due to internal pressure

12. _____ being the only one of its kind

13. _____ an overused expression

14. _____ to accept

15. _____ a flooded field where rice is grown

B Listen to the definitions, and fill in the blanks. Then choose the correct word. 🎧 💿 1-14

opera	Dewey Decimal System	oral plaque	portraiture	rice

1. This is a build-up of yellowish, sticky _____ that occurs _____ on our teeth.

2. This is a naturally occurring _____ that is generally grown in _____.

3. This is a form of drama that incorporates _____ and_____.

4. This is a system of _____ found in a _____.

5. This is a form of _____ that became popular during the _____.

Unit 2

Listening for Main Purpose

2 Listening for Main Purpose

Overview

■ Introduction

In order to understand the purpose of the listening passage, you must be able to recognize the reason why various topics are discussed or mentioned. This type of question often occurs in conversations rather than lectures. Just like main idea questions, the speakers may provide this information at the beginning of the passage, or it may be imparted during the course of the passage. If the latter is the case, then you must be able to generalize or determine the information based upon the content of the passage.

■ Question Types

1. Why does the student visit the professor?

2. Why does the student visit the registrar's office?

3. Why does the professor ask to see the student?

4. Why does the professor explain X?

■ Useful Tips

• Understand the reason for having the lecture or conversation.

• Listen very carefully to the ends of conversations.

• Determine the purpose by recognizing the solution to the problem.

• Avoid choosing answers that are either irrelevant to the passage or not covered during the entire course of the passage.

• Avoid nonspecific answers that are too general.

• Make good use of your notes.

Sample iBT Question

Why does the student visit the professor?

- (A) To inquire as to Professor Smith's whereabouts.
- (B) To ask about some different graduate schools.
- (C) To request a favor from the professor.
- (D) To submit a letter of recommendation to the professor.

Script

M1: Dr. Drexler, may I speak with you for a moment, please? You're not too busy right now, are you?

M2: No, not at all, Adrian. Come into my office, and have a seat... So, tell me... What's on your mind right now?

M1: Well, you may or may not know this, but I'm applying to several different graduate schools, so I was hoping that you would be able to write a few letters of recommendation that I could send out along with my applications.

M2: I'm honored that you've asked me, Adrian, and I'm more than happy to help you out, but don't you think you ought to ask Professor Smith instead? After all, he is your advisor, and he's the professor that you've worked with the longest in all of your years here. I would think that he would be able to write the best, most comprehensive letter of recommendation for you.

M1: Yes, sir. You're absolutely right. The only problem is that I can't get in touch with Professor Smith at this moment. Apparently, he is still at that conference somewhere in Europe, and I don't know when he's coming back. I left him a couple of voice messages, and I've e-mailed him several times, but he hasn't responded to any of them.

Correct Answer The answer to the above question is (C). The reason the student visited the professor is that he wanted Dr. Drexler to write some letters of recommendation for him, so he is asking the professor for a favor.

Practice with Conversations

A   Listen to part of a conversation between a student and a professor. 🔊 1-16

1. **Why does the student visit the professor?**

   Ⓐ She is upset with her grade in history class.
   Ⓑ She wants more information about the final examination.
   Ⓒ She is thinking about withdrawing from his course.
   Ⓓ She would like to rewrite her paper.

2. **How do HIT tutors help the undergraduate students?**

   Ⓐ They summarize the textbooks and give information on exams.
   Ⓑ They provide reports for the students.
   Ⓒ They do the projects for the students.
   Ⓓ They teach them in advance.

3. **What is the likely outcome of this conversation?**

   Ⓐ The student will drop the course.
   Ⓑ The student will give up her part-time job.
   Ⓒ The student will stay enrolled in the class.
   Ⓓ The student will become an HIT tutor.

• **cumulative (a)** total • **consult (v)** to ask someone for advice • **drop or drop out (v)** to quit something • **entire (a)** all of • **session (n)** a lesson or meeting • **tutoring (n)** informal teaching • **undergraduate (n)** a university student that has not earned a degree yet • **withdraw (v)** to quit

4. Listen to the conversation, and fill in the blanks to complete the conversation notes.

1) Student meets professor
2) Claims the book is too _____ so must - _____ the class
3) Professor says it is very _____ to drop
4) Professor says student's grades are _____
5) Student says she needs a high grade for _____
6) Professor recommends _____
   A) Is called _____
   B) Graduate students tutor students
   C) Is a _____ service
7) Student decides to look into the program

5. Complete the following summary with the words given below.

A student told her professor that she was thinking of (1)_____ from his history course because she had a part-time job, she didn't have enough time to study, and the textbook contained (2)_____ to read. The professor told her that it would be a shame if she dropped out of the course because she had already completed five weeks and had done well on the assignments. He also told her not to worry about failing the course. The student replied that (3)_____ about failing but that her concern was (4)_____ to attain a high grade. The professor then told her about the history tutoring program. He said that the tutors were graduate students who could probably do a good job of (5)_____ _____. Upon hearing this news, the student (6)_____ and told the professor that she would check out the History Department's website as soon as she got back to her computer.

| she wasn't worried | became excited | withdrawing |
| summarizing the textbook | it would be too difficult | too much material |

33

B   Listen to part of a conversation between a student and a manager. ⊙ 1-17

1. **Why does the student meet with the cafeteria manager?**

    Ⓐ To complain about the food in the cafeteria.
    Ⓑ To apply for a job.
    Ⓒ To request that the snack bar extend its hours.
    Ⓓ To get permission to study in the cafeteria late in the evening.

2. **According to the conversation, why does the student want to extend the snack bar's hours? Choose 2 answers.**

    Ⓐ Students from the dormitory like to hang out late at the snack bar.
    Ⓑ Students like the food at the snack bar.
    Ⓒ It is inconvenient to go out late at night to get a snack.
    Ⓓ Students want to eat more during exam week.

3. **What can be inferred from the conversation?**

    Ⓐ The snack bar is a popular place.
    Ⓑ The unionized employees are becoming too powerful.
    Ⓒ The snack bar has very cheap food.
    Ⓓ The manager of the cafeteria does not like this student.

• **appreciate (v)** to be thankful for • **complaint (n)** a negative comment • **custodian (n)** someone that is paid to clean a building • **extend (v)** to make longer • **hang out (v)** to spend time at • **petition (n)** a sheet of paper with a lot of names and signatures on it • **snack (n)** a short, small meal • **steady (a)** consistent

4. Listen to the conversation, and fill in the blanks to complete the conversation notes.

1) Student visits cafeteria manager

2) Student wants snack bar to _____
    A) Says students like to hang out there late and study
    B) Is too _____ to walk to _____

3) Manager understands student's argument
    A) Has to close early for _____
    B) Students cannot clean
    C) Only _____ members can clean

4) Students suggests selling _____ from 10 to 12

5) Manager agrees to do that during _____

5. Complete the following summary with the words given below.

A student visits the (1)_____ to talk about the hours of the snack bar in the cafeteria. The student said that many students enjoyed hanging out and working there at night. He said that the students were (2)_____ that the snack bar closed at 10:00 every day. He indicated it would be better if the snack bar stayed open until midnight. The manager replied that it was necessary to close the snack bar by 10:00 to (3)_____, who stop working at 10:30, time to clean up. He said that student employees (4)_____ to clean the snack bar. The student then (5)_____ that they keep the snack bar open during midterm exam week and only permit the sale of (6)_____ after 10:00. The student also showed the manager a petition. Upon hearing the student's suggestion and seeing the petition, (7)_____ to extend the snack bar's hours during the midterm exam week and possibly during final exam week, too.

allow the custodians	cafeteria manager	disappointed
packaged goods	suggested	the manager agreed
were not allowed		

C Listen to part of a conversation between two students.  1-18

1. Why does the man ask the woman so many questions about tutoring?

   Ⓐ He needs a tutor.
   Ⓑ He is interested in being a tutor.
   Ⓒ He wants to spend more time with her.
   Ⓓ She wants him to be a tutor.

2. How is the woman more qualified than the man to tutor math?

   Ⓐ She has a car and therefore does not have to rely on public transit.
   Ⓑ She has more university degrees than he has.
   Ⓒ She used to be a school teacher.
   Ⓓ She has more knowledge of math than he does.

3. Listen again to part of the conversation. Then answer the question.

   What does the woman mean when she says this?

   Ⓐ She thinks the pay for the job is too low.
   Ⓑ She needs another job.
   Ⓒ She likes high-paying jobs.
   Ⓓ She would rather have a full-time job.

• **calculus (n)** a type of mathematics • **capable (a)** having the ability to do something • **challenging (a)** difficult, but not too difficult • **fortunately (ad)** with good luck or having good luck • **gradually (ad)** slowly • **minimum (n)** the lowest amount • **relief (n)** a chance to relax • **trigonometry (n)** a type of mathematics

4. Listen to the conversation, and fill in the blanks to complete the conversation notes.

1) Two students are discussing _____

2) Woman says she works _____ on campus
    A) Receives $_____ an hour
    B) Tutors _____
    C) Is difficult but _____ and _____

3) Man asks about _____
    A) Does not major _____
    B) But did well in _____

4) Woman says must know all areas of math

5) Man says he probably should _____

5. Complete the following summary with the words given below.

Mark and Julie both attend the same university. Julie informed Mark that she had a part-time job as a math tutor, which pays a lot higher than (1)_____ for university students. Upon hearing this, Mark became very interested in this kind of work. He told Julie that he had completed a first-year university math course and felt he could tutor (2)_____ _____ and high school students. Julie told him that (3)_____ for him to teach math because he didn't have much experience in mathematics and math tutors were usually (4)_____ to know a lot more about math than their students. Plus, Mark is a psychology major, not a math major. Upon further discussion, Julie told Mark that math tutors had to teach all areas of math, including algebra, trigonometry, (5)_____, and calculus. When Mark heard this, (6)_____ that being a math tutor might not be a good idea because he was poor at calculus.

expected	first-year students	typical part-time jobs
it might be difficult	he suddenly realized	statistics

D   Listen to part of a conversation between a student and a professor. 1-19

1. **Why does the student speak with her professor?**
   - (A) To ask about a nursing job.
   - (B) To respond to her inquiry about volunteer work.
   - (C) To request her help in organizing a conference.
   - (D) To tell the professor about her work experience.

2. **Why does the student want the professor's help?**
   - (A) She does not have much experience.
   - (B) Most of her contacts are limited.
   - (C) The professor has plenty of spare time.
   - (D) The professor is eager to help the student.

3. **What can be inferred from the conversation?**
   - (A) The student wants the professor's full participation.
   - (B) The professor is eager to help the student.
   - (C) The professor is very busy.
   - (D) The student has lots of experience overseas.

- **accomplish (v)** to reach a goal or objective • **association (n)** a formal club, group, league, or organization
- **exclusively (ad)** only • **huge (a)** very big • **logistics (n)** the way something is organized or arranged
- **numerous (a)** many • **nursing major (n)** a student that studies nursing • **respond (v)** to answer

4. Listen to the conversation, and fill in the blanks to complete the conversation notes.

1) Student wants to speak with a professor   A) Had _____ many times
                                             B) Professor never _____

2) Professor had been _____

3) Student wants to set up an employment conference

4) Professor suggests using _____

5) Student doesn't want to do that   A) Thinks the center's contacts are _____
                                     B) Can't find good jobs through it

6) Student offers to do the work   A) Has many contacts
                                   B) Professor just has to do _____ work

7) Professor agrees to help

5. Complete the following summary with the words given below.

A university nursing student went to speak to her professor. She asked the professor to help
(1)_____. The professor didn't think the conference was a
(2)_____. She said she was too busy. She said this type of event should be
conducted through the Student Employment Center. She also indicated that the Nursing
Department had held employment conferences in the past and that all of these conferences
had been (3)_____. She said the students didn't (4)_____ and had
(5)_____ in organizing conferences. The student then advised the professor
not to worry about the above factors because she used to work for the Nursing Association and
had helped organize numerous nursing conferences. The professor was (6)_____
_____ to hear this and then agreed to make a few phone calls to help arrange the conference.

good idea   set up an employment conference
insufficient experience   pleasantly surprised
unsuccessful   do much work

Practice with Lectures

A Listen to part of a lecture in a zoology class.

Zoology

1. Why did the professor describe the harshness of the Arctic environment?
   - (A) To discourage the students from visiting it.
   - (B) To emphasize how impressive polar bears are.
   - (C) To explain why many animals there are dying.
   - (D) To let the students know how cold the Arctic is.

2. What is one difference between polar bears and brown bears?
   - (A) Polar bears eat more fish than brown bears.
   - (B) Unlike brown bears, polar bears eat meat.
   - (C) Polar bears are bigger than brown bears.
   - (D) Brown bears cannot swim.

3. What is the likely outcome of continued global warming?
   - (A) Polar bears will become very lonely animals.
   - (B) Polar bears will have to move to Antarctica.
   - (C) Polar bears will probably become extinct.
   - (D) Seals will move farther out to sea.

> • **amazingly (ad)** surprisingly • **camouflage (v)** to disguise one's appearance • **endangered (a)** in a dangerous situation • **extremely (ad)** very • **frequently (ad)** often • **harsh (a)** severe • **insulate (v)** to provide a warm layer of skin or clothing to help keep one warm • **roam (v)** to walk all over the place with no specific destination in mind

4. Listen to the lecture, and fill in the blanks to complete the lecture notes.

1) Professor discusses _____
   A) Live in Arctic in freezing _____
   B) Few species can survive there
   C) Roam the land and ice hunting
      - Eat seals, fish, and other food
   D) Have no natural _____

2) Shows pictures of polar bears
   A) Are bigger than _____ and _____ bears
   B) Can weigh up to _____
   C) Have _____ fur
   D) Are strong swimmers

3) Are becoming endangered
   A) Global warming decreases the amount of ice
   B) Bears have _____ time to hunt

5. Complete the following summary with the words given below.

Polar bears live in the (1)_____, which has an extremely (2)_____. It's one of the coldest places on Earth. The temperature in the Arctic frequently drops below minus 40 degrees centigrade. The polar bear, however, thrives in this kind of environment. The polar bear (3)_____ on land, swims in freezing sea water, and (4)_____ on sheets of ice while looking for (5)_____, which is its favorite food. Polar bears are very large. They have a very thick (6)_____ of fur and large front (7)_____ that allow them to swim far from land. Unfortunately, polar bears are an endangered (8)_____ because the Arctic is becoming too warm for them. The (9)_____ is disappearing, and so are the seals. The polar bear (10)_____.

roams	Arctic	paws
seals	harsh environment	floats
coat	species	population is decreasing
ice		

B Listen to part of a lecture in a geology class.  1-21

Geology

1. **Why did the professor discuss seismic waves?**

   Ⓐ To illustrate their history.

   Ⓑ To explain the causes of earthquakes.

   Ⓒ To explain why they are so dangerous.

   Ⓓ To illustrate the differences between various types of seismic waves.

2. **According to the lecture, which of the following describes surface waves? Choose 2 answers.**

   Ⓐ They are the fastest kind of seismic waves.

   Ⓑ They travel at half the speed of P waves.

   Ⓒ They are the most destructive type of seismic waves.

   Ⓓ They move at or near Earth's surface.

3. **What can be inferred from the lecture?**

   Ⓐ All earthquakes are dangerous.

   Ⓑ Not all earthquakes are dangerous.

   Ⓒ Earthquakes with body waves are the most dangerous.

   Ⓓ Earthquakes can be caused by sound waves.

• **amplitude (n)** the height of the wave • **catastrophic (a)** having a very harmful impact • **destructive (a)** causing damage • **duration (n)** period of time • **frequency (n)** how often something happens • **material (n)** content; an ingredient • **ripples (n)** small waves • **tremor (n)** small shaking

4. Listen to the lecture, and fill in the blanks to complete the lecture notes.

1) Professor discusses _____   A) Some cannot be felt on Earth
                                          B) Some are violent with _____

2) People feel seismic waves   A) Are similar to _____ and _____ waves
                                B) Can _____ and _____
                                C) Can change speed

3) Two major kinds of seismic waves   A) _____
                                          - P wave or primary wave
                                          - S wave or secondary wave
                                       B) _____
                                          - Move at Earth's surface
                                          - Are very destructive
                                          - Love wave and Rayleigh wave

5. Complete the following summary with the words given below.

Seismic waves are caused by earthquakes and (1)_____. Sometimes, it's possible to feel seismic waves (2)_____. If one feels shaking during an earthquake, what is felt are seismic waves. Seismic waves have similar properties to sound waves and light waves. The (3)_____ that one can feel are body waves. These might not be very powerful because they move (4)_____ Earth's surface. But because some of them travel very fast, they are the waves that a person feels first. Perhaps a person won't feel or (5)_____. If he does, he will feel them as a minor tremor. Some body waves travel slower and might cause more (6)_____ at Earth's surface. Surface waves travel at or near Earth's surface. They are usually more destructive than body waves because of their (7)_____, larger amplitude, and longer (8)_____. One type of body wave, when it reaches Earth's surface, might appear as a wave (9)_____, sometimes making it appear as though (10)_____ are moving up and down.

duration	hear them	during an earthquake
damage	first kinds of waves	cars
lower frequency	moving up and down	major explosions
deep inside		

C Listen to part of a lecture in an astronomy class. 1-22

Astronomy

1. Why did the professor compare Jupiter with Earth?

　Ⓐ To help describe how the planets formed.
　Ⓑ To help explain why Jupiter is dangerous.
　Ⓒ To help explain why Jupiter is so big.
　Ⓓ To help describe the difference between rocky and Jovian planets.

2. According to the lecture, which of the following describes Jupiter?
　Choose 2 answers.

　Ⓐ It is very cold.
　Ⓑ It has the Great Dark Spot.
　Ⓒ It is twice as massive as all of the other planets combined.
　Ⓓ It is very hot.

3. Listen again to part of the lecture. Then answer the question.
　Why does the professor say this?

　Ⓐ He wants to distinguish between Jovian planets and gas giants.
　Ⓑ He does not want to confuse the students.
　Ⓒ He wants the students to look in their textbooks.
　Ⓓ He wants to compare Jovian planets with gas giants.

- **bombard (v)** to quickly hit, shoot, or target something many times　• **blend (n)** a mixture　• **core (n)** the center of an object　• **diameter (n)** the distance across a circle　• **fixture (n)** something that is permanent　• **halo (n)** a circle of light　• **massive (a)** large in size　• **radiate (v)** to deflect away　• **reiterate (v)** to repeat

4. Listen to the lecture, and fill in the blanks to complete the lecture notes.

1) Professor discusses _____ A) Neptune, Uranus, Saturn, and Jupiter
                                        B) Are different from _____ and ____
                                        C) Are mostly composed of _____ and _____

2) Jovian planets do not have solid surfaces A) Are _____
                                              B) Can't land a spacecraft on them

3) Gives more facts about them A) Have many _____ and _____
                                B) Are very large

4) Weather patterns are very different A) Have violent _____
                                        B) Have many _____

5) Is probably no life on Jovian planets

5. Complete the following summary with the words given below.

There are two types of planets. One type is those with a $^{(1)}$_____ such as Earth and Mars. The other type is the gaseous planets, which are Neptune, Uranus, Saturn, and Jupiter. The biggest of these is Jupiter. The rocky planets and the gaseous planets are very different. For example, the $^{(2)}$_____ of a gaseous planet does not have a solid surface. Therefore, a spacecraft would be incapable of $^{(3)}$_____ such a planet. The Jovian planets have a $^{(4)}$_____ and moons. Jupiter has 63 moons. It's also the biggest planet in the solar system. In fact, it's $^{(5)}$_____ as all of the other planets combined! Jupiter has the Great Red Spot, a storm which is $^{(6)}$_____ 340 years old. Wind speeds on Jupiter often reach up to 600km/hr. Jupiter's innermost ring is 22,000km wide! And Jupiter is always covered by $^{(7)}$_____.

exterior	number of rings	at least
a layer of clouds	twice as massive	landing on
rocky core		

D Listen to part of a lecture in a climatology class. 1-23

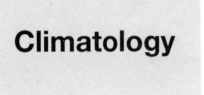

1. Why did the professor mention that 90% of India's water supply comes from monsoons?

  (A) To illustrate how heavy the rainfall is.
  (B) To inform the students that India has too much water.
  (C) To indicate that this weather phenomenon can be beneficial.
  (D) To illustrate why other countries do not receive much rainfall.

2. According to the lecture, which of the following describes monsoons? Choose 2 answers.

  (A) Monsoons are more common in the northern hemisphere.
  (B) India is almost 100% reliant on monsoon rains.
  (C) All monsoons have the same duration.
  (D) Monsoons are very common in the United States.

3. What aspect of monsoons does the professor mainly discuss?

  (A) The damage caused by them.
  (B) How they are caused by global warming.
  (C) The monsoon season in Asia.
  (D) Their positive aspects.

- **annual (a)** occurring every year • **ample (a)** plenty; a lot • **derive from (v)** to come from • **drenched (a)** extremely wet • **famine (n)** starvation • **moist (a)** wet • **porous (a)** having many holes • **reliant on (a)** dependent on • **urge (v)** to encourage, recommend, or suggest • **shabby (a)** old; broken-down

4.   Listen to the lecture, and fill in the blanks to complete the lecture notes.

1) Professor discusses _____
   A) Are annual weather phenomena
   B) Are heavy rains
   C) Occur in _____ places
2) Can be beneficial
   A) Supply _____% of India's water
   B) Essential for _____
3) Can be harmful
   A) Can cause _____
   B) Inconvenience people in cities
4) Are hard to _____

5.   Complete the following summary with the words given below.

Monsoons are an (1)_____ weather phenomena that occur (2)_____. More specifically, they're very heavy rains which originate from moist air masses that move inland from the ocean. Typically, cool air (3)_____ reaches warm dry air above India, causing it to rain throughout South Asia. Monsoons can be destructive, (4)_____ and subsequent famines. But unlike most natural weather phenomena, they also have a beneficial impact. For example, monsoon rains supply about 90% of India's total water supply. They're essential for crops. Poor subsistence farmers are totally reliant on (5)_____ for their livelihoods. Too little rain may result in famine. The precise dates and duration of monsoons are (6)_____ to predict. Monsoons are more common in the northern hemisphere, where there are more large landmasses, than in the southern hemisphere, which is mostly comprised of sea water.

these rains	primarily in Asia	over the ocean
causing flooding	annual	impossible

Integrated Listening & Speaking

Listen to a different version of the previous lecture, and say the answers out loud. 🔘 2-01

1) Professor discusses polar bears

    A) Live in Arctic in freezing temperature

    B) Few species can survive there

    C) Roam the land and ice hunting

      - Eat seals, fish, and other food

    D) Have no natural enemies

2) Shows pictures of polar bears

    A) Are bigger than brown and black bears

    B) Can weigh up to 1,600lbs

    C) Have thick, white fur

    D) Are strong swimmers

3) Are becoming endangered

    A) Global warming decreases the amount of ice

    B) Bears have less time to hunt

1. What do polar bears look like?

_____

2. What do polar bears like to eat?

_____

3. Why are polar bears an endangered species?

_____

B Listen to a different version of the previous lecture, and say the answers out loud. ⊙ 2-02

1) Professor discusses monsoons

   A) Are annual weather phenomena
   B) Are heavy rains
   C) Occur in various places

2) Can be beneficial

   A) Supply 90% of India's water
   B) Essential for crops

3) Can be harmful

   A) Can cause flooding
   B) Inconvenience people in cities

4) Are hard to predict

1. What causes monsoons to occur in India?

   _____

2. How do monsoons benefit farmers?

   _____

3. Why are most monsoons in the northern hemisphere?

   _____

Listen to part of a conversation between a student and a student center employee. 2-03

1. **Why did the employee ask the student if he had a driver's license?**

    (A) She was worried that the employer had hired the wrong person.

    (B) She was worried that the student might not be able to do the job.

    (C) The job requires a lot of driving.

    (D) The student told her he preferred to be a taxi driver.

2. **According to the conversation, what does a media assistant do?**

    (A) Picks up and delivers movies, videos, and many edited films.

    (B) Usually works in an office.

    (C) Makes movies.

    (D) Travels to other countries to deliver things.

3. **Listen again to part of the conversation. Then answer the question.** 🎧

    What can be inferred from the woman's comments?

    (A) This is not the first time that Bestviews has hired a media assistant from the university.

    (B) Bestviews is a very successful business.

    (C) The job might be dangerous.

    (D) The student will be working primarily on educational films.

4. **Why does the student visit the student center?**

    (A) To schedule an interview for a job.

    (B) To find out some job requirements.

    (C) To receive the results of his application.

    (D) To ask questions about Bestviews.

5. **What will the student probably do next?**

    (A) Meet with Emily.

    (B) Contact his supervisor.

    (C) Start working at his job.

    (D) Find another job.

Listen to part of a lecture in an astronomy class. 🔘 2-04

Astronomy

1. Why did the professor mention how the Nile supplied the plains with water and rich soil?

   Ⓐ To show why the original Egyptian calendar was important.
   Ⓑ To show why the Egyptians needed another calendar.
   Ⓒ To show why the Egyptians needed a third calendar.
   Ⓓ To show that most Egyptians were farmers.

2. Why were the first two calendars NOT in sync?

   Ⓐ The Egyptians did not understand mathematics.
   Ⓑ One calendar was a few hours shorter than the other.
   Ⓒ The Egyptians did not have computers.
   Ⓓ One calendar was a few days shorter than the other.

3. Listen again to part of the lecture. Then answer the question. 🎧

   How did the original calendar become a more accurate predictor?

   Ⓐ The Egyptians calculated the duration of the Nile's floods.
   Ⓑ The Egyptians stopped using it to predict floods.
   Ⓒ The Egyptians began to use it only for predicting floods.
   Ⓓ The Egyptians started to use the stars to help with their predictions.

4. What aspect of calendars does the professor mainly discuss?

   Ⓐ The similarities between the Chinese and Egyptian calendars.
   Ⓑ The uses of the different calendars kept by the Egyptians.
   Ⓒ The manner in which the Egyptians calculated days and months.
   Ⓓ The development of the Egyptian lunar calendar.

5. According to the professor, what did the Egyptians use their calendars for? Choose 2 answers.

   Ⓐ Noting when to begin their days.
   Ⓑ For farming purposes.
   Ⓒ For predicting various weather changes.
   Ⓓ For keeping track of the reigns of all previous rulers.

6. What is the professor's opinion of the Egyptian calendar based on star movements?

   Ⓐ He thinks it was rather bizarre.
   Ⓑ He believes it was practical.
   Ⓒ He considers it too complicated.
   Ⓓ He thinks it was unnecessary.

Vocabulary Review

A Choose and write the correct word that matches each definition

camouflage	steady	initiate	reveal	respond
drenched	capable	gradually	extend	petition
anatomy	transparent	insulate	blend	ripples

1. _____ to disguise something

2. _____ very wet

3. _____ a mixture

4. _____ to start

5. _____ to answer

6. _____ able to be seen through

7. _____ to show or expose

8. _____ able to do something

9. _____ to provide a warm layer

10. _____ to make longer

11. _____ small waves

12. _____ slowly

13. _____ a list of names and signatures

14. _____ consistent

15. _____ a detailed description of a body

B Listen to the definitions, and fill in the blanks. Then choose the correct word. 🎧 ⊙ 2-05

polar bears	monsoon	seismic waves	Jupiter	Jovian planets

1. This weather phenomenon is a _____ that occurs when cool, moist air over the ocean reaches _____ above the Asian continent.

2. _____ are examples of these planets. Their exteriors are gaseous.

3. These waves move _____ whenever there is an earthquake or major explosion.

4. These large creatures are very comfortable living in _____.

5. This is _____ in the solar system.

54

Unit 3

Listening for Major Details

3 Listening for Major Details

Overview

■ Introduction

In order to answer detail questions correctly, you must both understand and remember various details and facts given in the listening passage. The details asked about are often related to the main idea. They may be examples or may expand upon the main topic in the form of supporting statements. The majority of questions asked about details are concerned with major, not minor, details.

■ Question Types

1. According to the professor, what is one way that X can affect Y?

2. What are X?

3. What resulted from the invention of the X?

4. According to the professor, what is the main problem with the X theory?

■ Useful Tips

• Be sure to take excellent notes with regards to details. Make good use of your notes on details.

• Listen very carefully to the major details, not the minor details, which are given in the passage.

• Answers to detail questions are often paraphrased sentences, not the exact words as they appeared in the passage.

• When you are not positive about the correct answer, look at the answer choices, and determine which of them most closely resembles the main idea of the passage.

Sample iBT Question

According to the professor, which part of the Statue of Liberty has a gold leaf coating?

Ⓐ The robe.
Ⓑ The torch flame.
Ⓒ The crown.
Ⓓ The stone tablet.

Script

The second monument I'd like to discuss is the Statue of Liberty. This monument, also known as Liberty Enlightening the World, is a statue of a woman dressed in a robe and wearing a crown while holding a stone tablet in her left hand and a flaming torch in her right hand that was given to the United States by the Parisian-based Franco-American Union in 1885. The statue was given to the United States by the French as a gesture of friendship and goodwill between the two nations. The Statue of Liberty stands on Liberty Island in New York Harbor as a welcome to all visitors and immigrants and returning Americans. If anyone has ever seen this monument, it is a welcoming sight to behold! The statue is made of pure copper, with the exception of the torch flame, which has a coating of gold leaf. Etched on the tablet that the woman is holding is the text July IV MDCCLXXVI, which was the date of the United States' Declaration of Independence, July 4, 1776. The Statue of Liberty was constructed by two Frenchmen, the sculptor Frederic Auguste Bartholdi and the architect Alexandre Gustave Eiffel, who was also the designer of the Eiffel Tower.

Correct Answer The correct response to the above question is (B). The statue is made of copper, but the torch flame has a coating of gold leaf.

Practice with Conversations

A Listen to part of a conversation between a student and an advisor. ⊙ 2-07

1. During the conversation, in what class did the student say he met his friend?

   Ⓐ Geology.
   Ⓑ Psychology.
   Ⓒ Chemistry.
   Ⓓ Anthropology.

2. What reason does Mr. Jones give the student for not being able to switch roommates?

   Ⓐ He forgot to get signed permission.
   Ⓑ It is the middle of a semester.
   Ⓒ His roommate refuses to switch.
   Ⓓ Mr. Jones does not like the student.

3. What is the likely outcome of this conversation?

   Ⓐ The student will try to convince his current roommate to be more understanding.
   Ⓑ The student's grades will suffer.
   Ⓒ The student will start studying in the library.
   Ⓓ The student's new roommate will be David.

• **upheaval (n)** a strong change • **exception (n)** a decision that is against the general rule • **signature (n)** a person's signed name on a document • **invite (v)** to ask a person to attend an event • **compromise (n)** the settlement of differences when two parties offer a change in their needs • **proof (n)** evidence that shows something is true
• **interruption (n)** something that causes a break in the middle of something

4. Listen to the conversation, and fill in the blanks to complete the conversation notes.

1) Student speaks with advisor
   A) Has problem with _____
      - Has different hours than roommate
      - Doesn't like roommate's _____
   B) Wants to change roommates
2) Advisor says is _____ to change
3) Student has already found _____
4) Advisor refuses
   A) Student complains that grades are _____ and can't study
   B) Advisor suggests studying in _____
5) Advisor agrees to _____ the roommate switch

5. Complete the following summary with the words given below.

A student goes to speak to his advisor because he is unhappy with his (1)_____.
The advisor asks the student what is wrong, and the student says that he wants to change roommates because the one he is currently living with keeps a different schedule than himself. The student complains that his roommate stays up late and (2)_____ when he is trying to sleep. This causes him to sleep (3)_____, so when he gets up in the morning to study, he is too tired. The student also complains that when he wishes to have friends over, his roommate is not as understanding and tends to complain. The student says that his studies are suffering and asks to switch roommates. The advisor tells the student that he is sorry but the college does not allow students to switch roommates (4)_____.
The student tells his advisor that he understands but he thinks he has found himself a perfect roommate – a student he met in (5)_____ who keeps the same schedule. The advisor considers this and says he will allow the student to change roommates if he gets (6)_____ from his friend and from the other roommates agreeing to this. The advisor concludes by pointing out that difficult living situations can teach the student a lot about compromising.

halfway through the semester	poorly	chemistry class
plays loud music	living situation	signatures

B   Listen to part of a conversation between a student and a professor. 2-08

1. What class is the student interested in taking for no credit?
   - (A) Modern Theater.
   - (B) Shakespeare.
   - (C) Theater History.
   - (D) Dance in Theater.

2. Why would the professor like the student to wait and take her class next semester?
   - (A) The professor would like her to be able to participate in class.
   - (B) The professor has no more room in his current class.
   - (C) The student will learn more in next semester's class.
   - (D) The college does not allow students to take classes for no credit.

3. What can be inferred from the conversation?
   - (A) The student is very irresponsible.
   - (B) The professor does not like the student.
   - (C) Major classes should be taken for credit.
   - (D) The student should take at least twenty credits every semester.

• **currently (ad)** at the present time • **secure (v)** to get hold of something • **audit (v)** to attend a class but not receive credit or a grade • **regarding (prep)** in relation with something else • **audience (n)** a group of people at an event • **participate (v)** to take part in something

4. Listen to the conversation, and fill in the blanks to complete the conversation notes.

1) Student goes to speak with professor
2) Wants to take his _____ class
3) Professor suggests she wait until _____
4) Student wants to _____ class
   A) Can attend class
   B) But does not get _____
5) Professor believes is not a good idea
   A) Cannot participate in _____
   B) Should get credit for _____
6) Student agrees to take class later

5. Complete the following summary with the words given below.

A student goes to her professor's office because she wishes to take the professor's (1)_____ _____ this semester even though she is already taking (2)_____. The professor tells the student that eighteen credits is already a lot of work and asks the student to wait until next semester to take the class. The student says she wants to be a (3)_____ _____ and worries that she should take the class now. The student asks the professor if she can audit this semester's theater history class for no credit. The professor says that she can although he wonders if the student will be okay with the fact that she (4)_____ to participate in the discussions during class. The professor also points out that the school recommends that they take all of their major classes for credit. The student says she did not consider this and decides to take the theater history class for credit the (5)_____.

following semester	will not be able	theater history class
theater history major	eighteen credits	

C Listen to part of a conversation between a student and a registration clerk. 2-09

1. **How much was the student's library fine?**

   (A) Fifty cents.
   (B) Five dollars.
   (C) Six dollars.
   (D) Ten dollars.

2. **Why must the student hurry to the library to get his receipt?**

   (A) The library clerk has an appointment she needs to get to.
   (B) In-person registration ends at 4:00 p.m.
   (C) The library clerk hates giving out receipts.
   (D) Daniel needs to have the receipt by the morning.

3. **Listen again to part of the conversation. Then answer the question.**

   What does the clerk imply when he says this?

   (A) He thinks the student is lying.
   (B) He thinks the student usually returns books late to the library.
   (C) He thinks the student might be confused about the fine.
   (D) He thinks the student is confused about the location of the library.

- **specify (v)** to mention in detail • **distinctly (ad)** unmistakably • **reminisce (v)** to remember past experiences
- **receipt (n)** written acknowledgment of having paid for something • **fine (n)** something paid as a penalty
- **update (v)** to make something current

4. Listen to the conversation, and fill in the blanks to complete the conversation notes.

> 1) Student has trouble registering for class
>   A) Cannot use _____
>   B) Wants to know the problem
> 2) Clerk says student has unpaid _____
> 3) Student claims to have paid
>   A) Clerk says _____ record is not in the system
>   B) Student realizes that library clerk did not record it
> 4) Must register for classes today
> 5) Student decides to go to library and pay _____
> 6) Will register later from _____

5. Complete the following summary with the words given below.

A student approaches the registration clerk because he is having trouble registering online. Whenever the student tries to (1)_____, he receives a notice that he must see a clerk to proceed. The registration clerk checks his computer and finds that the reason the student cannot register is that (2)_____. The student tells the clerk that he paid the fine and that the incident stands out in his mind because the woman he paid was someone he knew in his past. The clerk tells the student that the only way to resolve the issue is to (3)_____ from the library, but he (4)_____ because in-person registration (5)_____ and online registration (6)_____. To give himself a little more time, the student decides he will get the library receipt after dinner and then (7)_____.

must hurry	he has not paid a library fine	ends at 4:00 p.m.
register online	get a receipt	complete his registration
ends at 10:00 p.m.		

D Listen to part of a conversation between a student and a professor. 2-10

1. What is the first reason the student gives the professor for doing so poorly in his class?

   Ⓐ She did not receive many of the assignments.
   Ⓑ She is having trouble understanding the concepts.
   Ⓒ She has a new boyfriend and has been distracted.
   Ⓓ She dislikes physics.

2. What did the professor just do recently that could help the student?

   Ⓐ He cleaned out his office.
   Ⓑ He bought new textbooks for the students.
   Ⓒ He hired a part-time tutor.
   Ⓓ He cut down on the amount of homework assignments.

3. What can be inferred from the conversation?

   Ⓐ If you are having trouble in a class, you should tell the professor as soon as possible.
   Ⓑ Lab groups never work out.
   Ⓒ The professor's class was too difficult.
   Ⓓ The student should drop her physics class.

• **remedy (v)** to mend or fix • **salvage (v)** to save • **concept (n)** an idea • **extend (v)** to lengthen • **curious (a)** eager to learn or know • **suffer (v)** to endure pain or grief • **familiar (a)** easy to recognize because of prior experience

4. Listen to the conversation, and fill in the blanks to complete the conversation notes.

1) Student meets professor
2) Student has problems in _____ class
   A) Professor suggests getting _____
3) Student has problem with _____
4) Professor suggests _____
5) Student apologizes for not asking for help sooner

5. Complete the following summary with the words given below.

A physics professor scheduled a meeting with one of his students because he was
(1)_____ in his class. The professor asked his student if she could list
any reasons why she thought she might be having so much trouble in his class. The student
admitted that she was having trouble (2)_____, and, even though she
was staying up late to study, she was still doing poorly. The professor told her that he had just
hired a (3)_____ who would be more than happy to help her. The student then went
on to say that she was also having trouble with her (4)_____. They were leaving her to
do parts of the lab that she did not understand on her own and would then (5)_____ with
her efforts. The professor promised to switch her to a different lab group and also allowed her to
hand in her (6)_____ at a later date so she would have a chance to catch
up on the material.

part-time tutor   upcoming physics project
lab partners   learning the new concepts
become upset   concerned about her grades

Practice with Lectures

A   Listen to part of a lecture in a dramatics class.   ⊙ 2-11

Dramatics

1. In what city was the Globe Theater built?

    (A) Greece.

    (B) London.

    (C) Delphi.

    (D) Rome.

2. Why was it important to have the amphitheater be round in shape?

    (A) To help harness the sound.

    (B) To allow the audience to enter and leave quickly .

    (C) To help cut the cost of admission.

    (D) To keep the weather from interfering.

3. How does the professor organize the information about theaters?

    (A) From humorous to informative.

    (B) Not seriously.

    (C) From complex to simple.

    (D) In chronological order.

• **balcony (n)** a raised gallery in a theater   • **slope (n)** ground that has a natural incline or decline   • **spectator (n)** a person who watches   • **resonate (v)** to cause to sound again   • **harness (v)** to gain control of   • **octagonal (a)** eight-sided   • **erect (v)** to raise   • **drawback (n)** a disadvantage   • **replica (n)** a copy

4. Listen to the lecture, and fill in the blanks to complete the lecture notes.

1) Professor discusses _____

2) Originated in _____

3) First theaters were _____
   A) Built into _____
   B) Were round
   C) _____ and Theater of Dionysus
   D) Couldn't be used in _____ weather

4) William Shakespeare's Globe Theater was famous
   A) Was much improved over _____
   B) Burned down but was later rebuilt

5. Complete the following summary with the words given below.

(1) _____ and Western drama were first developed by the (2)_____. The Greeks constructed what were known as (3)_____. These were (4)_____ in shape with high wooden seats built into the (5)_____ so that an audience could better see and hear a performance. Two of the earliest and most famous Greek theaters were the theater at Delphi, known as the Attic Theater, and the Theater of Dionysus in (6)_____. The Greeks used very few (7)_____ for their dramas, and the plays were always performed in the (8)_____. By Elizabethan times, however, theater architecture had evolved. Shakespeare's Globe Theater, for instance, was (9)_____ in shape with three-story-high walls and an elevated stage. The (10)_____ was for standing room only. Some of the developments featured such things as (11)_____ on the stage floor and rigging in the wings. In 1613, fire damaged the Globe Theater, but, during the mid 1990s, an exact replica was made in the city of (12)_____.

trapdoors	London	octagonal
ancient Greeks	Athens	theater architecture
props	open air	hillsides
pit	amphitheaters	round

B   Listen to part of a lecture in a literature class. ⊙ 2-12

Literature

1. What novel by Pearl S. Buck was made into a motion picture?

    Ⓐ *The Patriot*.
    Ⓑ *The Child Who Never Grew*.
    Ⓒ *Chinese Culture*.
    Ⓓ *The Good Earth*.

2. According to the professor, where did Pearl S. Buck spend the better part of the first forty years of her life?

    Ⓐ In Nanking.
    Ⓑ In China.
    Ⓒ In Pennsylvania.
    Ⓓ At Cornell University.

3. Listen again to part of the lecture. Then answer the question.

   What did Pearl S. Buck likely mean when she said this? 🎧

    Ⓐ She was not religious.
    Ⓑ She did not trust her fellow human beings.
    Ⓒ She thought that humans were naturally greedy.
    Ⓓ She had experienced many bad relationships in her life.

• **interpreter (n)** a person who translates languages   • **hysterectomy (n)** surgery to remove a woman's uterus
• **impoverished (a)** very poor   • **humanitarian (a)** having concern for other people   • **span (v)** to extend over or across   • **tutor (n)** a person who instructs another privately   • **seek (v)** to go in search of something or someone
• **candor (n)** sincerity; honesty

4. Listen to the lecture, and fill in the blanks to complete the lecture notes.

1) Professor discusses _____
   A) Born in West Virginia but moved to _____
   B) Spent almost _____ years in China
   C) Went to college, got married, and had different jobs

2) Had an eventful private life

3) Published _____
   A) Sold _____ copies in its first years
   B) Describes life of Wang Lung

4) Won the _____ for literature

5) Published over eighty works

5. Complete the following summary with the words given below.

Pearl S. Buck was a great American literary figure who was born in West Virginia to two (1)_____. (2)_____ after her birth, Pearl's family moved to (3)_____. Pearl grew up speaking both (4)_____and Chinese, and in the (5)_____, she enrolled at Randolph-Macon Women's College in (6)_____. In 1917, Pearl married John Lossing Buck, and the two of them settled in (7)_____ in China, where Pearl worked as a (8)_____ and also acted as an interpreter for her husband. Pearl and John had two children. Carol, their first child, was born with considerable birth defects, and their second daughter, Janice, (9)_____ since Pearl underwent a hysterectomy after the birth of Carol. Pearl and John's marriage did not last, and in the year 1935, she divorced her husband and married her (10)_____, Richard Walsh. They moved back to the United States. In the year 1931, she wrote her most famous novel, *The Good Earth*, which sold nearly two million copies and earned her the (11)_____. Pearl continued writing until her death in 1973. During her life, she wrote over eighty works of literature and even won the Nobel Prize.

Anhwei Province	publisher	three months
China	year 1910	Presbyterian missionaries
Virginia	English	teacher
Pulitzer Prize	was adopted	

C   Listen to part of a lecture in a Latin class. 🔘 2-13

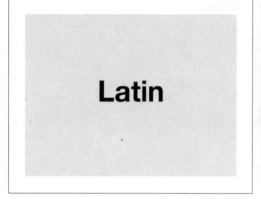

1. **What two consonants can sometimes be used as vowels?**

   Ⓐ A and C.

   Ⓑ Y and W.

   Ⓒ D and T.

   Ⓓ X and W.

2. **Why does the letter I have a long sound in the word pine?**

   Ⓐ There is no letter S in the word.

   Ⓑ The P is silent.

   Ⓒ There is an E at the end of the word.

   Ⓓ I always makes a long sound.

3. **What is the Etruscan alphabet?**

   Ⓐ It is a complicated alphabet with 38 characters.

   Ⓑ It is another name for the Roman alphabet.

   Ⓒ It is an early form of the Latin alphabet with 23 characters.

   Ⓓ It is the most widely used alphabet in the world.

• **pronunciation (n)** the act of saying a word   • **inscription (n)** words impressed, cut, or painted onto stone
• **exception (n)** something that does not follow a general rule   • **frustrate (v)** to disappoint or thwart   • **convey (v)** to communicate   • **distinct (a)** not identical; separate   • **observation (n)** the act of noticing something

4. Listen to the lecture, and fill in the blanks to complete the lecture notes.

1) Professor discusses _____
   A) Also called _____
   B) Based on Etruscan alphabet
   C) Has _____ letters
      - Five vowels
      - Twenty-one _____
2) Were no long or short vowels in Latin
3) Describes rules for _____
4) Are both _____ and _____ to the rules

5. Complete the following summary with the words given below.

The Latin alphabet, also known as the (1)_____, initially contained only (2)_____ letters but later developed into the modern alphabet, which has (3)_____ letters. Each letter in the alphabet represents a phoneme, the (4)_____ of sound within a language. The modern alphabet is made up of (5)_____ vowels and twenty-one consonants, although the letters Y and W can sometimes (6)_____. Each of the vowels can exhibit either a (7)_____ sound, depending on how the word is spelled or if the word ends with an E. Consonants can exhibit different sounds as well, depending on which letters precede and follow them in a word.

smallest unit	five	act as vowels
twenty-three	Roman alphabet	twenty-six
long or short		

D   Listen to part of a lecture in an entomology class. ⊙ 2-14

1. **What is another name for swarmer white ants?**

   Ⓐ Workers.
   Ⓑ Alates.
   Ⓒ Termites.
   Ⓓ Nymphs.

2. **Why must worker white ants feed all the other white ants?**

   Ⓐ The worker ants have the largest appetites.
   Ⓑ Soldier white ants do not have time to eat.
   Ⓒ The worker white ants have special bacteria in their stomach.
   Ⓓ The king white ant forces the worker white ants to feed him.

3. **What can be inferred from the lecture?**

   Ⓐ All white ants should be exterminated, even in the wilderness.
   Ⓑ White ants are better than carpenter ants.
   Ⓒ Soldier white ants are more important than queen white ants.
   Ⓓ White ants are highly organized insects that can be very destructive.

• **subterranean (a)** below ground   • **nymph (n)** the young of an insect   • **regurgitate (v)** to expel undigested food
• **pheromone (n)** a chemical that attracts the opposite sex   • **exterminator (n)** a person that eliminates insects
• **refrain (v)** to stop   • **considerable (a)** worthy of attention   • **gather (v)** to bring together in one group
• **groom (v)** to clean or otherwise tend to something   • **invade (v)** to enter forcefully

4. Listen to the lecture, and fill in the blanks to complete the lecture notes.

1) Professor discusses _____
   A) Is another name for _____
   B) Resembles ant but is closer to _____
2) Live in colonies
   A) Different kinds of _____
   B) Have different duties
      - Workers feed others and care for the nest
      - Queen lays _____
      - Soldiers _____ the nest
      - Alates become kings and queens in future colonies
3) Are difficult to _____
4) Can cause much damage to structures

5. Complete the following summary with the words given below.

White ants are a form of (1)_____ that are mainly found in Australia and feed on (2)_____, which causes them to live either underground or (3)_____. They live in a highly organized colony with each different type of white ant serving a particular function within the nest. The king and queen white ant are responsible only for the (4)_____ _____, or nymphs, as they are called. Soldier white ants are responsible for protecting the colony from intruders. Worker white ants have many tasks, from building and maintaining the colony to (5)_____ all the termites. It is the worker white ants' responsibility to feed all the others because they are the only white ants to have special (6)_____ _____ in their stomach. Finally, the swarmers, or alates, are the future kings and queens of other colonies, as they have reproductive capabilities. White ants cause considerable (7)_____ to buildings and homes in Australia. The best way to deal with white ants is to steer clear of them in the wild and to call an (8)_____ if they are in a home or office.

digestive bacteria	cellulose	damage
reproduction of young	termite	exterminator
in damp timber	grooming and feeding	

Integrated Listening & Speaking

A Listen to a different version of the previous lecture, and say the answers out loud. 🔊 2-15

1) Professor discusses white ant
   A) Is another name for termite
   B) Resembles ant but is closer to cockroach

2) Live in colonies
   A) Different kinds of termites
   B) Have different duties
      - Workers feed others and care for the nest
      - Queen lays eggs
      - Soldiers protect the nest
      - Alates become kings and queens in future colonies

3) Are difficult to exterminate

4) Can cause much damage to structures

1. Why do white ants cause so much destruction to homes and buildings?

   _____

2. How would you describe the physical characteristics of a white ant?

   _____

3. What is a responsibility of the soldier white ants?

   _____

B   Listen to a different version of the previous lecture, and say the answers out loud. 🔊 2-16

1) Professor discusses development of theater

2) Originated in ancient Greece

3) First theaters were amphitheaters
   A) Built into hillside
   B) Were round
   C) Attic Theater and Theater of Dionysus
   D) Couldn't be used in bad weather

4) William Shakespeare's Globe Theater was famous
   A) Was much improved over amphitheaters
   B) Burned down but was later rebuilt

1. What is an advantage of having round and octagonal-shaped theaters?

    _____

2. Where is the Globe Theater located?

    _____

3. In ancient Greece, where did the audience sit when they were watching a performance?

    _____

Listen to part of a conversation between a student and a professor.

1. According to the professor, what is one way to examine the wedding scene in the play *A Midsummer Night's Dream*?

   Ⓐ Look at another play with a wedding in it.

   Ⓑ Compare it to factual information about marriage traditions.

   Ⓒ Compare this play to others by William Shakespeare.

   Ⓓ Imagine if there were no wedding scene in the play.

2. What kind of play is *A Midsummer Night's Dream*?

   Ⓐ A history.

   Ⓑ A comedy.

   Ⓒ A tragedy.

   Ⓓ A romance.

3. Listen again to part of the conversation. Then answer the question.

   What does the character Bottom convince his friends to do?

   Ⓐ Watch the 1999 film version of *A Midsummer Night's Dream*.

   Ⓑ Make wedding cakes for the other characters.

   Ⓒ Write an essay about Shakespeare.

   Ⓓ Put on a play.

4. What is the professor's attitude toward the student?

   Ⓐ She is very encouraging.

   Ⓑ She is not very helpful.

   Ⓒ She is somewhat aloof.

   Ⓓ She is rather critical.

5. Why does the professor mention Michael Hoffman?

   Ⓐ To name the author of a book on Shakespeare she recommends.

   Ⓑ To declare that his work on Athenian Law is critical.

   Ⓒ To criticize his interpretation of Shakespeare's works.

   Ⓓ To associate him with a cinematic production of a Shakespearean play.

Listen to part of a lecture in a geology class. 2-18

Geology

1. **In what year was the construction of the Erie Canal completed?**

   Ⓐ 1818

   Ⓑ 1825

   Ⓒ 1852

   Ⓓ 1925

2. **What is the function of a lock in a canal system?**

   Ⓐ It allows boats to go diagonally through the canal.

   Ⓑ It allows boats to go uphill and downhill.

   Ⓒ It is a place to dock a boat.

   Ⓓ It is another name for a captain on a ship.

3. **Listen again to part of the lecture. Then answer the question.**

   A vessel can be no wider than how many feet to pass through the Erie Canal?

   Ⓐ 4

   Ⓑ 30

   Ⓒ 40

   Ⓓ 44

4. **What is the main topic of the lecture?**

   Ⓐ The creation of the canal.

   Ⓑ The function of the locks in the canal.

   Ⓒ The importance of the canal.

   Ⓓ A physical description of the canal.

5. **Why does the professor explain the canal's dimensions?**

   Ⓐ To show the maximum size for any boat passing through it.

   Ⓑ To comment on the size of boats built in the nineteenth century.

   Ⓒ To explain some of the engineering feats it took to build the canal.

   Ⓓ To account for the fact that the canal is still being used in modern times.

6. **Why does the professor mention the waterways in New York?**

   Ⓐ To prove that the Erie Canal's construction was important.

   Ⓑ To prove why shipping was so important to New York.

   Ⓒ To explain how Lake Erie and the Hudson River are connected.

   Ⓓ To note how extensive the Erie Canal actually is.

Vocabulary Review

Choose and write the correct word that matches each definition.

nymph	brilliance	reminisce	upheaval	gather
drawback	harness	hysterectomy	tutor	unique
slope	impoverished	invade	remedy	salvage

1. _____ to save

2. _____ to remember past experiences

3. _____ very poor

4. _____ surgery to remove a woman's uterus

5. _____ ground that has a natural incline or decline

6. _____ to gain control of

7. _____ the young of an insect

8. _____ a strong change

9. _____ solitary in type

10. _____ to mend or fix

11. _____ excellence

12. _____ a disadvantage

13. _____ to enter forcefully

14. _____ a person who instructs another privately

15. _____ to bring together in a group

B Listen to the definitions, and fill in the blanks. Then choose the correct word. 🎧 ⊙2-19

Globe Theater	subterranean	consonant	Pearl S. Buck	amphitheater

1. This is one of _____ characters in the Latin alphabet.

2. This was built _____ with three stories. It was first built in London.

3. This term means living _____ and is a characteristic of the white ant.

4. This was _____ first created by the ancient Greeks.

5. This woman won the Pulitzer Prize for her work _____.

80

PART 2

Pragmatic Understanding

Pragmatic Understanding questions test understanding of certain features that go beyond basic comprehension. Generally, two question types test pragmatic understanding: Function of What Is Said and Speaker's Attitude. Function of What Is Said questions test whether you can understand the underlying intentions of what is said. Speaker's Attitude questions test whether you can understand a speaker's attitude or opinion that has not been directly expressed. Pragmatic Understanding questions typically involve a replay of a small portion of the listening passage.

Unit 4

Understanding the Function of What Is Said

4 Understanding the Function of What Is Said

Overview

■ Introduction

These questions determine whether or not you understand the speaker's intentions. You must often determine the speaker's intentions by understanding the context of the passage surrounding the sentence in question. By analyzing the passage as a whole, you can determine the speaker's intentions. These questions typically replay a part of the listening passage.

■ Question Types

1. What does the professor imply when he says this? (replay)

2. What can be inferred from the professor's response to the student? (replay)

3. What is the purpose of the woman's response? (replay)

4. Why does the student say this? (replay)

■ Useful Tips

- Practice recognizing the unspoken meanings of words.

- Make notes on the context of the passage.

- Recognize what tone of voice the speakers are using in the passage.

Sample iBT Question

Listen again to part of the conversation. Then answer the question.
What can be inferred from the professor's response to the student?

- (A) He is happy the student's mother made him work at the orphanage.
- (B) He is pleased to have met the student's mother at the orphanage.
- (C) He does not want the student to disappoint his mother again.
- (D) He believes the student should work at the orphanage some more.

Script

M1: Hmm… You also worked at an orphanage for two summers?

M2: Well, ah… actually, that, ah… that was a volunteer job. My mother works there. She made me do that.

M1: Well, thank God for your mother! When you go home tonight, give her a big hug. And then tomorrow tell the interviewers you worked at an orphanage. What did you do there?

M2: Well, I helped them take the children on field trips and special outings. Also, I helped organize special events at the orphanage. For example, baseball games, soccer games, and birthday parties. Some of the children were disabled, so I taught them to play wheelchair basketball. Sometimes, I took the blind children for a walk.

Correct Answer The answer to the above question is (A). The professor is happy the student's mother made him work at the orphanage because now he has some valuable work experience.

Practice with Conversations

A   Listen to part of a conversation between a student and a professor. ⊙ 2-21

1.   Listen again to part of the conversation. Then answer the question.

   What can be inferred when the student says this? 🎧

   Ⓐ He hates making business cards.
   Ⓑ He thinks making business cards requires no skill.
   Ⓒ He does not know what a business card is.
   Ⓓ He is very lazy.

2.   **What can be inferred about the student?**

   Ⓐ He thinks he is smarter than the professor.
   Ⓑ He does not always follow directions.
   Ⓒ He has already designed a business card.
   Ⓓ He feels the professor misunderstands him.

3.   Listen again to part of the conversation. Then answer the question. 🎧

   What does the student mean when he says this? 🎧

   Ⓐ He does not want to waste time designing a business card.
   Ⓑ He thinks the professor does not like him.
   Ⓒ The student is trying to get out of doing a difficult project.
   Ⓓ The student thinks business cards are quite beneficial.

• **beneficial (a)** helpful   • **conduct (v)** to do   • **design (v)** to create or draw something   • **elaborate (a)** having lots of details or information   • **essential (a)** required; needed   • **purchaser (n)** a buyer   • **simultaneously (ad)** at the same time

4. Listen to the conversation, and fill in the blanks to complete the conversation notes.

    1) Professor wants to see student's _____
    2) Student did _____ instead
    3) Professor says student did _____
    4) Student thinks business cards are _____
    5) Professor disagrees
       A) Cards are good for _____
       B) Are basic but _____
    6) Student agrees to do the business card assignment

5. Complete the following summary with the words given below.

    In this conversation, the professor asked the student if he could look at the student's business card. But the student was working on (1)_____. He was designing a cover for a (2)_____. The professor told the student that the assignment was to design a basic business card. The student suggested that (3)_____ was perhaps a waste of time and that he wanted to work on something more elaborate. He said that business cards were not (4)_____. The professor replied that business cards were a valuable marketing tool and also very important for establishing contacts and for (5)_____. The professor insisted that the student work on the business card and told the student there would be plenty of opportunities later on to work on (6)_____. The student agreed to do so.

designing business cards	networking
another project	a project of his choice
an important marketing tool	car magazine

B Listen to part of a conversation between a student and an administrator. ⊙ 2-22

1. Listen again to part of the conversation. Then answer the question.

   What can be inferred from the administrator's response to the student?

   Ⓐ She expects the student to attend orientation.
   Ⓑ She believes the student has no money.
   Ⓒ She thinks the student loves parties.
   Ⓓ She thinks the student is a senior.

2. Listen again to part of the conversation. Then answer the question.

   Why does the student say this?

   Ⓐ To explain that she is not inexperienced.
   Ⓑ To show the administrator that she needs lots of help.
   Ⓒ To tell the administrator about her old school.
   Ⓓ To get her credits transferred from her old school.

3. What can be inferred from the conversation?

   Ⓐ The student might begin studying before the semester starts.
   Ⓑ The student has already graduated from another university.
   Ⓒ The administrator attended the same orientation program when she was a student.
   Ⓓ Most transfer students do not attend orientation.

---

* **adjust (v)** to get used to; to become accustomed to • **arrange (v)** to organize something in a certain way
* **coupon book (n)** a book with many coupons in it • **freshman (n)** a first-year student • **itinerary (n)** a schedule
* **orientation program (n)** a program for new members • **perhaps (ad)** maybe; possibly • **syllabus (n)** an outline for a course • **transfer student (n)** a student who has changed schools

4. Listen to the conversation, and fill in the blanks to complete the conversation notes.

    1) Student visits administrator
       A) Asks for _____ and _____
       B) Administrator gives hero a big package
    2) Student says won't be around for _____
       A) Administrator describes events
       B) But student has _____
    3) Student says is _____ with campus already
    4) Administrator offers to provide extra help

5. Complete the following summary with the words given below.

    An administrator gave a student a package containing various items, (1)_____ _____ for the orientation program and an orientation itinerary. Upon hearing about the (2)_____, the student informed the administrator that she would not be going to the program. The administrator was very surprised to hear this because, in her view, the program was very valuable. The student explained to the administrator that she had already (3)_____ during orientation week and that it would be impossible for her to attend. She also advised the administrator that her brother, who graduated from the same university, could show her (4)_____ if necessary. Because the student could not attend the orientation, the administrator agreed to (5)_____ whatever helpful information she could get to help the student prepare for the (6)_____.

around campus	booked a vacation	including a name tag
gather	orientation	upcoming semester

C Listen to part of a conversation between a student and a professor. 2-23

1. Listen again to part of the conversation. Then answer the question.

   What can be inferred about the student?

   (A) She presumes that the professor is unaware that her major is not psychology.
   (B) She enjoys the classes that she is taking on European banking this semester.
   (C) She had once majored in psychology but changed her major to commerce.
   (D) She intends to take more banking classes when she goes to study in France.

2. What is the purpose of the student's visit to the professor?

   (A) The student is hoping for help in finding a job in France.
   (B) The student must drop the class because of her trip to France.
   (C) The student wants to ask the professor about his experience in France.
   (D) The student is having a serious problem in the professor's class.

3. What is the likely outcome of this conversation?

   (A) The professor will ask his friend how the student should get in touch with him.
   (B) The student will not have any contacts in France when she goes there.
   (C) The student will call Frank right away.
   (D) The student will not be able to go to France.

- **complain (v)** to indicate unhappiness or displeasure • **contact (v)** to speak with or write to • **hook up with (v)** to connect with; to meet • **major (n)** an area of specialized study • **mention (v)** to say • **recognize (v)** to remember having seen something • **suggestion (n)** recommendation • **wonder (v)** to ask oneself a question • **wonderful (a)** very good

4. Listen to the conversation, and fill in the blanks to complete the conversation notes.

> 1) Student visits professor's office
>
> 2) Says is looking for job in _____
>   A) Knows professor lived in France
>   B) Wants help from professor
>   C) Wants to work at _____
>
> 3) Professor doesn't know _____
>
> 4) Professor knows _____ who worked in France
>   A) Thinks friend may help
>   B) Offers to give _____

5. Complete the following summary with the words given below.

(1) _____ that she was planning to look for a job in France. The professor told her that (2) _____. He asked her what kind of job she was looking for. She replied that she wanted a banking job. He told her that (3) _____ were difficult work. But the student was (4) _____, was studying European banking, and could speak French. However, she needed advice on where she could stay in Paris and how (5) _____ there. The professor told her that he couldn't answer those two questions but said he would contact his friend, a businessman in France, and (6) _____ for the student to contact him.

arrange	banking jobs
he lived in France as a teenager	she could find a job
a student told her professor	a commerce major

D Listen to part of a conversation between a student and a janitor. ⊙ 3-01

1. Listen again to part of the conversation. Then answer the question.

    What can be inferred from this part of the conversation?

    Ⓐ The student is in no hurry.
    Ⓑ The file is no longer in the building.
    Ⓒ The janitor is unwilling to admit that he has seen the student before.
    Ⓓ The student is desperate to get into the building.

2. Why did the student not use her passport to enter the building?

    Ⓐ It was in her purse.
    Ⓑ Her passport had expired.
    Ⓒ It was in the dormitory.
    Ⓓ The janitor insisted that she had to show her ID card.

3. What can be inferred from the conversation?

    Ⓐ The student had her purse stolen.
    Ⓑ The janitor does not want to make any mistakes.
    Ⓒ The janitor thinks the student is probably a thief.
    Ⓓ The student is trying to steal a file.

• **foyer (n)** an entrance hall • **ID card (n)** an identification card • **retrieve (v)** to go back and get something one has forgotten • **temporary (a)** lasting for a short period of time; not permanent • **urgent (a)** important that needs to be done immediately • **appreciate (v)** to be thankful for • **attend (v)** to be at; to go to • **proper (a)** correct; appropriate • **strict (a)** inflexible; not lenient

92

4. Listen to the conversation, and fill in the blanks to complete the conversation notes.

    1) Janitor won't let student in building without _____
    2) Student lost _____ with ID card in it
    3) Needs _____ in building
    4) Janitor requires proper ID like _____ or _____
    5) Student offers to give ID number and go in with _____
    6) Janitor accepts offer

5. Complete the following summary with the words given below.

    A student tried to enter a building to (1)_____. However, the janitor would not let her into the building because she didn't have her ID card. (2)_____ _____ she had lost her purse and the ID card was in the purse. The janitor said she could use (3)_____, but the student said her driver's license was (4)_____, too. Then the janitor suggested that she get her passport, but the student said that the passport was in (5)_____ and she couldn't get into the dormitory without her ID card. (6)_____ _____, the janitor agreed to let the student into building if she gave him her ID number and she got (7)_____ with an ID card to go in with her.

retrieve an important file	the dormitory	in her purse
the student told him	another person	eventually
her driver's license		

VOLUME   HELP   OK   NEXT

A   Listen to part of a lecture in a literature class. ⊙ 3-02

Literature

1.   Listen again to part of the lecture. Then answer the question.

     What does the professor imply when he says this? 🎧

     Ⓐ Wordsworth was a satirical poet.
     Ⓑ Wordsworth created a new trend in poetry.
     Ⓒ Wordsworth was a hopeless romantic.
     Ⓓ Wordsworth was influenced by a new trend in poetry.

2.   Which theme would typify romanticist poetry?

     Ⓐ Death.
     Ⓑ Love.
     Ⓒ Nature.
     Ⓓ Politics.

3.   Why does the professor mention *To a Butterfly*?

     Ⓐ To name one of Wordsworth's best poems.
     Ⓑ To contrast it with the poem *Rainbow*.
     Ⓒ To state a typical example of Wordsworth's work.
     Ⓓ To give an example of a romanticist poem.

• **aesthetic (a)** relating to beauty   • **ascend (v)** to climb or go up   • **genre (n)** a kind of art or style   • **leap (v)** to jump
• **major (a)** main; most important   • **transcend (v)** to go through or beyond   • **typify (v)** to do what is normal, usual, or expected   • **vividly (ad)** clearly

4. Listen to the lecture, and fill in the blanks to complete the lecture notes.

1) Professor reads _____ to class
   A) Students like it
   B) Is about _____
2) Is poem by William Wordsworth
   A) Not _____
   B) _____ genre
3) Describes romanticism
   A) _____ movement
   B) Nature is healing and spiritual force
4) Gives titles of other similar poems

5. Complete the following summary with the words given below.

The professor read a poem to his students. The poem was *Rainbow*, written by William Wordsworth, a (1)_____ who began writing in the late 18th century. The poem typifies the romanticists' style in that (2)_____. Romanticism was a back-to-nature movement. The poems were (3)_____ and quite vivid in their descriptions of nature and its beauty. This (4)_____ the previous genre, which was satirical and placed more emphases on (5)_____ and less on emotion and nature. Wordsworth himself lived in a lake area, where he spent most of his (6)_____ enjoying nature. His love for nature undoubtedly influenced his writing style.

contradicted	it describes nature	romanticist
adulthood	truth and reason	emotional

B Listen to part of a lecture in a geology class. 3-03

Geology

1. Listen again to part of the lecture. Then answer the question.

   What can be inferred about the professor when he says this?

   (A) He does not enjoy the hot weather of the Nile.
   (B) He is planning another trip to the Amazon soon.
   (C) He enjoys spending time outside of his office.
   (D) He would like to take his students on a trip to the Nile.

2. Listen again to part of the lecture. Then answer the question.

   What does the professor imply when he says this?

   (A) The Amazon River is more easily accessible than the Nile.
   (B) The Nile River is not a very interesting place to visit.
   (C) The Amazon is much less expensive to visit.
   (D) The Nile is the longest river in the world.

3. What can be inferred from the lecture?

   (A) The professor has been to Nigeria in Africa.
   (B) The professor has been to Antarctica.
   (C) The professor has been to China.
   (D) The professor has been to the North Pole.

> • **basin (n)** the entire area of a river, including nearby land and streams • **canopy (n)** a covering • **chilling (a)** scary • **consider (v)** to think about • **creature (n)** a type of life form • **ecosystem (n)** an entire community of living organisms in a certain area • **electrifying (a)** very exciting • **immense (a)** very many or very much • **species (n)** a type of plant, animal, or insect • **varied (a)** having different types

4. Listen to the lecture, and fill in the blanks to complete the lecture notes.

1) Professor compares _____ and _____ Rivers   A) Has done work in both places
                                                  B) _____ students to visit the Amazon

2) Describes the Amazon   A) Has _____
                          B) Has much _____ of life
                          C) Has a varied _____

3) Describes animals there   A) Jaguar – large, powerful cat
                             B) Giant otter – _____ long
                             C) Piranhas, dolphins, and anacondas

4) Has thick _____   A) Many kinds of trees
                           B) Some are very tall

5. Complete the following summary with the words given below.

The Amazon River is (1)_____ in the world, but the Amazon basin and its (2)_____ are the largest on the planet. It is an extremely interesting place to visit and contains more life than any other place on Earth. This can be contrasted with the Nile River. Although the Nile is longer, it has less wildlife and less plant life. It's (3)_____ mainly by dry desert. The Amazon is home to 500 species of mammals, one third of the world's bird population, hundreds of reptiles, 175 different kinds of lizards, up to 300 million types of insects, and (4)_____. The trees are so dense that their treetops form a canopy. The Amazon is home to such (5)_____ as the jaguar, the most powerful cat in the western hemisphere, 20 species of piranha, 300-pound dolphins, and the anaconda. The treetop (6)_____ is nine times bigger than Texas and home to millions of (7)_____. Some scientists believe this canopy alone may contain half of the world's animal species!

canopy	undiscovered species	creatures
surrounded	the second longest river	immense vegetation
tropical rain forest		

C Listen to part of a lecture in a culture class. ⊙ 3-04

Culture

1. Listen again to part of the lecture. Then answer the question.

   What can be inferred from the professor's comments when he says this? ∩

   Ⓐ The professor is a Native American.
   Ⓑ The professor is a Native Canadian.
   Ⓒ The professor can imitate snakes and buffalos.
   Ⓓ Nature has a continuing impact on native North American culture.

2. Listen again to part of the lecture. Then answer the question.

   Why does the student ask this? ∩

   Ⓐ She wants to know if natives can control the weather.
   Ⓑ She is comparing natives to their image in Western movies.
   Ⓒ She wants to learn how to do a rain dance.
   Ⓓ She thinks native dances are silly and foolish.

3. Listen again to part of the lecture. Then answer the question. ∩

   What can be inferred about the student when she says this? ∩

   Ⓐ She is very knowledgeable about Native Americans.
   Ⓑ She is surprised there are still so many Native Americans.
   Ⓒ She is most interested in the diets of Native Americans.
   Ⓓ She wants to learn more about Native American powwows.

   • **assimilate (v)** to become the same as others • **attire (n)** clothing • **imitate (v)** to act like someone or something else • **indigenous (a)** native • **mainstream (n)** the main group in a population • **misconception (n)** a misunderstanding based on false information • **traditional (a)** of old style

4. Listen to the lecture, and fill in the blanks to complete the lecture notes.

1) Professor discusses _____
   A) Student thinks doesn't exist anymore
   B) Professor disagrees
2) Describes _____
   A) Shows photos
   B) Are social event with _____ and _____
   C) Are many kinds of _____
   D) Can last from _____ to _____
   E) Can be very _____ events

5. Complete the following summary with the words given below.

Native American culture has not disappeared, and Native Americans have not become totally assimilated into (1)_____. They have retained some of their culture. An example of this is powwows. A powwow is a gathering of Native Americans or native (2)_____. Sometimes they are major socializing events with singing, dancing, and people playing drums. They often have booths where people can buy food, supplies, arts, and crafts. Some of the food is (3)_____. They may perform a number of dances such as the crow hop and the (4)_____. Most of these dances are played with (5)_____. These dances often originate from the days of the plains Indians. These can be very formal events (6)_____ _____ a year in advance, with sponsorship, promoters, masters of ceremonies, and judges.

mainstream culture	the owl dance	Canadians
drum music	indigenous	organized by committees

D Listen to part of a lecture in a botany class. ⊙ 3-05

Botany

1. Listen again to part of the lecture. Then answer the question.

   What can be inferred when the professor says this? 🎧

   (A) Branches do not have cambium.
   (B) Cambium causes the fungal infection.
   (C) Cambium causes a wound in the tree.
   (D) Chestnut blight is more likely to harm a wounded tree.

2. Listen again to part of the lecture. Then answer the question.

   What does the professor imply when she says this? 🎧

   (A) The foundation is not concerned with preserving trees.
   (B) The foundation wants to sell American chestnut trees.
   (C) The foundation is most concerned with apple trees.
   (D) The foundation is concerned with preserving chestnut trees.

3. What can be inferred from the lecture?

   (A) The chestnut bark disease probably originated in China.
   (B) The chestnut bark disease has been eliminated.
   (C) Someday, the American chestnut tree might number in the millions.
   (D) The American chestnut will soon become extinct.

• **extinct (a)** no longer existing • **breedind (n)** the activity of creating new offspring • **gene (n)** something inherited with DNA and RNA • **progeny (n)** offspring of plants and animals • **resistant (a)** immune to • **susceptible (a)** vulnerable; likely to suffer hardship • **thwart (v)** to slow down or stop something • **twig (n)** a small branch • **wipeout (v)** to eliminate completely

4. Listen to the lecture, and fill in the blanks to complete the lecture notes.

1) Professor discusses _____
   A) Spread through _____ and _____
   B) Belongs to _____ and _____ family
   C) Has many uses

2) Almost became extinct by _____

3) Chestnut blight kills many trees

4) American Chestnut Foundation tries to save trees
   A) Are creating _____ .
   B) Hoping to make _____ trees

5. Complete the following summary with the words given below.

Until about 100 years ago, there were millions of American chestnut trees throughout eastern North America. (1)_____ reached up to 150 feet tall and were a valuable source of timber. They were also (2)_____ of chestnuts. But, in the early 1900s, a disease known as chestnut blight (3)_____ the forests of eastern North America, wiping out the (4)_____. Only a few of these trees still exist today. However, the tree is not totally extinct, and the American Chestnut Foundation has started (5)_____ to revive these trees. They accomplish this by breeding Chinese trees resistant to the disease with susceptible American trees. And then they breed the hybrids with more American trees, which pass on two resistant genes to the progeny. (6)_____ until eventually the percentage of American genes in the hybrids is very high and one of the progeny receives four resistance genes, making it (7)_____ to the blight fungus.

some of these trees	the process is repeated	a wonderful supply
swept across	fully resistant	American chestnut trees
a breeding program		

Integrated Listening & Speaking

A Listen to a different version of the previous lecture, and say the answers out loud. ⊙ 3-06

1) Professor compares Nile and Amazon Rivers
   A) Has done work in both places
   B) Encourages students to visit the Amazon

2) Describes the Amazon
   A) Has a rain forest
   B) Has much diversity of life
   C) Has a varied ecosystem

3) Describes animals there
   A) Jaguar – large, powerful cat
   B) Giant otter – over six-feet long
   C) Piranhas, dolphins, and anacondas

4) Has thick vegetation
   A) Many kinds of trees
   B) Some are very tall

1. How would you describe the Amazon River basin?

   _____

2. Where do most of the Amazon's species live?

   _____

3. Which percentage of Earth's species live in the Amazon's rain forest?

   _____

B   Listen to a different version of the previous lecture, and say the answers out loud. ⊙ 3-07

1) Professor reads poem to class
   A) Students like it
   B) Is about rainbows

2) Is poem by William Wordsworth
   A) Not satire
   B) Romanticism genre

3) Describes romanticism
   A) Back-to-nature movement
   B) Nature is healing and spiritual force

4) Gives titles of other similar poems

1.   How would you describe romanticist poetry?

   _____

2.   Name one poem that typified romanticism.

   _____

3.   What kind of person was Wordsworth?

   _____

TOEFL iBT Practice Test

Listen to part of a conversation between a student and a professor.

1. Listen again to part of the conversation. Then answer the question. 🎧

   What does the professor imply when he says this? 🎧

   Ⓐ The student will graduate in another month.

   Ⓑ The professor presumes that the student is wealthy.

   Ⓒ The professor does not think that becoming a teacher is a good choice.

   Ⓓ The professor will be sad to see the student leave the university.

2. **Why does the professor mention a sponsor?**

   Ⓐ To prove that the student can win the competition.

   Ⓑ To show his willingness to support the student.

   Ⓒ To explain that many people want to sponsor the student.

   Ⓓ To encourage the student to attend graduate school.

3. Listen again to part of the conversation. Then answer the question. 🎧

   Why does the professor suggest that the student study history or journalism?

   Ⓐ These areas will result in the highest paying jobs.

   Ⓑ He feels these are subjects that require a lot of writing.

   Ⓒ The student has no aptitude for math and science.

   Ⓓ These are the types of subjects that will help the student become mayor someday.

4. **What are the speakers mainly discussing?**

   Ⓐ The student's need to attend graduate school.

   Ⓑ The professor's desire to see the student succeed.

   Ⓒ The student's potential as a writer.

   Ⓓ The upcoming writing competition.

5. **What is the professor's opinion of the student?**

   Ⓐ The professor feels the student is the best one he has ever had.

   Ⓑ He is convinced that the student can become a bestselling author.

   Ⓒ He believes the student will win any writing contest he enters.

   Ⓓ He is confident that the student has the ability to succeed in writing.

Listen to part of a lecture in an architecture class. 3-09

Architecture

1. Listen again to part of the conversation. Then answer the question.

   What can be inferred when the professor says this?

   Ⓐ There will be at least two more lectures next week.

   Ⓑ There will be an exam during the next class.

   Ⓒ He will not speak in detail about the Empire State Building during the current lecture.

   Ⓓ The Golden Gate Bridge and the Hoover Dam were designed by the same architect.

2. **What did Gordon Kaufman do?**

   Ⓐ He made the original design of the Hoover Dam.

   Ⓑ He simplified the original design of the Hoover Dam.

   Ⓒ He designed the town near the Hoover Dam.

   Ⓓ He added an overhanging balcony.

3. Listen again to part of the lecture. Then answer the question.

   What can be inferred about the architect Gordon Kaufman?

   Ⓐ He was not respected as an architect.

   Ⓑ He was an influential architect.

   Ⓒ His suggestions were highly controversial.

   Ⓓ His style was not very influential.

4. **What aspect of the Hoover Dam does the professor mainly discuss?**

   Ⓐ Its design.

   Ⓑ Its construction.

   Ⓒ Its completion.

   Ⓓ Its surrounding infrastructure.

5. **Why does the professor mention third world nations?**

   Ⓐ To give a description of America in a previous time.

   Ⓑ To say that the dam could not have been built in one country.

   Ⓒ To state how they were harmed by the completion of the dam.

   Ⓓ To say that the dam's design has been copied by them.

6. **Which of the following are features of the Hoover Dam? Choose 2 answers.**

   Ⓐ Art Deco sculptures on the outer towers.

   Ⓑ Towers with simple appearances.

   Ⓒ Tunnels leading to the towers.

   Ⓓ An ornamental control panel.

Vocabulary Review

A Choose and write the correct word that matches each definition.

essential	indigenous	thwart	infant	perhaps
simultaneously	beneficial	complain	retain	purchaser
gesture	arrange	mention	retrieve	exchange

1. _____ a baby or small child

2. _____ a buyer

3. _____ at the same time

4. _____ native

5. _____ necessary; required

6. _____ to stop or slow something down

7. _____ helpful

8. _____ to keep or keep the same

9. _____ to communicate with body movements

10. _____ to go get something and bring it back

11. _____ maybe

12. _____ to organize something in a certain way

13. _____ to say something to someone

14. _____ to tell someone one is unhappy about something

15. _____ to trade one thing for another

B Listen to the definitions, and fill in the blanks. Then choose the correct word. 🎧 ⊙ 3-10

powwow	romanticist	gestures	the Amazon River	chestnut blight

1. William Wordsworth wrote this type of _____ that _____described the _____of nature.

2. This is the _____ river in the world and home to the world's largest _____rain forest.

3. This is a _____ of North American _____ people.

4. In the early 1900s, this _____ spread throughout the forests of eastern North America, _____ almost all of the American chestnut trees.

5. This is a form of _____ through _____.

Unit 5

Understanding the Speaker's Attitude

5 Understanding the Speaker's Attitude

Overview

■ Introduction

These questions determine whether or not you understand the attitude or opinion of the speaker. These questions ask about the speaker's feelings, likes and dislikes, and the reasons for the emotions the speaker displays. These questions often ask about the speaker's degree of certainty. These questions typically replay a part of the listening passage.

■ Question Types

1. What can be inferred about the student?

2. What is the professor's attitude toward X?

3. What is the professor's opinion of X?

4. What can be inferred about the student when she says this? (replay)

5. What does the woman mean when she says this? (replay)

■ Useful Tips

• Recognize the tone of voice, intonation, and sentence stress that the speakers use throughout the passage.

• Distinguish between referencing and giving personal opinions.

• Avoid choosing answers that are not connected with the passage's general tone.

• Make notes on the context of the passage.

• Take note of adjectives and verbs of feeling.

Sample iBT Question

Listen again to part of the conversation. Then answer the question.
What does the professor mean when he says this?

- Ⓐ The student has not been turning in her homework lately.
- Ⓑ The student has been copying someone else's homework.
- Ⓒ The student should get some assistance with her homework.
- Ⓓ The student is not doing very well on her homework.

Script

W: Hi, Professor Smith. Do you have a minute?

M: Of course, Sally. What can I help you with?

W: Well, I wanted to talk to you about my grade in your calculus class.

M: Okay. Give me a second to find your information on this spreadsheet. Here it is. It looks like you're lagging behind on your homework assignments. Hmm, and you've also missed quite a number of classes so far this semester. Is everything okay?

W: Well, I've been having a hard time this semester because I broke up with my boyfriend. We've been seeing each other for a bit, but he recently moved away from here. It's been hard trying to keep focused on school.

M: I'm sorry to hear that. It's certainly hard when someone important in our lives moves away. Coping with the end of a relationship can be difficult for anyone.

Correct Answer The correct answer to the above question is (D). When the professor says that the student is lagging on her homework, it means that she is not doing well on her assignments and is therefore getting lower grades on them.

Practice with Conversations

A Listen to part of a conversation between a student and a housing office secretary. ⊙ 3-12

1. Listen again to part of the conversation. Then answer the question.

   What can be inferred about the student when she says this?

   Ⓐ She is sad because she is being fined.
   Ⓑ She is angry that she is being fined.
   Ⓒ She is sorry for having a halogen lamp.
   Ⓓ She is worried about paying the fine.

2. What reason does the secretary give for why the student cannot have a halogen lamp in her room?

   Ⓐ Halogen bulbs can get very hot and have been known to start fires.
   Ⓑ Halogen lamps do not go with the dorm décor.
   Ⓒ Halogen lamps are too expensive for students.
   Ⓓ The secretary had a bad experience with one of her own halogen lamps.

3. Listen again to part of the conversation. Then answer the question.

   What can be inferred about the secretary when she says this?

   Ⓐ She is very strict.
   Ⓑ She is quite reasonable.
   Ⓒ She does not like dealing with careless students.
   Ⓓ She knows the school needs money from student fines.

   • **disregard (v)** to pay no attention to • **clause (n)** a provision in a contract • **cautious (a)** showing hesitation or carefulness • **hazard (n)** a danger or risk • **minor (a)** not serious • **responsible (a)** accountable for something

4. Listen to the conversation, and fill in the blanks to complete the conversation notes.

1) Student asks secretary about _____
   A) Doesn't understand why she was fined
   B) Is _____ and _____
2) Secretary explains fine is for _____
3) Student doesn't understand
4) Secretary says halogen lamps are _____
   A) A halogen lamp once caused fire at school
   B) Must follow the rules
5) Student won't have to pay fine if buys _____

5. Complete the following summary with the words given below.

A student goes into the housing office and (1)_____ she has received. The secretary checks her computer to find that the student has been fined for keeping a (2)_____ in her dorm room. The student is shocked by this news. She does not understand how having a lamp could result in a fine. She tells the secretary that she is a very responsible student. The secretary explains that, although the student may be cautious, halogen lamps (3)_____ because the bulbs heat up to such a high degree. The secretary suggests that the student (4)_____ as soon as possible. The student asks whether she can keep the lamp if she is very careful where she places it, but the secretary (5)_____ _____. The student then complains that the fine is too high, so the secretary offers to waive the fine if the student goes out and buys a new lamp immediately and then (6)_____ _____ the receipt.

pose a fire danger	stands by the school rules	halogen lamp
inquires about a fine	buy a new lamp	brings the secretary

B Listen to part of a conversation between a student and a professor. 3-13

1. Listen again to part of the conversation. Then answer the question.

   What can be inferred about the student's feeling when he finds out that there are 200 students coming?

   Ⓐ He is angry.
   Ⓑ He is nervous and worried.
   Ⓒ He is happy and enthusiastic.
   Ⓓ He is confused and depressed.

2. What did the professor say was an optional activity for visiting students?

   Ⓐ Visiting the recreation center.
   Ⓑ Sitting in on a lecture.
   Ⓒ Joining the football team.
   Ⓓ Giving an impromptu speech.

3. What can be inferred from the students' visit?

   Ⓐ The college wants to make students feel as welcome as possible.
   Ⓑ College officials do not really care about welcoming visiting students.
   Ⓒ Only girls should volunteer to lead host groups.
   Ⓓ David will probably get sick on orientation day.

- **inquire (v)** to ask • **entail (v)** to cover • **prospective (a)** potential or likely • **mandatory (a)** necessary ; required
- **drama (n)** a play • **consider (v)** to think about • **orientation (n)** an introduction to show people new surroundings
- **logistics (n)** the planning and coordination of an event

4. Listen to the conversation, and fill in the blanks to complete the conversation notes.

1) Student talks to professor about _____
   A) Will host _____
   B) Professor is pleased

2) Professor explains student's duties
   A) Show prospective students _____
   B) Answer any questions
   C) Be _____ and _____

3) Student says is not good with big crowds

4) Professor says will only have to escort _____ students

5) Student may have to help prospective students sit in on various classes

5. Complete the following summary with the words given below.

A student wants to volunteer to help (1)_____ at his college, so he visits his professor to see how he can apply for this. The student's professor tells the student that he would be responsible for leading a small group of students (2)_____ around campus. The professor also says that the students (3)_____ of sitting in on a class of their choice, but this is (4)_____. The student says he will accept the job, so the professor gives him the final details, which are to have each of his students attend at least (5)_____ _____ orientations, either on (6)_____ afternoon or (7)_____, at night.

Monday	not obligatory	on a tour
have the option	Thursday	one of two mandatory
host visiting students		

C Listen to part of a conversation between a student and a post office clerk. ⊙ 3-14

1. Listen again to part of the conversation. Then answer the question.

   What can be inferred about the student?

   Ⓐ She is frustrated with the post office.
   Ⓑ She is indecisive about what to do with her mail.
   Ⓒ She is happy to speak with the post office worker.
   Ⓓ She feels angry that they will not hold her mail indefinitely.

2. **What is the advantage of forwarding mail to Spain?**

   Ⓐ She will win a prize that is sponsored by the post office.
   Ⓑ She will get to stay in Spain for an extra month.
   Ⓒ The post office clerk will get a raise.
   Ⓓ She will not have to wait three months before she receives her school mail.

3. Listen again to part of the conversation. Then answer the question.

   Why does the student say this?

   Ⓐ She wants to get good advice from the clerk.
   Ⓑ She wants to know what the clerk thinks of her idea.
   Ⓒ She wants the clerk to imagine what it would be like to study in Spain.
   Ⓓ She wants to know if there are any other options.

• **indefinitely (ad)** for a period of time with no fixed limit • **urgent (a)** requiring immediate action • **cancel (v)** to stop something • **storage (n)** a space for keeping things • **handle (v)** to manage something • **subscription (n)** the regular reception of published material

4. Listen to the conversation, and fill in the blanks to complete the conversation notes.

1) Student visits _____
   A) Is going to Spain for _____
   B) Is worried about _____

2) Clerk explains choices
   A) Can have mail forwarded
   B) Or can hold mail for _____

3) Clerk recommends holding mail if she won't receive anything urgent

4) Student agrees with clerk
   A) Fills out form
   B) Must cancel _____

5. Complete the following summary with the words given below.

A student goes into the school post office because she is (1)_____ for three months and is (2)_____ about what will happen to her mail during that time. The student asks the post office clerk about her options. The clerk tells the student that she either has the option of having her mail (3)_____ or can have the post office hold her mail. The only provisions are that if the student chooses to have her mail held, the post office can only hold it for (4)_____, and they cannot hold the (5)_____for her, as it would take up too much space. The student tells the clerk that because she does not have anything urgent coming to her in the mail, she would like to have her mail held. She tells the clerk that she currently receives the school newspaper but will (6)_____ since she does not read it regularly.

| school newspaper | concerned | up to three months |
| forwarded to Spain | cancel her subscription | leaving the country |

D Listen to part of a conversation between a student and a professor. 3-15

1. Listen again to part of the conversation. Then answer the question.
    What is the professor's attitude toward classroom attendance?

    (A) It is not an important part of the grading process.
    (B) It is an important part of the student's grade.
    (C) It is impossible to have high test scores with poor attendance.
    (D) It is offensive for a student to miss too many classes.

2. **What can be inferred about the student by his response to the professor?**

    (A) He is very respectful to his professors.
    (B) He is confused by the class grading policy.
    (C) He is angry that the tests were too easy.
    (D) He is determined to raise his grade.

3. **What can be inferred from the conversation?**

    (A) Test scores are not the only reflection of a student's learning.
    (B) Class discussions are a waste of time.
    (C) John should drop all of his biology classes.
    (D) Professor Higgins should assign more tests.

* **baffled (a)** confused * **apparent (a)** obvious * **conduct (v)** to lead or guide * **analogy (n)** a similarity between two like features of two separate things * **comparable (a)** similar to something else * **anticipate (v)** to expect something beforehand * **apply (v)** to put to use * **amoeba (n)** a one-celled organism

4. Listen to the conversation, and fill in the blanks to complete the conversation notes.

1) Student visits professor to talk about _____
    A) Got _____ and doesn't know why
    B) Says did well on tests
2) Professor consults grades
    A) Agrees that test scores were _____
    B) Says attendance was _____
3) Student questions _____
4) Professor says it is _____
    A) Can participate in class discussions
    B) Can learn things not in the book
    C) Can get _____ in labs
5) Student realizes importance of going to class

5. Complete the following summary with the words given below.

A student makes an appointment with his professor because he is ⁽¹⁾_____ by his final score in her class. The student points out that he received ⁽²⁾_____ on the last few tests, so he cannot understand why his final grade was so low, especially when he enjoyed learning about so many of the concepts. The professor checks her records to find that the student did receive good test scores but failed to attend ⁽³⁾_____. The student does not see how this is a ⁽⁴⁾_____. The student believes that if his test scores are good, it proves he is ⁽⁵⁾_____. The professor points out that what the student is missing when he does not attend classes are ⁽⁶⁾_____, evidence of new and cutting-edge research, and important hands-on experience in labs, which can be applied to the ideas and research of the current time.

a third of her classes	confused	learning all of the material
very good test scores	problem	lively discussions

Practice with Lectures

A   Listen to part of a lecture in a biology class. 3-16

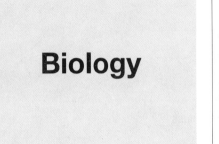   

Biology

1. **What is the professor's opinion toward the student who discussed her uncle's glioma?**

   Ⓐ He was annoyed that she spoke too much.
   Ⓑ He was happy that she was not sad about her uncle's death.
   Ⓒ He was thankful that she shared her experience with the class.
   Ⓓ He was unhappy because she sidetracked his lecture plans.

2. **According to the professor, what is one way a glioma can affect the body?**

   Ⓐ It can cause the human body to gain weight rapidly.
   Ⓑ It can invade neighboring cells and organs.
   Ⓒ It can cause the body to shut down.
   Ⓓ It can cause the body to lose its sense of feeling.

3. **Listen again to part of the lecture. Then answer the question.**

   What does the professor mean when he says this?

   Ⓐ He regrets saying that the student's uncle will probably die.
   Ⓑ He does not care about the student's feelings.
   Ⓒ He scolds the student on her insensitivity.
   Ⓓ He wants information, but he does not want to offend the student.

• **enlighten (v)** to reveal • **aggressive (a)** strongly energetic • **pathologic (a)** dealing with diseases • **succumb (v)** to submit • **disregard (v)** to pay no attention to; to ignore • **clarify (v)** to free from confusion • **combat (v)** to fight • **prompt (v)** to move to action

4. Listen to the lecture, and fill in the blanks to complete the lecture notes.

1) Professor mentions _____ A) Are _____
                                 B) Affect _____
                                 C) Arise from glial cells
                                    - Are not _____
                                    - Provide _____ and _____ to neurons
2) Can classify gliomas   A) Low grade is less _____
                          B) High grade is more aggressive
3) Discuss _____ tumors
4) Student mentions uncle's glioma A) Had astrocytoma
                                    B) Died after _____
5) Can treat glioma with radiation therapy and chemotherapy

5. Complete the following summary with the words given below.

Gliomas are tumors of the central nervous system associated with (1)_____. A glial
cell is a cell that provides nourishment and support to neurons within the (2)_____
_____. There are several different types of gliomas, depending on what type of glial
cell the tumor is associated with. For example, ependymomas (3)_____.
Gliomas are also classified as high grade or low grade upon diagnosis. A high-grade glioma is
(4)_____, and the prognosis for the patient tends not to be good. On the other hand,
a low-grade glioma is a (5)_____ tumor that is often 100% treatable. One type of
high-grade glioma, astrocytoma, also has a numbered grading system, with 1 being the least
aggressive form and 4 indicating the most aggressive form. Symptoms of a glioma present in
the body can range from headaches to vomiting to experiencing (6)_____.
Surgery, chemotherapy, and (7)_____ are all common treatments of gliomas.

less aggressive	radiation	glial cells
affect ependymal cells	numbness in the extremities	very aggressive
central nervous system		

B Listen to part of a lecture in a climatology class. 3-17

Climatology

1. According to the professor, what is one way a Martian Dust Devil can affect terrestrial technology?

　(A) It can replicate terrestrial technology.
　(B) It can reprogram terrestrial technology.
　(C) It can threaten terrestrial technology.
　(D) It can augment terrestrial technology.

2. How does a dust devil differ from a tornado?

　(A) A dust devil forms an updraft, and a tornado forms a downdraft.
　(B) A tornado and a dust devil are the same thing.
　(C) A dust devil is generally larger than a tornado.
　(D) A tornado is stationary.

3. What can be inferred about Martian Dust Devils?

　(A) They are not worth studying.
　(B) There is much to be learned about them.
　(C) Evidence of them implies that they also exist on Neptune.
　(D) Astronauts should stop traveling to the moon.

• **phenomenon (n)** something that is impressive or extraordinary • **prevalent (a)** widespread • **momentum (n)** speed of movement • **sustain (v)** to support • **terrestrial (a)** pertaining to land • **crucial (a)** extremely important • **threat (n)** a declaration of intent to harm someone or something • **swirl (v)** to move around in a whirling motion • **harmless (a)** without the power to cause injury; safe

4. Listen to the lecture, and fill in the blanks to complete the lecture notes.

1) Professor discusses _____
   A) Is a weather phenomenon
   B) Is similar to _____
   C) Forms an updraft when hot air rises quickly into _____
   D) Is common in _____
2) Professor describes creation in detail
   A) Hot air quickly rises and passes through cooler air
   B) The air _____ and makes a _____ effect
   C) Looks like a _____
3) Mars has large dust devils
4) Scientists learned about them from _____

5. Complete the following summary with the words given below.

Dust devils are formed when (1)_____ near the ground (2)_____ into cooler, low pressure air. The quickly-rising hot air (3)_____ that forms into a funnel-shaped column of air capable of moving along the ground due to (4)_____. Dust devils on Earth are relatively small and harmless while the Martian Dust Devils, as evidenced by satellite pictures, can be up to fifty times wider and (5)_____ than their earthbound cousins. Some concern arose regarding the safety of terrestrial space equipment on Mars should a dust devil form and destroy the equipment due to its size and power. However, there was an instance when a Martian Dust Devil actually (6)_____ on a space robot.

ten times higher	air speed and friction	very hot air
cleaned the solar panels	creates a swirling motion	forms an updraft

C Listen to part of a lecture in a sociology class. 3-18

1. What can be inferred about how the professor feels toward artisan-made pants?

   (A) The professor wants the artisan to take a lot of time to make his pants.
   (B) The professor would prefer a pair of quickly made factory pants.
   (C) The professor only wears skirts.
   (D) The professor would choose not to pay the artisan.

2. What resulted from the invention of the cotton mill?

   (A) Everyone owned cheaper pants.
   (B) Artisans could not find jobs.
   (C) Cotton production became a mechanized industry.
   (D) People soon owned many pairs of pants.

3. How does the professor organize the information about the Industrial Revolution?

   (A) From general to specific.
   (B) From present conditions to historical conditions.
   (C) As a question-and-answer session.
   (D) From types of inventions to social effects.

• **capitalism (n)** an economic system in which investment, ownership, and profit are in the private sector • **culminate (v)** to reach the highest point • **utilize (v)** to put to use • **proliferation (n)** a rapid increase • **lament (v)** to express grief • **prior (a)** earlier in time; previous • **harsh (a)** physically uncomfortable • **model (n)** an example used for comparison • **slightly (ad)** a little

4. Listen to the lecture, and fill in the blanks to complete the lecture notes.

1) Professor discusses _____ A) Began in England in _____
                                          B) Spread around the world
                                          C) Based on _____ and _____
                                          D) Replaced manpower with _____

2) Mentions steam engine A) Helped make transportation _____
                          B) Made faster manufacturing machines
                          C) Thomas Savery and Richard Trevithick worked on _____

3) Britain changed greatly A) Manchester became _____ city
                            B) Roller spinning machine created
                            C) Richard Awkright made _____

4) Modern cities created A) New laws made to _____ people
                          B) Communist writings became popular

5. Complete the following summary with the words given below.

The Industrial Revolution refers to the technological, (1)_____, and cultural changes
that took place in (2)_____ in the late eighteenth century. Prior to this period, goods and
services were provided through (3)_____. The development of the steam engine
revolutionized manufacturing forever by (4)_____ to do the job of men and at
a much faster rate. Factories sprang up and grew into what we now know as modern cities
as people left their rural homes and flocked to the cities for work. Trade unions sprang up to
(5)_____ from harsh laws and intolerable conditions. Transportation was
also changed forever with the invention of the (6)_____. Now, people and
goods could be transported across the country at a much faster rate. Many British historians and
philosophers at the time wrote manifestos concerning the state of the working class in England
and how the (7)_____ would change their lives forever.

protect the working class   man or horsepower
steam engine locomotive   Britain
socioeconomic   allowing machinery
Industrial Revolution

D   Listen to part of a lecture in a biology class.

1. What is the professor's attitude toward the fact that the crocodile does not eat the Egyptian Plover bird?

    Ⓐ Disgust.

    Ⓑ Amazement.

    Ⓒ Sadness.

    Ⓓ Anger.

2. According to the professor, how does the Oxpecker have relationships with certain African animals? Choose 2 answers.

    Ⓐ As a parasite.

    Ⓑ As a symbiont.

    Ⓒ As a host.

    Ⓓ As a predator.

3. According to the professor, what is one way the Oxpecker can affect African mammals?

    Ⓐ It can open wounds and drink the animal's blood.

    Ⓑ It can massage muscles and make the animal comfortable.

    Ⓒ It can help the animal survive dangerous diseases.

    Ⓓ It can help the animal to find food when it is hungry.

> • **intimate (a)** very personal or close   • **merge (v)** to join   • **lethal (a)** deadly   • **predator (n)** an organism that exists by eating other organisms   • **parasite (n)** an organism that lives off of another organism   • **unlikely (a)** not liable to happen   • **scenario (n)** an outline of what might happen   • **famous (a)** well known

4. Listen to the lecture, and fill in the blanks to complete the lecture notes.

1) Professor defines _____
   A) Two _____ organisms interact intimately or merge into one
   B) Larger one is host
   C) Smaller is _____
2) Discusses mutualism
   A) Relationship where both partners profit
      - Egyptian Plover bird and crocodile
      - Goby _____ and _____
3) Sometimes mutualism is not always _____ to one party
   A) Oxpecker and some large animals

5. Complete the following summary with the words given below.

Mutualism is defined as a (1)_____ in which two differing organisms (2)_____ from a close relationship. An example of mutualism is the relationship between the Egyptian Plover bird and the crocodile, where the Egyptian Plover (3)_____ off of the crocodile's body. The Egyptian Plover benefits from the relationship by getting an easy meal, and the crocodile benefits from the relationship by having (4)_____ removed from its body. Mutualism can sometimes (5)_____, however, if one of the organisms begins harming the other. For example, a different kind of bird, the Oxpecker, normally enjoys a relationship of mutualism with certain African land mammals. However, once in a while, the Oxpecker (6)_____ from the mammals to drink and so therefore benefits when the mammal does not.

potentially fatal parasites	eats the parasites	benefit
form of symbiosis	will draw blood	merge into parasitism

Integrated Listening & Speaking

Listen to a different version of the previous lecture, and say the answers out loud. 3-20

1) Professor mentions gliomas
   A) Are tumors
   B) Affect central nervous system
   C) Arise from glial cells
     - Are not neurons
     - Provide support and nutrition to neurons

2) Can classify gliomas
   A) Low grade is less aggressive
   B) High grade is more aggressive

3) Discuss malignant tumors

4) Student mentions uncle's glioma
   A) Had astrocytoma
   B) Died after eighteen months

5) Can treat glioma with radiation therapy and chemotherapy

1. What is a glial cell and what function does it provide?

_____

2. What does the term low-grade mean when used as part of a diagnosis for gliomas?

_____

3. Name two possible choices for treatment of gliomas.

_____

B Listen to a different version of the previous lecture, and say the answers out loud. 🔊 3-21

1) Professor defines symbiosis

   A) Two dissimilar organisms interact intimately or merge into one
   B) Larger one is host
   C) Smaller is symbiont

2) Discusses mutualism

   A) Relationship where both partners profit
     - Egyptian Plover bird and crocodile
     - Goby fish and shrimp

3) Sometimes mutualism is not always beneficial to one party

   A) Oxpecker and some large animals

1. If you come down with a cold, is your relationship with the virus considered mutualism or parasitism, and why?

   _____

2. In the case of the Egyptian Plover and the crocodile, how is the Plover bird benefiting from the relationship?

   _____

3. When is the relationship between the Oxpecker bird and a buffalo not an example of mutualism but one of parasitism?

   _____

Listen to part of a conversation between a student and a professor. 4-01

1. **What is the professor's opinion of Erika?**

    Ⓐ He thinks she needs to study a lot harder.

    Ⓑ She is one of his worst students.

    Ⓒ He thinks she should study in London.

    Ⓓ She is one of his best students.

2. **What advice in particular does the professor offer the student in her search for a graduate school?**

    Ⓐ He wants Erika to apply only to schools near her home.

    Ⓑ He wants Erika to consider applying to schools in different places.

    Ⓒ He wants Erika to study in London.

    Ⓓ He tells Erika to forget the idea of graduate school.

3. **Listen again to part of the conversation. Then answer the question.** 🎧

    What is the professor's attitude towards London?

    Ⓐ He thinks it is an exciting city.

    Ⓑ He thinks it is a dirty and dangerous city.

    Ⓒ He found it to be boring.

    Ⓓ He thinks it is much too expensive.

4. **Which of the following jobs is the student considering?**

    Choose 2 answers.

    Ⓐ Psychologist.

    Ⓑ Counselor.

    Ⓒ Elementary school teacher.

    Ⓓ College professor.

5. **Why does the student visit the professor?**

    Ⓐ To receive a letter of recommendation from him.

    Ⓑ To inquire about her academic future.

    Ⓒ To seek information on what jobs are available.

    Ⓓ To get his opinion on life in a large city like London.

Listen to part of a lecture in a life science class. 4-02

Life Science

1. What is the professor's attitude towards the extinction of plants?

   (A) It is natural.
   (B) It is not so bad if an invasive plant becomes extinct.
   (C) It should be prevented as much as possible.
   (D) It is caused by irresponsible gardeners.

2. According to the professor, how can purple loosestrife affect other plant species?

   (A) It can produce beautiful blossoms.
   (B) It can appear from nowhere.
   (C) It can spread too quickly and widely and choke off other plants.
   (D) It can cause diseases in certain animals.

3. According to the professor, in what way should humans deal with introduced and endemic plant species?

   (A) Whether endemic or exotic, the preservation of all species should be a priority.
   (B) Endemic plants are better than exotic plants.
   (C) Exotic plants are better than endemic plants.
   (D) All plants should be eradicated.

4. Why does the professor explain the Norway maple?

   (A) To complain about how it has spread through North America.
   (B) To explain why Scandinavians brought it with them.
   (C) To give an example of a harmless naturalized plant.
   (D) To state that it has harmed several native species.

5. How is the discussion organized?

   (A) By providing examples of the effects of naturalized plants.
   (B) By giving definitions of both naturalized and endemic plants.
   (C) By describing various naturalized plants in North America.
   (D) By discussing the reasons why people introduce non-native species.

6. What does the professor imply about national parks?

   (A) They can be quickly overcome by non-native plants.
   (B) They need non-native plants to feed their animal populations.
   (C) They can be testing grounds for the introduction of non-native plants.
   (D) They have helped keep various plants from becoming extinct.

Vocabulary Review

A Choose and write the correct word that matches each definition.

cadence	lament	extraneous	model	diagnosis
aggressive	terrestrial	apply	responsible	urgent
minor	clause	harmless	merge	momentum

1. _____ a provision in a contract

2. _____ to join

3. _____ speed of movement

4. _____ pertaining to land or ground

5. _____ determining the nature of a disease

6. _____ having or showing the potential to cause harm

7. _____ the rhythmic flow of words

8. _____ not necessary

9. _____ requiring immediate action

10. _____ to express grief

11. _____ to put to use

12. _____ not serious

13. _____ accountable for something

14. _____ without the power to cause injury

15. _____ an example used for a comparison

B Listen to the definitions and fill in the blanks. Then choose the correct word. 🎧 ⊙ 4-03

dust devil	exotic species	mutualism	trade union	glial cell

1. This is a form of _____ in which _____ both benefit from a close relationship.

2. This is the term used for a plant that is being introduced into _____.

3. This is found in the _____ and provides _____ and support to neurons.

4. This is created when very hot air _____ from the ground and forms a _____column.

5. This was something created during _____ to protect men, women, and children working _____.

PART 3

Connecting Information

Connecting Information questions test your ability to integrate information from different parts of the listening passage to make inferences, to draw conclusions, to form generalizations, and to make predictions. To choose the right answer, these question types require you to make connections between or among pieces of information in the text and to identify the relationships among the ideas and details.

Unit 6

Understanding Organization

6 Understanding Organization

Overview

■ Introduction

In order to answer these questions correctly, you must either recognize how the entire listening passage is organized or recognize how different portions of the passage are related to one another. These questions ask you to recognize the importance of information like topic changes, exemplifying, digressing, and inducing introductory and concluding remarks. These questions test whether you understand how a part of the passage is related to the passage as a whole. These questions often occur in lectures rather than conversations, and they sometimes ask for more than one answer.

■ Question Types

1. How does the professor organize the information about X that he presents to the class?

2. How is the discussion organized?

3. In what order does the speaker describe the topic?

4. Why does the professor discuss X?

5. Why does the professor mention X?

■ Useful Tips

• The questions often include the following patterns:
  – giving examples
  – contrasting
  – comparing
  – classifying / categorizing
  – describing causes and effects
  – explaining in chronological order

• Listen very carefully to recognize when there is a transition in the sequence.

• Take note of the transitional words and the relationships between the contents.

Sample iBT Question

Why does the professor mention the harsh Arctic environment?

(A) To explain why polar bears have no natural enemies anywhere.
(B) To show how strong the polar bear is to be able to survive there.
(C) To prove that the Arctic is one of the coldest places on Earth.
(D) To describe the kinds of animals that can survive in the Arctic.

Script

Now, you're probably aware that the Arctic is an extremely harsh environment and one of the coldest places on Earth. But let me remind you of what it's really like in the Arctic, especially in late December or early January. The temperature frequently drops below minus 40 degrees centigrade and sometimes gets even colder! Combine that with strong winds, little or no sunlight, and very little vegetation, and what you get is an environment in which very few species are capable of surviving. The polar bear, however, thrives in this kind of environment. The polar bear spends his time roaming throughout the Arctic, walking on land and ice, swimming in freezing sea water and floating on sheets of ice while looking for seals, fish, and other food. Their favorite food is seals, which they find along the edges of the ice, in holes in the ice, and under cracks in the ice. They have no natural enemies in this environment, which is perfectly suited for them.

Correct Answer The correct answer to the above question is (B). The professor describes the harshness of the environment to show the strength of the polar bear in being able to survive there.

Practice with Conversations

A Listen to part of a conversation between a student and a professor. 4-05

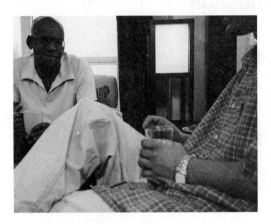

1. **What can be inferred about the student?**

   Ⓐ He is going to graduate soon.
   Ⓑ He has excellent grades.
   Ⓒ He is not close to many professors.
   Ⓓ He has already completed his research project.

2. **What does the professor ask the student to send him? Choose 2 answers.**

   Ⓐ A letter of recommendation.
   Ⓑ A resume.
   Ⓒ An abstract of his research project.
   Ⓓ A list of physics courses taken.

3. **Listen again to part of the conversation. Then answer the question.**

   What does the professor imply when he says this?

   Ⓐ He does not have time to write a letter for the student.
   Ⓑ Professor Smith is a better writer than he is.
   Ⓒ He does not know the student as well as Professor Smith.
   Ⓓ He only likes to write letters for his advisees.

• **apply for (v)** to write a letter or fill in a form in order to get something • **recommendation (n)** suggestion or advice
• **conference (n)** an organized meeting on a particular subject

4. Listen to the conversation, and fill in the blanks to complete the conversation notes.

1) Student wants to speak with professor

2) Asks professor to write _____ for graduate school
   A) Professor says he is not _____
   B) Thinks Professor Smith would be better

3) Student can't contact Professor Smith

4) Professor agrees to write _____
   A) Doesn't know student well
   B) Asks for _____
      - _____
      - List of physics classes taken

5) Student promises to send _____

6) Student wants to attend current school for _____

5. Complete the following summary with the words given below.

A student goes to a professor and asks to speak with him for a few minutes. The professor
(1)_____ as to what's on the student's mind. The student wants the professor to write
some letters of (2)_____ for him. The professor believes the student's advisor,
Professor Smith, would be a better choice, but the student is unable to contact Professor Smith,
who is (3)_____ at a conference. The professor agrees to write the letters but
says that he needs the student's personal information, including a (4)_____ and list of
classes taken. The student says that he will send the information by (5)_____ when he
goes home. He then (6)_____ that he would love to attend his current school for
graduate work and hopes that he will be accepted.

mentions	inquires	resume
recommendation	e-mail	out of the country

B   Listen to part of a conversation between a student and a librarian.  4-06

1. Why does the librarian mention that all books are treated equally in the library?
   - Ⓐ The student thinks that most books are not important.
   - Ⓑ The student does not want to pay the late fee.
   - Ⓒ The student argued that her overdue book was not important.
   - Ⓓ The student wants to be excused for returning a book late.

2. According to the librarian, what must the student do before she can check out the article she needs?
   - Ⓐ Get a disability card.
   - Ⓑ Pay a $10 late fee.
   - Ⓒ Return every book she has checked out.
   - Ⓓ Read a book on weightlifting instead of psychology.

3. What is the librarian's opinion of the student's disability?
   - Ⓐ She does not believe it is real.
   - Ⓑ She thinks it is very sad.
   - Ⓒ She thinks it is a lie to gain sympathy.
   - Ⓓ She thinks it is not the reason the book was overdue.

> • **disabled (a)** having a physical disability; handicapped   • **impairment (n)** a disability; something that causes disadvantages   • **"Let it slide." (phr)** Ignore it.; Don't worry about it.   • **psych (n)** psychology   • **reserve (v)** to book something ahead of time   • **ridiculous (a)** stupid; very unfair

4. Listen to the conversation, and fill in the blanks to complete the conversation notes.

1) Student wants to borrow _____ for class
2) Has _____ so can't borrow material
3) Must pay ____ dollars
4) Says does not have the money
   A) Claims she is _____
   B) Shouldn't have to pay fine
5) Student finally _____
6) Borrows _____

5. Complete the following summary with the words given below.

A student asked a librarian to borrow an article which was on reserve. However, the librarian noticed that the student had (1)_____ and told the student that she had to pay the fine, which was ten dollars, before (2)_____ out the article. The librarian said the student had returned a library book one week late. (3)_____ _____ to waive the fine and (4)_____ as to why she should waive it. Among the reasons were the facts that the student had a (5)_____ and the book was not very important. The librarian (6)_____ that the student had to pay the fine. The student then reluctantly paid the ten-dollar fine.

hearing disability	she would be allowed to sign
gave her several reasons	an outstanding fine
the student asked the librarian	insisted

C Listen to part of a conversation between a student and a professor. 4-07

1. Why does the professor mention that he stayed up past his bedtime?
    - (A) He says it is the reason he made a grading mistake.
    - (B) It is too late for him to speak to students.
    - (C) He makes fewer mistakes late at night.
    - (D) The student tried to call him at night.

2. According to the professor, what is the position of the student's grade in the class?
    - (A) It is the lowest grade in the class.
    - (B) It is an average grade.
    - (C) It is a decent grade but not the best.
    - (D) It is the highest grade in the class.

3. Listen again to part of the conversation. Then answer the question.
    What is the professor's attitude in this part of the conversation?
    - (A) He is very angry with the student.
    - (B) He is joking around.
    - (C) He does not trust the student.
    - (D) He is very formal towards the students.

- **error (n)** a mistake • **grade (n)** a score • **hesitate (v)** to pause • **inconvenience (n)** an annoyance; a bother
- **nonsense (n)** silliness • **quantum (n)** an amount of energy in nuclear physics

4. Listen to the conversation, and fill in the blanks to complete the conversation notes.

1) Student asks to speak with professor
   A) Says made mistake on _____
   B) Professor doesn't believe him

2) Student shows the scores

3) Professor can't find student on _____

4) Was looking at _____

5) Professor agrees grade was _____

6) _____ for error

5. Complete the following summary with the words given below.

A student went to his professor's office to tell him that (1)_____ that the professor (2)_____ when he calculated the student's quantum physics grade. The student said that (3)_____ the professor's spreadsheet, his grade was only a 72, but his midterm score was an 85, and his quiz score was a 90. Therefore, he felt his grade should have been higher than a 72. The (4)_____ told him that he sometimes makes mistakes (5)_____. He asked for the student's ID number but couldn't find the student on the class list. Eventually, the professor realized that he was looking at the wrong list. Then (6)_____ and confirmed that student's statements were correct. He informed the student that (7)_____ should have been 86. He apologized for the mistake and told the student that he did the grades late at night.

professor	he found the right list	had made a mistake
he suspected	the correct grade	calculating grades
according to		

D Listen to part of a conversation between a student and a librarian. ⊙ 4-08

1. Why does the librarian mention the returned books section?

   Ⓐ She is certain that the book the man wants is there.
   Ⓑ She wants the man to put all of his overdue books there.
   Ⓒ She believes the book the man is looking for may be there.
   Ⓓ She is going to go look for a book there for the man.

2. Why does the student go to speak with the librarian?

   Ⓐ To renew some of his books.
   Ⓑ To pay a fine on overdue books.
   Ⓒ To ask about a book's availability.
   Ⓓ To request a book's call number.

3. What is the librarian's attitude toward the student?

   Ⓐ She is not particularly interested.
   Ⓑ She likes joking about everything.
   Ⓒ She is eager to be of assistance.
   Ⓓ She is pleased he has renewed his books.

• **due (a)** expected; scheduled • **relief (n)** comfort; ease • **crucial (a)** vital; important • **fascinating (a)** captivating; gripping

4. Listen to the conversation, and fill in the blanks to complete the conversation notes.

1) Student visits _____
   A) Asks to _____ books
   B) Hopes he does not have to _____

2) Librarian renews his books

3) Student asks about another book
   A) Needs it for _____
   B) Is expensive so does not want to _____

4) Librarian finds that book is available
   A) Gives man _____
   B) Tells him what to do if _____

5. Complete the following summary with the words given below.

A student goes to the library (1)_____ some of his books. He asks the librarian if he needs to bring the books with him, but she tells him that is not necessary. He gives her (2)_____, and she calls his name up on the computer. She then renews the student's books for him. The student then proceeds to ask a question about a book that he needs to complete (3)_____. He says that the book is currently (4)_____, and, because it is so expensive, he does not want to purchase it. The librarian checks (5)_____ and notices that the book was returned that day. She gives the man the book's call number and then tells him that if the book is not (6)_____, he should tell her, and then she will go find the book in the returned books section.

to renew	his ID card	his research project
checked out	its availability	on the shelves

Practice with Lectures

A Listen to part of a lecture in an economy class. 4-09

Economy

1. How does the professor organize the lecture?
   - (A) By comparing domestic trade with foreign trade.
   - (B) By comparing two types of trade.
   - (C) By comparing the characteristics of two types of trading policies.
   - (D) By discussing one type of trade.

2. Which is least likely to be true about free trade?
   - (A) It will apply to both goods and services.
   - (B) It will apply to goods but not services.
   - (C) It will keep prices down but also reduce domestic wages.
   - (D) It will keep prices down but result in the loss of domestic jobs.

3. What is the likely outcome of adopting protectionist policies?
   - (A) Consumers will pay lower prices for foreign goods.
   - (B) The country will probably lose jobs to foreign competition.
   - (C) The prices of most goods will rise.
   - (D) Trade will increase between countries.

• **dump (v)** to throw away • **import (n)** something brought in from another country • **manufacture (v)** to make • **nation (n)** a country • **outsource (v)** to delegate work outside a company • **prevent (v)** to stop something before it happens • **quota (n)** a numerical limit • **regulations (n)** rules • **subsidy (n)** economic funding or assistance

4. Listen to the lecture, and fill in the blanks to complete the lecture notes.

1) Professor discusses _____
   A) Is free flow of _____
   B) Lets people buy and sell anything
   C) Will create _____ for both partners

2) Free trade has different meanings to people

3) Describes protectionism
   A) Prevents people from _____
   B) Can include _____

4) Describes advantages of free trade
   A) Cheap _____
   B) Outsource jobs
   C) Improve _____ of developing nations

5. Complete the following summary with the words given below.

Free trade is the free flow of goods and services between nations. Some of the characteristics of free trade are the (1)_____, quotas, subsidies, and various other regulations that limit the free (2)_____. Free trade agreements usually involve some (3)_____. Protectionism is government restraint on trade between two nations. It is one nation's efforts to prevent its own people from trading. Such protective measures include tariffs, restrictive quotas, government regulations, anti-dumping laws, and subsidies. (4)_____ of free trade is that it keeps prices down, but, (5)_____, a big disadvantage is that it might cause many (6)_____ to suffer economically, domestic jobs to disappear, and domestic wages to decrease. Foreign businesses, especially in poorer countries, can provide the same (7)_____ at a cheaper price because of lower labor costs.

protective policies	absence of tariffs	domestic businesses
one major advantage	at the same time	goods and services
flow of business		

B Listen to part of a lecture in an art class. 4-10

1. How does the professor organize the lecture?
   - (A) She discusses the technology of the camera in detail.
   - (B) It is organized from the least important events to the most important events.
   - (C) It is organized from the most important events to the least important events.
   - (D) It is organized in chronological order.

2. Who was the first to make multiple copies of the same image?
   - (A) Joseph Nicéphore Niépce.
   - (B) Louis Daguerre.
   - (C) William Henry Talbot.
   - (D) Frederick Scott Archer.

3. Which of the following statements can be inferred from the lecture?
   - (A) The ancient Greeks could have invented cameras but they had no use for them.
   - (B) Today, the oldest existing photographs were probably taken after 1900.
   - (C) Today, it is impossible for us to look at the first photographic image of 1814.
   - (D) Today it is no longer possible to darken silver nitrate.

- **accomplish (v)** to achieve • **capture (v)** to catch • **be composed of (phr)** be made of • **expose (v)** to uncover, reveal, or show • **jeopardize (v)** to put in danger • **immerse (v)** to be put completely into • **instant (a)** immediate • **practical (a)** useful • **resemble (v)** to look the same as; to look like • **snowball (v)** to spread; to become greater

4. Listen to the lecture, and fill in the blanks to complete the lecture notes.

1) Professor gives _____
   A) _____ and _____ philosophers described its principles
   B) Isaac Newton discovered light was made of _____
   C) Johann Heinrich Schulze learned light could _____ silver nitrate
   D) Joseph Nicéphore Niépce created first photographic image

2) Louis Daguerre experiments with photography
   A) Captured an image that _____
   B) Developed photographic plates

3) William Henry Talbot developed _____ process

4) Frederick Scott Archer invented Collodion process

5) Cameras first mass-marketed in _____

6) More inventions later

5. Complete the following summary with the words given below.

The history of photography is a long one. In the fourth and fifth centuries B.C., Greek and Chinese philosophers were already (1)_____ the basic principles of cameras. In 1727, Johann Heinrich Schulze discovered that (2)_____ would darken silver nitrate. Finally, in 1814, a Frenchman, Joseph Nicéphore Niépce, created a photographic image, but it wasn't very practical because it needed to be exposed to light for (3)_____ and the image quickly faded. In 1833, his business partner, Louis Daguerre, became the first to capture a permanent image. He accomplished this by immersing the image (4)_____. Also, he developed (5)_____, which significantly reduced the required exposure time to thirty minutes. In 1841, William Henry Talbot (6)_____ a process that (7)_____ to have multiple copies of the same image. Finally, in 1851, Frederick Scott Archer invented the Collodion process, in which images (8)_____ of light exposure.

at least eight hours	in salt	photographic plates
only required a few seconds	familiar with	exposure to light
invented	made it possible	

C Listen to part of a lecture in an archeology class. 4-11

Archeology

1. How does the professor organize the lecture?

   Ⓐ By comparing North American excavations with Eastern excavations.
   Ⓑ By comparing two types of excavations.
   Ⓒ By discussing the history of excavations.
   Ⓓ By discussing the different types of rescues.

2. According to the professor, what is one way that land development can affect archeological sites?

   Ⓐ It always helps to uncover valuable artifacts.
   Ⓑ It can destroy valuable archeological sites.
   Ⓒ It is an inexpensive way to practice archeology.
   Ⓓ It does not affect archeological sites.

3. How is the discussion organized?

   Ⓐ By geographic region.
   Ⓑ As random, general information.
   Ⓒ From theory to practice.
   Ⓓ By class, or types of archeology.

• **artifact (n)** a relic • **erosion (n)** a process by which something is broken down • **inevitable (a)** bound to happen
• **imminent (a)** looming • **reconstruct (v)** to put together again • **remains (n)** remnants • **peril (n)** serious danger
• **source (n)** an origin • **urgent (a)** needing to be done soon

4. Listen to the lecture, and fill in the blanks to complete the lecture notes.

1) Professor describes _____
   A) Study of _____ and _____
   B) Examine _____
   C) Must dig for them

2) Describes rescue archeology
   A) Survey _____
   B) Must excavate quickly
   C) Is common in _____

3) Thousands of digs throughout world
   A) Many in _____
   B) Mentions Pompeii

5. Complete the following summary with the words given below.

Ancient cultures left little or no written history, but archeologists can learn a lot about these cultures by examining (1)_____ such as buildings, tools, graves, and artifacts. These remains are our chief (2)_____ of prehistoric and ancient cultures. Archeologists get their information by (3)_____. One kind of archeology is rescue archeology, which is the (4)_____ threatened by land development. Usually, development is imminent, so archeologists must urgently excavate before the bulldozers move in. Many sites also suffer (5)_____, which adds to the peril of the situation. In such a case, excavation becomes an exercise in damage control. Sometimes excavation can be done at a relaxed pace (6)_____. This is called research excavation. During this type of excavation, archeologists have more resources and can excavate more fully. Right now, there are thousands of digs taking place (7)_____. The countries where ancient civilizations were located tend to have the most archeological sites.

with no deadlines	ancient remains	digging or excavating
examination of sites	a lot of erosion	all over the world
source of knowledge		

D Listen to part of a lecture in an art class. 4-12

1. How does the professor begin his lecture?
   - (A) By asking students which is the most glamorous form of art.
   - (B) By asking students to compare ceramics with architecture.
   - (C) By asking students if there are any art forms they have not yet discussed.
   - (D) By asking students to comment on a specific plate.

2. According to the professor, where is most kitchenware produced?
   - (A) In ceramics studios.
   - (B) In ancient civilizations.
   - (C) In factories.
   - (D) By students in university art classes.

3. What can be inferred from the lecture?
   - (A) Pottery began about 1,200 years ago.
   - (B) Pottery began thousands of years ago.
   - (C) Twentieth-century pottery is completely different than ancient pottery.
   - (D) During the prehistoric age, man was incapable of developing pots.

* **decorative (a)** used for decoration or adornment • **devote (v)** to dedicate time or attention • **durability (n)** strength
* **glaze (v)** to paint or coat something and give it a shiny appearance • **modify (v)** to change • **non-porous (a)**
having no holes or gaps • **practical (a)** useful • **refined (a)** polished • **utilitarian (a)** useful

4. Listen to the lecture, and fill in the blanks to complete the lecture notes.

1) Professor describes _____
    A) Are objects made from _____
    B) Often called _____
    C) Are used as _____
    D) Oldest form of art
2) Describes manufacturing process
    A) Create pot with _____ and _____
    B) Heat clay in kiln
    C) Hardens
    D) Glazed before _____

5. Complete the following summary with the words given below.

Generally, ceramic arts, which are sometimes referred to as pottery, are pieces made from a (1)_____ of inorganic non-metallic materials and heat. The most common ingredient is clay, but it's usually mixed with (2)_____. Typically, pottery is something people have used their entire lives: kitchenware. It usually has utilitarian purposes, but sometimes it's designed purely for decorative reasons. It's very durable, and (3)_____. Many pieces date back to the age of prehistoric man. Much of the kitchenware seen in the stores (4)_____. However, many pots are made in old-fashioned, modest studios. And they're made by hand. The potter starts with a hunk of clay, (5)_____, and then heats it up in a kiln. (6)_____. Pots and other ceramic arts are usually heated at an extremely high temperature, but they're always glazed before the final firing, which gives them a refined look and makes it non-porous. Artists may add a final touch to it as well.

various minerals	combination
this hardens the clay	it's the oldest form of art
shapes it with his hands	is mass produced in factories

Integrated Listening & Speaking

A Listen to a different version of the previous lecture, and say the answers out loud. 4-13

1) Professor discusses free trade
   A) Is free flow of goods and services
   B) Lets people buy and sell anything
   C) Will create wealth for both partners

2) Free trade has different meanings to people

3) Describes protectionism
   A) Prevents people from trading
   B) Can include tariffs

4) Describes advantages of free trade
   A) Cheap manufacturing
   B) Outsource jobs
   C) Improve economies of developing nations

1. How would you describe free trade?

   _____

2. Which type of trade is more likely to result in higher domestic prices?

   _____

3. What are the advantages of protectionism?

   _____

B   Listen to a different version of the previous lecture, and say the answers out loud. ⊙ 4-14

1) Professor describes ceramics
   A) Is objects made from clay
   B) Often called pottery
   C) Is used as kitchenware
   D) Oldest form of art

2) Describes manufacturing process
   A) Create pot with potter's wheel and hands
   B) Heat clay in kiln
   C) Hardens
   D) Glazed before firing again

1.   What do people often use pottery for?

_____

2.   What are the steps to making a pot?

_____

3.   What does glazing do?

_____

TOEFL iBT Practice Test

Listen to part of a conversation between a student and a clerk.

1. According to the student, why didn't he buy this book earlier in the semester?

   Ⓐ He did not have enough money.
   Ⓑ He could not find the book.
   Ⓒ He did not know he needed this book.
   Ⓓ He did not have time to read it before.

2. According to the clerk, how can limited shelf space affect their stock of books?

   Ⓐ It does not affect it at all.
   Ⓑ They send unsold books back to the publisher.
   Ⓒ They sell old books very cheaply.
   Ⓓ They cannot carry many popular books.

3. Listen again to part of the conversation. Then answer the question.

   What can be inferred from the woman's statements? 🎧

   Ⓐ You can buy anything online.
   Ⓑ Some online stores have the best textbooks.
   Ⓒ Some online stores sell more than just textbooks.
   Ⓓ The best places to buy everything, including textbooks, are online stores.

4. Why does the clerk mention her sister?

   Ⓐ To say that she can help the student find the book.
   Ⓑ To point out the way that she acquires her books.
   Ⓒ To note her association with Spider Books.
   Ⓓ To state that she can get him some materials online.

5. What will the student probably do next?

   Ⓐ Purchase the book online.
   Ⓑ Order the book from the publisher.
   Ⓒ Look for the book in Bargain Books.
   Ⓓ Make a visit to Spider Books.

Listen to part of a lecture in a zoology class. 4-16

1. How did the professor organize the lecture?

    (A) He began with general information about hibernation and moved toward specific information about bears.

    (B) He focused on general information about hibernation.

    (C) He focused on specific information about bears.

    (D) He began with specific information about bears and moved to general information about hibernation.

2. According to the professor, how do some hibernators practice predictive dormancy?

    (A) They hibernate as the days grow longer.

    (B) They hibernate all year round.

    (C) They hibernate as the days decrease in length.

    (D) They only hibernate when they do not have enough food.

3. Listen again to part of the lecture. Then answer the question.

    What can be inferred about the professor's comment?

    (A) It is highly unlikely that people can see gray squirrels in the winter.

    (B) People can expect to see gray squirrels in the winter.

    (C) People can expect to see chipmunks during the winter.

    (D) Chipmunks are non-hibernators.

4. In the course of the lecture, the professor mentions both torpor and deep hibernators. Which of the following animals are torpor hibernators, and which are deep hibernators?

	Torpor Hibernators	Deep Hibernators
(A) Raccoons		
(B) Toads		
(C) Skunks		
(D) Woodchucks		

5. What is the main topic of the lecture?

    (A) Why bears are not true hibernators.

    (B) The characteristics of various hibernators.

    (C) The details of predictive dormancy.

    (D) The various kinds of deep hibernators.

6. What is true hibernation?

    (A) A state of complete inactivity for a long period of time.

    (B) A condition of sensing winter approaching and acting accordingly.

    (C) A state of unconsciousness that lasts for a short period of time.

    (D) A condition where the animal can rouse itself from dormancy.

Vocabulary Review

A Choose and write the correct word that matches each definition.

subsidize	erosion	reconstruct	incinerator	disabled
jeopardize	dwindle	resemble	durable	furor
upset	make	quantum	snowball	accomplish

1. _____ anger

2. _____ to provide economic assistance

3. _____ to put in danger

4. _____ to look the same as

5. _____ to put back together

6. _____ something that burns things

7. _____ to decrease or get smaller

8. _____ unable to do things because of a physical problem

9. _____ slowly break down because of nature

10. _____ long-lasting

11. _____ unhappy

12. _____ to manufacture

13. _____ to achieve

14. _____ to spread

15. _____ an amount of energy

B Listen to the definitions, and fill in the blanks. Then choose the correct word. 🎧 ⊙4-17

| archeology | excavation | pottery | recycling | photography | free trade |

1. This is the _____ of a big hole to expose _____ and other findings so that we can _____ ancient cultures.

2. This activity _____ and _____ and reduces _____ gas emissions.

3. This is a government policy that allows people to _____ whatever they want with whomever they want, without any _____.

4. This art is _____ and other materials. Usually, _____ a very hot kiln.

5. This technology slowly developed _____ but finally started to _____ in the 19th century.

6. _____ is the study of _____ by _____ ancient remains.

Connecting Content

7 Connecting Content

Overview

■ Introduction

In order to answer these questions correctly, you must identify the relationships between various ideas in the listening passage. Sometimes these ideas are stated openly; other times they must be inferred. These questions sometimes ask you to classify items into categories, identify a sequence of events or the steps involved in a process, or specify the relationship between various ideas in a manner that was not presented in the passage. Other questions may ask you to make inferences about information in the passage and then make a prediction, come to a conclusion, or extrapolate some other information.

■ Question Types

1. What is the likely outcome of doing procedure X before procedure Y?

2. What can be inferred about X?

3. What does the professor imply about X?

■ Useful Tips

• Pay attention to the way that you take your notes.

• Take note of the category words, their characteristics, and examples.

Sample iBT Question

What can be inferred about the student's roommate?

Ⓐ His grades are not very good.

Ⓑ He does not enjoy his classes.

Ⓒ He is a very selfish individual.

Ⓓ He has more friends than the student.

Script

M2: Hi, Mr. Jones. I was wondering if I could speak to you for a moment.

M1: Certainly, Bobby. What seems to be the trouble?

M2: Well, I really like my classes and everything, but I am having some trouble with my roommate. The problem is that we have completely different schedules. I like to go to bed early and then get up in the morning to do my studying. My roommate likes to stay up late and then sleep through the morning. This wouldn't be too much of a problem if he were quiet when I am trying to sleep, but at night he likes to play loud music and talk on the telephone. I try to be as patient as possible with him, but when the shoe is on the other foot, he is not as understanding. For example, one night I invited a few of my friends over so we could work on a project. My roommate got upset when they wouldn't leave by eleven in the evening, but then the very next night, he invited his friends over, and they stayed up talking until two a.m.! I just want to live with someone who keeps the same schedule as me.

Correct Answer The right answer to the above question is (C). The student's roommate only thinks about his own situation, so this makes him very selfish.

Practice with Conversations

A   Listen to part of a conversation between a student and a professor. 🔊 4-19

1. **What does the professor imply about ascending too quickly?**

   Ⓐ It is only dangerous to babies and handicapped people.
   Ⓑ It can affect people who are in good physical condition.
   Ⓒ It is most dangerous to children who are not with their mothers.
   Ⓓ It affects animals more than humans in most cases.

2. **According to the professor, how can acclimatization affect the body?**

   Ⓐ It can cause a heart attack.
   Ⓑ It can deprive the body of fluids.
   Ⓒ It can make a person go crazy.
   Ⓓ It can cause altitude sickness.

3. **Listen again to part of the conversation. Then answer the question.**

   What does the professor imply when he says this? 🎧

   Ⓐ He does not mind patiently explaining the subject.
   Ⓑ He is irritated by dimwitted students.
   Ⓒ He thinks the student is causing him a lot of trouble.
   Ⓓ He is afraid of boring the student with a long explanation.

• **ascend (v)** to climb or go upward   • **strenuous (a)** vigorous   • **hydrate (v)** to take in water   • **replenish (v)** to make full or complete again   • **nausea (n)** sickness of the stomach; queasiness   • **reduce (v)** to make less or smaller   • **accompany (v)** to go along with someone

4. Listen to the conversation, and fill in the blanks to complete the conversation notes.

1) Student wants to speak to professor
   A) Had problem understanding lecture
   B) Professor offers _____

2) Discusses _____
   A) Occurs in people _____
   B) Caused by lack of _____
   C) Can cause feelings of _____ or _____

3) Some are acclimatized to it

4) _____ helps prevent it

5. Complete the following summary with the words given below.

A student asked his professor to help him (1)_____ from an earlier lecture. The lecture was about high altitude sickness. The professor started by defining high altitude sickness as an illness that occurs when people (2)_____ too quickly. People tend to feel ill because they are not breathing as many (3)_____ as they normally do. If a person were on a plane that was flying at 12,000 feet, he would be taking in (4)_____ oxygen molecules with each breath. This depletion in oxygen intake can cause the person to feel dizzy or nauseous. The professor then told the student about some of the (5)_____ in high altitudes. The person could start to ascend from no more than 10,000 feet and ascend slowly. The professor also pointed out the benefits of drinking plenty of fluids and (6)_____ for the first twenty-four hours after flying.

ways to acclimatize	understand a concept
40% fewer	oxygen molecules
ascend into the atmosphere	of refraining from strenuous activity

B Listen to part of a conversation between a student and a housing office clerk. (○ 4-20)

1. According to the student, why does she have to remain for one more semester?

   Ⓐ She has to do student teaching.
   Ⓑ She does not have enough credit.
   Ⓒ She does not have any other place to go.
   Ⓓ She loves the dorm so much.

2. What reason does the office clerk give the student as to why the foreign student should be given the dormitory room?

   Ⓐ The female student has been on campus longer.
   Ⓑ The foreign student does not know the area.
   Ⓒ The foreign student receives better grades.
   Ⓓ The female student's best friends live in the dorm.

3. What can be inferred about incoming foreign students?

   Ⓐ They should be made to feel as welcome as possible.
   Ⓑ They should have to fend for themselves on campus.
   Ⓒ They cause the most damage to dorm rooms.
   Ⓓ They are the most important students on campus.

• **allocate (v)** to set apart for a particular purpose • **upgrade (n)** an improvement • **spiteful (a)** full of malice or ill intent • **desperate (a)** having an urgent need • **initially (ad)** at the beginning • **forfeit (v)** to lose something; to give up • **extend (v)** to make longer • **mistake (n)** an error

4. Listen to the conversation, and fill in the blanks to complete the conversation notes.

1) Student visits _____
   A) Wants to _____
   B) Gives personal information
2) Clerk says can't stay there because of _____
3) Student becomes upset
4) Clerk refuses to kick _____ out
5) Student _____ situation

5. Complete the following summary with the words given below.

A student stops by the housing office to let the clerk know that she needs to remain in her dorm room for an (1)_____ because she forgot she had to (2)_____.
The clerk checks the computer and finds that her room has already been allocated to a (3)_____ _____ for next semester, so the student must (4)_____ arrangements.
(5)_____ since she feels she should be able to remain in her room since she is a senior. The clerk kindly informs her that the reason the university puts foreign students in dorm rooms is to try to (6)_____ in a new country and on a new campus.
The clerk suggests that she find an off-campus house with one of her friends. The student understands the clerk's point of view and mentions a friend she knows that (7)_____.

this angers the student	extra semester
help them get comfortable	needs a roommate
complete her student teaching	foreign student
find new housing	

C   Listen to part of a conversation between a student and a music hall official. ◉ 4-21

1. **What compromise does the officer offer the student?**

   Ⓐ The officer tells the student to drop out of the big concert.
   Ⓑ The officer cancels the construction.
   Ⓒ The officer allows the student to practice in the theater building.
   Ⓓ The entire concert is canceled.

2. **Why would the construction workers coming in after hours be an inconvenience for the students living next door?**

   Ⓐ All of the students next door want to take construction classes.
   Ⓑ The noise of the construction would keep the students up all night.
   Ⓒ The construction workers are taking the students' parking spaces.
   Ⓓ The students next door are all theater majors.

3. **At first, what is the attitude of the officer towards the student?**

   Ⓐ He will do anything to help the student prepare for the concert.
   Ⓑ He does not care one bit about the student's problem.
   Ⓒ He cannot understand why the student is so upset.
   Ⓓ He pities the student, but he is being practical.

• **inconvenience (n)** something that causes discomfort or trouble • **guarantee (n)** a promise or assurance • **prior (a)** earlier in time or order; beforehand • **utilize (v)** to make use of • **mobile (a)** able to move • **pushy (a)** self-assertive • **polish (v)** to make exact or better • **convenient (a)** suitable or agreeable • **crew (n)** a group of people working together for one purpose

4. Listen to the conversation, and fill in the blanks to complete the conversation notes.

1) Student complains about _____
   A) Construction causes noise
   B) Can't concentrate on _____
2) Official says workers can't stop construction
3) Student needs to _____
4) Official offers to let student use _____ for one week
5) Student agrees

5. Complete the following summary with the words given below.

A student storms into Lincoln Music Hall and (1)_____ on duty that she (2)_____ herself practicing the piano because there are construction workers in the building (3)_____. The officer apologizes but tells her that the upgrades on Lincoln Hall (4)_____ before the big concert and that the construction workers are only booked for (5)_____. The student says that she requires a full (6)_____ of practice on her Bach piece and simply cannot have that much noise. The official offers her a (7)_____. He will give her (8)_____ to use the piano in the theater building for one week while the construction workers finish their job. The student agrees to this compromise and thanks the official.

six weeks	cannot hear	complains to the official
one week	making too much noise	are necessary
written permission	compromise	

D Listen to part of a conversation between a student and a student office clerk. ⊙ 4-22

1. What is the likely outcome of failing to attend a school field trip without calling to cancel?

   Ⓐ The student will be required to attend the field trip next semester.
   Ⓑ The student can never successfully apply for the field trip again.
   Ⓒ The student's field trip application will be denied.
   Ⓓ The student will be exempt from the field trip.

2. Why was it important that the student call to let the science office know that he could not make the trip?

   Ⓐ The field trip is so popular that the office allows everyone to have a fair chance to attend.
   Ⓑ The science office loves to hear about sick students.
   Ⓒ The science office gets reimbursed by the university if sick students do not attend.
   Ⓓ The workers at Inglewood Forest only allow fifty students on a field trip at one time.

3. What implication is the science office clerk making when she tells the student to get to the bus stop early?

   Ⓐ She wants the student to be first in line because she does not like female students.
   Ⓑ She thinks the student will have a good chance of filling a vacancy provided he gets there on time.
   Ⓒ The office clerk believes the field trip will be cancelled.
   Ⓓ The office clerk has never gone to Inglewood Forest.

• **forfeit (v)** to lose something as a result of a fault • **crucial (a)** extremely important • **consolation (n)** the act of offering comfort • **vacancy (n)** an unoccupied place • **preferential (a)** given special consideration • **delete (v)** to erase • **attend (v)** to be present; to go to • **basis (n)** the base upon which something rests

4. Listen to the conversation, and fill in the blanks to complete the conversation notes.

1) Student visits office worker
   A) Needs to _____
   B) But application was _____
2) Worker says student _____ last time
3) Student never called to cancel
   A) Trip is _____
   B) If didn't cancel last time, cannot go on trip
4) Student needs trip to_____
5) Can show up early in case other student doesn't _____

5. Complete the following summary with the words given below.

A student went into the science office because he (1)_____ why his application to attend the Inglewood Forest field trip had been denied. The office clerk informed him that the reason he was denied was that he had (2)_____ for the same field trip last term but (3)_____ on that day. The student explained that he did not attend the trip because he had the flu. The clerk told him that because he had not bothered to (4)_____ the science office, he had (5)_____ to go on the trip. The student told the clerk that he needed to attend the field trip in order to graduate and that there (6)_____ he could go. The clerk said that she was sorry, but the only way he would have a chance at going was to (7)_____ on the day of the trip and hope to (8)_____ left by another student.

forfeited his chance	had not shown up	must be a way
call in and inform	could not understand	fill a vacancy
submitted an application	wait at the bus stop	

Practice with Lectures

A   Listen to part of a lecture in a psychology class. ⊙ 5-01

1. For each situation, check the appropriate box indicating whether the person or thing exerted a positive or negative use of inhibition.

Situation	Positive display	Negative display
(A) Bobby keeps eating even though he is full.		
(B) Eric jumps into a fast moving river after his ball.		
(C) There is a fire, so Sue calls the fire department.		
(D) Mike refuses to take a bath for fear of drowning.		
(E) Lucy resists the temptation to steal candy from a store.		

2. According to the professor, what is one way inhibition can affect a person positively?

   Ⓐ It can lead the person into a dangerous situation.
   Ⓑ It cannot affect the person positively.
   Ⓒ It can help the person find food when he is hungry.
   Ⓓ It can keep the person out of a dangerous situation.

3. What does the professor imply about inhibition?

   Ⓐ It can be learned by all creatures, from insects to humans.
   Ⓑ It is a negative quality in all creatures.
   Ⓒ It can be viewed as good or bad depending on the situation.
   Ⓓ It can cause physical harm.

• **bash (v)** to strike very hard   • **deem (v)** to believe   • **obtain (v)** to acquire   • **exert (v)** to put into use; to make an effort
• **perish (v)** to die   • **detrimental (a)** damaging   • **gratification (n)** great satisfaction   • **peers (n)** friends; equals

4. Listen to the lecture, and fill in the blanks to complete the lecture notes.

1) Professor describes _____
   A) Can be positive or _____
   B) Provides different examples
      - _____ going after food behind window
      - Boy and burning building

2) Humans can think about _____
   A) Describes shy girl at school
      - Doesn't talk, so can't make friends – _____
      - Doesn't talk to stranger, so is safe – _____

5. Complete the following summary with the words given below.

Inhibition is a mental state in which a person either stops or is hesitant (1)_____
with a particular action. An example of inhibition is a housefly that repeatedly bashes itself
against a window (2)_____ on the other side. It is the (3)_____ to try to get to
the food, and the fly's lack of inhibition keeps it from (4)_____ to obtain the
food. In this case, a lack of inhibition is (5)_____; however inhibition can also be
seen as a good thing. It can help human beings find a better method of (6)_____.
For example, a child may want to chase a ball that bounces into the street, (7)_____
_____. However, if the child should pause to look both ways, then her inhibition would
allow her to (8)_____.

finding another method	problem solving	make a safer choice
to follow through	fly's instinct	to get the food
risking the child's safety	viewed as negative	

B Listen to part of a lecture in a zoology class. 🔵 5-02

1. In the chart below, indicate which characteristics are true of each different type of whale by checking the appropriate boxes.

Type	Teeth	Baleen	Migrates
(A) Humpback Whale			
(B) Sperm Whale			
(C) Killer Whale			
(D) Blue Whale			

2. Why do whales migrate to warmer waters?

   Ⓐ To avoid whaling ships.
   Ⓑ To eat.
   Ⓒ To breed and give birth.
   Ⓓ To attack dolphins.

3. What can be inferred about a whale's intelligence?

   Ⓐ Whales panic in stressful situations and generally are killed.
   Ⓑ A whale uses its intelligence to adapt to stressful situations.
   Ⓒ Whales are able to learn the human alphabet.
   Ⓓ Whales are the least intelligent creature in the ocean.

• **migration (n)** a number of animals moving in unison • **distinct (a)** different in nature • **distinguish (v)** to recognize as different • **formation (n)** a particular arrangement of different parts • **gorge (v)** to stuff with food • **sieve (n)** a container used to separate large parts from smaller parts • **activity (n)** a specific action • **typical (a)** showing a particular characteristic

4. Listen to the lecture, and fill in the blanks to complete the lecture notes.

> 1) Professor discusses _____   A) Humpback whale
>   B) _____ whale
>
> 2) Mentions baleen   A) Filters water from _____
>   B) Made of keratin
>
> 3) Toothed whales   A) Sperm whale
>   B) _____ whale
>   C) _____ whale
>
> 4) Whale migration   A) For food
>   B) For _____
>
> 5) Whale intelligence   A) Have very large brains
>   B) Are social
>   C) Communicate through _____

5. Complete the following summary with the words given below.

The mammals known as whales can be divided into two main groups: (1)_____ and those with teeth. Baleen is a sieve-like structure made of (2)_____ that filters out plankton for baleen whales to eat. Two types of baleen whales are the (3)_____ and the humpback whale. Toothed whales, such as the (4)_____ and the killer whale, prey on larger animals such as fish or squid. Whales also migrate. They migrate into warmer waters (5)_____, and then they migrate into colder waters (6)_____. One would think that the energy spent for these mass migrations would not be worth it; however, once whales are in their feeding waters, they are able to gorge to their hearts' content. Whales are very intelligent and will often (7)_____ to try to avoid danger.

> to breed and give birth   those with baleen   blue whale
> sperm whale   to feed   keratin
> work together in groups

C   Listen to part of a lecture in a culture class. 🔊 5-03

Culture

1. **What can be inferred about the Statue of Liberty?**

   Ⓐ It is considered to be the only important symbol in the United States.
   Ⓑ It includes a popular family style restaurant.
   Ⓒ It is considered a very important site by American citizens.
   Ⓓ Every American citizen visits this site once in their lifetime.

2. **What function did the Statue of Liberty serve for the first sixteen years of its life in New York Harbor?**

   Ⓐ A prison.
   Ⓑ An amusement park ride.
   Ⓒ A museum.
   Ⓓ A lighthouse.

3. **How does the professor organize the information about American landmarks?**

   Ⓐ Individually.
   Ⓑ Chronologically.
   Ⓒ By most famous to least famous.
   Ⓓ By cost.

- **origin (n)** the beginning   • **conceive (v)** to think; to create   • **visage (n)** the face   • **persuade (v)** to convince
- **precarious (a)** uncertain; unstable   • **frigate (n)** a fast military and cargo ship   • **dedicate (v)** to set apart for some purpose   • **icon (n)** a representation of something well known   • **tourist (n)** a person traveling for pleasure
- **construct (v)** to build or make   • **immigrant (n)** a person who goes to live in a different country

4. Listen to the lecture, and fill in the blanks to complete the lecture notes.

1) Professor mentions _____
   A) In South Dakota
   B) _____ of four U.S. presidents
   C) Made to increase _____
   D) Took fourteen years to finish

2) Professor discusses Statue of Liberty
   A) Woman in robe wearing _____
   B) Given to U.S. by _____
   C) In New York Harbor
   D) Has many _____
   E) Very recognizable American icon

5. Complete the following summary with the words given below.

Two famous monuments in the United States are Mount Rushmore and the Statue of Liberty. Mount Rushmore is located in (1)_____ and is a large sculpture of four United States presidents that is etched into the (2)_____ of the tallest peak in the (3)_____. The four presidents represented in the sculpture are George Washington, Thomas Jefferson, Theodore Roosevelt, and Abraham Lincoln. The monument was conceived by a man named Doane Robinson who was trying to think of a way to (4)_____ to the Black Hills region. A sculptor by the name of Gutzon Borglum and his four hundred workers completed Mount Rushmore in 1941. The Statue of Liberty is a monument of a woman wearing a robe and crown while (5)_____ and a flaming torch. She was given to the Americans by the French in 1884 as a (6)_____ and goodwill. One of the designers of the Statue of Liberty was Alexandre Gustave Eiffel, the same man who designed the Eiffel Tower in Paris, France. The Statue of Liberty is made of (7)_____ and stands on an island in the middle of (8)_____.

gesture of friendship	Black Hills	South Dakota
pure copper	New York Harbor	granite hillside
bring more tourists	holding a stone tablet	

D   Listen to part of a lecture in a history class.   5-04

1. **What can be inferred about the early Greek tyrants?**

    (A) They were not supported by the poor.
    (B) They were supported by the elite they opposed.
    (C) They were opposed by the elite.
    (D) They ruled without any problems.

2. **What resulted from the rise of tyranny in ancient Greece?**

    (A) The word today means a kind, helpful leader.
    (B) The word is not used anymore.
    (C) The word is used to describe all leaders now.
    (D) The word now refers to a leader who rules with absolute power.

3. **What can be inferred about the nature of words and language from the lecture?**

    (A) The meanings of words never change.
    (B) The dictionary is open to interpretation.
    (C) The meanings of words often evolve along with human civilizations.
    (D) The Roman alphabet is better than the Greek alphabet.

• **brutal (a)** savage or cruel   • **aristocrat (n)** a person born of nobility   • **bribe (n)** money or consideration promised with an intent of corrupting behavior   • **conjure (v)** to produce   • **negative (a)** unfavorable   • **lofty (a)** elevated in style or tone   • **aspiration (n)** a strong desire   • **appealing (a)** attracting interest or desire   • **rural (a)** of the country; not of the city   • **connotation (n)** the associated meaning of a word

4. Listen to the lecture, and fill in the blanks to complete the lecture notes.

1) Professor describes _____ in ancient Greece
   A) Past definition is different from current one
   B) Aristocrats secured power by _____
   C) Was during _____

2) Describes ancient Greece
   A) Democracy starting
   B) Mostly _____
   C) Aristocrats overthrow them

3) Mentions populists
   A) Type of _____
   B) Try to stand up for _____
   C) Want _____

5. Complete the following summary with the words given below.

The term tyranny is defined as the (1)_____ of power by one (2)_____ _____ over a group of people. Although the current term has negative connotations, the first tyrants were not harsh rulers but were in fact a group of aristocrats (3)_____ _____ who wished to represent the (4)_____ who were being undervalued and (5)_____ by the elite. Some of these populists gained control and became known as tyrants because their method of amassing support from the poor or slaves (6)_____ with money or promises of freedom.

known as populists	unjust exercising	mistreated
poor people	was to bribe them	absolute ruler

Integrated Listening & Speaking

Listen to a different version of the previous lecture. And say the answers out loud. 🎧 5-05

1) Professor mentions Mount Rushmore

   A) In South Dakota
   B) Sculptures of four U.S. presidents
   C) Made to increase tourism
   D) Took fourteen years to finish

2) Professor discusses Statue of Liberty

   A) Woman in robe wearing crown
   B) Given to U.S. by France
   C) In New York Harbor
   D) Has many symbols
   E) Very recognizable American icon

1. In what U.S. state is Mount Rushmore located?

   _____

2. What does Mount Rushmore represent?

   _____

3. The Statue of Liberty is a statue of a woman. What two things is she holding?

   _____

B Listen to a different version of the previous lecture. And say the answers out loud. ⊙ 5-06

1) Professor describes tyranny in ancient Greece

   A) Past definition is different from current one
   B) Aristocrats secured power by helping poor
   C) Was during archaic period

2) Describes ancient Greece

   A) Democracy starting
   B) Mostly monarchies
   C) Aristocrats overthrow them

3) Mentions populists

   A) Type of tyrant
   B) Try to stand up for poor people
   C) Want equal representation

1. How did tyrants gain the support of the poor or the slaves?

_____

2. In what way did the tyrants evolve so that today's definition of them is no longer seen as positive?

_____

3. Where did tyranny originate?

_____

TOEFL iBT Practice Test

Listen to part of a conversation between two students.

1. Why does Mark mention role play?

   (A) It is not offered in his class.
   (B) They role play in class to prepare for job interviews.
   (C) It is his favorite part of the class.
   (D) It is not a useful exercise.

2. What can be inferred about Nancy?

   (A) She does not feel comfortable speaking in front of people.
   (B) She is a great public speaker.
   (C) She could be the host of a television talk show.
   (D) She will not be able to take this class.

3. Listen again to part of the conversation. Then answer the question.

   What is the man's attitude toward the woman?

   (A) He thinks she is a poor public speaker.
   (B) He does not think this class will help her.
   (C) He wants to help her get into this class.
   (D) He is hoping she will quit the class and date him.

4. What will the woman probably do next?

   (A) Contact Professor Smith.
   (B) Prepare for an interview.
   (C) Apply for the class.
   (D) Go out for a meal.

5. What are the speakers mainly discussing?

   (A) The concepts and skills taught in the man's class.
   (B) The man's ability to learn much in his class.
   (C) The chances of the woman being able to attend the class.
   (D) The importance of first impressions and good interviews.

Listen to part of a lecture in an education class. 5-08

Education

1. According to John Dewey's philosophy, what would be the best way to learn how to make a pancake?

   Ⓐ Listen to a teacher recite the ingredients and recipe.

   Ⓑ Gather the ingredients and recipe and try to make a pancake.

   Ⓒ Listen to a lecture about pancakes given by an actual chef.

   Ⓓ Buy nice skillets to make pancakes.

2. What does the professor imply about John Dewey's philosophy of progressive education?

   Ⓐ It is better than the rote learning teaching philosophy.

   Ⓑ It is not a good teaching philosophy and best forgotten.

   Ⓒ It is an outdated philosophy of education.

   Ⓓ The history of this philosophy is not important.

3. According to the professor, what is one way that humans can learn better?

   Ⓐ Humans learn better by participating in real-life activities.

   Ⓑ Humans learn better by memorizing information.

   Ⓒ Real-life activities distract people from learning.

   Ⓓ People should do half activities and half memorization.

4. Listen again to part of the lecture. Then answer the question. 🎧

   What does the woman imply when she says this? 🎧

   Ⓐ Dewey copied the laboratory processes for his learning approaches.

   Ⓑ She does not need to learn this since she studied it in the laboratory.

   Ⓒ She was not aware that she has already been using Dewey's methods.

   Ⓓ The laboratory process is much simpler than the methods Dewey used.

5. What aspect of John Dewey does the professor mainly discuss?

   Ⓐ His personal life.

   Ⓑ His teaching philosophy.

   Ⓒ His connection with educational progressives.

   Ⓓ His five-step approach to learning.

6. Why does the professor explain educational progressivism?

   Ⓐ To give Dewey's five-step process for learning.

   Ⓑ To explain Dewey's thoughts on how people learn best.

   Ⓒ To summarize Dewey's philosophy of education.

   Ⓓ To connect it with Dewey's personal biography.

Vocabulary Review

A Choose and write the correct word that matches each definition.

persuade	pushy	inconvenience	gorge	obtain
distinguish	tourist	encompass	upgrade	tedious
perish	connotation	visage	conjure	peers

1. _____ to surround or include

2. _____ friends

3. _____ to acquire

4. _____ to convince

5. _____ something that causes discomfort or trouble

6. _____ an improvement

7. _____ to die

8. _____ to produce

9. _____ the face

10. _____ to recognize as different

11. _____ a person traveling for pleasure

12. _____ the associated meaning of a word

13. _____ to stuff with food

14. _____ long and tiresome

15. _____ self-assertive

B Listen to the definitions, and fill in the blanks. Then choose the correct word. 🎧 ⊙ 5-09

Mount Rushmore	progressive education	bioclimatology	inhibition	tyrant

1. This is a philosophy of teaching and learning that _____ a hands-on approach and integration into _____.

2. This is a monument in South Dakota that features the _____ of four American _____ _____.

3. This concept _____ what happens when _____ from reacting instinctively.

4. This was a type of ruler that gained _____ by promising them money.

5. This is a field of science that looks at _____ people have on _____.

Unit 8

Making Inferences

Making Inferences

Overview

■ Introduction

In order to answer these questions correctly, you must come to conclusions based upon facts given in the listening passage. You must take the information given and determine a future outcome. These questions may ask about various things like a simple process, a cause and effect, or a comparison and contrast.

■ Question Types

1. What does the professor imply about X?

2. What will the student probably do next?

3. What can be inferred about X?

4. What does the professor imply when he says this? (replay)

■ Useful Tips

• Try to come to a conclusion about the details you hear while you are taking notes.

• Try to generalize about the information you hear.

• Think about what is inferred by the speakers.

• Concentrate on answer choices that use words which do not appear in the passage.

Sample iBT Question

What will the student probably do next?

- (A) Call her friend immediately.
- (B) File a complaint about the janitor.
- (C) Continue looking for her ID card.
- (D) Wait for her friend to arrive.

Script

M: Then I can't help you.

W: Oh, please don't say that! You have to help me!

M: There's nothing I can do. I know you. I've seen you here many times, but I'm simply not allowed to let you in without proper identification.

W: Okay, wait…! I have an idea. I just remembered something… Can I just give you my ID number?

M: Hmm… I don't know.

W: …Look! My friend will be picking me up in a minute. How about you let her in with her ID card and let me go in with her. I'll give you my ID number. Is that okay?

M: Where's your friend? I don't see her.

W: She's going to pick me up. She'll be here in a minute.

M: Okay… Uh, if she has proper identification, I'll let you do that.

W: Oh, thank you! I really appreciate it.

 Correct Answer The correct answer is (D) . The student says that her friend will be meeting her soon, so she will likely just wait for her friend to arrive.

Practice with Conversations

A   Listen to part of a conversation between a student and a bookstore manager. ○ 5-11

1. **What can be inferred from the conversation?**

    (A) A 25% buyback system has always been the store's policy.

    (B) There is only one person working in the store.

    (C) The manager paid the student more than 25% for the used textbooks.

    (D) Most of the used books in the store do not look brand new.

2. **Why were the textbooks in good condition?**

    (A) The student just bought them a few days ago.

    (B) The student never read them.

    (C) The student took very good care of them while reading them.

    (D) The student received the books directly from the publisher.

3. **Listen again to part of the conversation. Then answer the question.** ᨏ

    What does the manager imply when he says this? ᨏ

    (A) He is apologizing for trying to cheat the student.

    (B) He is advising the student to go to another bookstore.

    (C) He is being fair to the inexperienced student.

    (D) He is trying to tell the student that his books are worthless.

• **across the board (ad)** the same for everything   • **bargain (n)** a good price   • **buck (n)** a dollar   • **consider (v)** to think about   • **get rid of (v)** to put away; to throw away   • **obsolete (a)** old; outdated   • **rip-off (v)** to cheat

4. Listen to the conversation, and fill in the blanks to complete the conversation notes.

> 1) Student goes to _____
>   A) Wants to sell _____
>   B) Has never read them
> 2) Wants to sell them for _____
> 3) Manager offers lower price
>   A) Will pay _____% of the original price
>   B) Student wants _____%
> 4) Manager explains bookstore policy
> 5) Student takes _____% price

5. Complete the following summary with the words given below.

A student brought a (1)_____ into a bookstore and spoke to the manager. The manager expressed surprise that the books were almost new. The student told him the books cost him $430 but he would sell them for $300. The manager replied that he could only pay 25% of the (2)_____ for the books. He said a 25% buyback system was the policy for all books. (3)_____ why the policy was only 25%. The manager replied that most of the customers were (4)_____ to pay more than 50% for used books, so, in order to make a profit, the store couldn't afford to pay more than (5)_____ for the books. The student understood and agreed to sell them for $110.

box of textbooks	the student asked	unwilling
original purchase prices	25%	

B Listen to part of a conversation between a student and a librarian.  5-12

1. What can be inferred from the conversation?

   Ⓐ Library workers like CDs that contain reference information.
   Ⓑ The library does not have a deposit box.
   Ⓒ The librarian feels the student should be more careful.
   Ⓓ The librarian likes baseball game CDs.

2. What can be inferred about the librarian?

   Ⓐ He is not willing to help the student.
   Ⓑ He is a kind and helpful person.
   Ⓒ He has the woman's brother's CD.
   Ⓓ He did not try very hard to find the CD.

3. According to the librarian, what is one possible place the CD ended up?

   Ⓐ It could be in one of the library computers.
   Ⓑ It could be in the trash.
   Ⓒ It could be at his house.
   Ⓓ It could be tossed in with the other library materials.

- **atlas (n)** a book of maps • **charge (v)** to ask a person for money • **deposit (v)** to put into; to drop into
- **drop-off (v)** to leave something or someone somewhere • **fine (n)** a penalty • **generic (a)** general; not specific
- **miscellaneous (a)** not belonging to any category • **notice (v)** to see, read, or hear • **toss (v)** to throw lightly or carelessly

4. Listen to the conversation, and fill in the blanks to complete the conversation notes.

    1) Student goes to library to _____

    2) Had lost game CD earlier
       A) Was her brother's
       B) Think she dropped it off at _____

    3) Librarian said had not been reported

    4) Gets _____

    5) Will call if finds _____

5. Complete the following summary with the words given below.

    A student went to the library to return a CD. She told the librarian that (1)_____ she had accidentally returned her brother's CD, which looked like the CD (2)_____
    _____. She said she wanted to get her brother's CD back if possible. The librarian said that (3)_____. He checked the miscellaneous basket, but it wasn't there. He told her that possibly (4)_____ had noticed the CD yet. The student then gave him (5)_____
    _____ and phone number. The librarian said that if anybody came across the CD, he would call her. She asked him about the fine for returning the library's CD so late. The librarian told her that (6)_____ for the CD. She thanked him.

nobody	a week earlier
she borrowed from the library	he had not seen it
he wasn't going to charge her	her name

C Listen to part of a conversation between a student and a professor. 5-13

1. What can be inferred from this conversation?

   (A) The student wants to become a cook.
   (B) The student wants to become a chef.
   (C) The student wants to become a social worker.
   (D) The student wants to work at an orphanage.

2. Why did the professor tell the student to give his mom a big hug?

   (A) He thinks the student is lucky to have a mother.
   (B) He thinks the orphanage was great work experience.
   (C) He owns an orphanage.
   (D) He is an orphan and wishes he had a mother.

3. What does the professor imply about the student's orphanage experience?

   (A) It will really impress the interviewers.
   (B) The student should not mention the experience.
   (C) That experience will show that the student is a real team player.
   (D) Volunteer jobs are not important for getting a real job.

• **co-worker (n)** someone one works with • **graduate (v)** to finish school or university • **hire (v)** to employ • **interviewee (n)** the person being interviewed • **orphanage (n)** a home for children with no parents • **reject (v)** to say no; to refuse • **resume (n)** a document describing one's educational background and work experience

4. Listen to the conversation, and fill in the blanks to complete the conversation notes.

1) Student tells professor about _____
   A) Doesn't like _____
   B) Got rejected by _____

2) Professor encourages student
   A) Says to talk about KFC experience
   B) Says don't volunteer negative experience

3) Student volunteered at _____
   A) Professor says to talk about that
   B) Is good _____

5. Complete the following summary with the words given below.

A student (1)_____ for some advice for his job interview. It was for a social work position. The student said (2)_____. When the professor asked why, the student replied that (3)_____ in social work and he hadn't done an interview in six years. He said he had an interview at McDonald's but wasn't hired. The professor told him not to mention that at the interview. The student also told the professor (4)_____ as a cook. He said he enjoyed the job and got along well with everyone. The professor was happy to hear this. He said the employers probably already understood that he had little work experience, but they might be looking for a bright, (5)_____ who was a good team player and easy to get along with. The student mentioned he had volunteered at an orphanage. The professor was very pleased. He advised the student to talk a lot about that experience.

asked his professor	he didn't have any experience	he was nervous
he worked at KFC	smiling person	

D Listen to part of a conversation between a student and a professor. 5-14

1. **Listen again to part of the conversation. Then answer the question.**

    What does the professor imply when she says this?

    (A) The student's answer about Franklin's work in France was correct.
    (B) The student failed the midterm exam.
    (C) The student is in danger of failing this class.
    (D) The student's answer about Franklin's work in France was incorrect.

2. **What did the professor advise the student to do?**

    (A) Study more often and stop missing so many classes.
    (B) Form a study group with some of her classmates.
    (C) Stop missing so many classes.
    (D) Be at least a little familiar with each topic.

3. **How many questions were on the exam?**

    (A) Two.
    (B) Three.
    (C) Four.
    (D) Several.

• **adjustment (n)** a change   • **assume (v)** to think something is true   • **congress (n)** a nation's legislature   • **flee (v)** to run away; to escape   • **hostilities (n)** warlike violence   • **overrun (v)** to defeat or take over   • **vague (a)** unclear and confusing   • **support (n)** assistance   • **tactic (n)** a plan or strategy

4. Listen to the conversation, and fill in the blanks to complete the conversation notes.

1) Professor wants to speak to student
   A) Concerned about _____
   B) Said she didn't understand _____

2) Professor goes over _____
   A) Explains first question
   B) Explains second question
   C) Explains third question

3) Professor tells student to _____

5. Complete the following summary with the words given below.

A professor asked her student why she failed her exam. The student told the professor that (1)_____ because she didn't understand two of the topics. There were three questions on the exam. Each one was (2)_____. The student said she understood (3)_____. She said there were only two topics she didn't understand and, by coincidence, (4)_____ on the exam were about the two she didn't understand. The professor told the student that her class participation was good and that (5)_____ on her assignment. The professor went over the exam questions with the student and told her (6)_____ to study all of the topics at least a little and to meet with her before (7)_____ for some more guidance.

two of the three questions	she failed	the final exam
most of the topics	next time	an essay question
she did well		

199

Practice with Lectures

A Listen to part of a lecture in an art class. 5-15

1. **What can be inferred about the term Eskimos?**

   Ⓐ Inuit people do not want to be called Eskimos.

   Ⓑ Inuit people prefer to be called Eskimos.

   Ⓒ The word Eskimos is interchangeable with Inuit.

   Ⓓ It is against the law to call Inuit people Eskimos.

2. **According to the passage, where do the Inuit live?**

   Ⓐ All over Canada.

   Ⓑ In Arctic Canada.

   Ⓒ In the Arctic regions of Russia, Alaska, Canada and Greenland.

   Ⓓ With the Eskimos of Alaska and Northern Canada.

3. **Listen again to part of the lecture. Then answer the question.**

   What does the professor imply when he says this? 🎧

   Ⓐ Alaskans are related to the Eskimos.

   Ⓑ One should not call an Inuit person an Eskimo.

   Ⓒ Russians are not real Eskimos.

   Ⓓ Eskimos originated in Greenland.

• **authentic (a)** real; not artificial • **carving (n)** a sculpture • **derogatory (a)** insulting • **flourish (v)** to grow fast and healthily • **humorous (a)** funny • **incorporate (v)** to include as part of • **miniature (a)** very small • **nomadic (a)** always moving • **perception (n)** belief as to what is true • **primitive (a)** very old style; simple

4. Listen to the lecture, and fill in the blanks to complete the lecture notes.

> 1) Professor discusses _____
>   A) Live in _____
>   B) Mostly associated with _____
>   C) Have many kinds of _____
> 2) Inuit sculptures
>   A) Becoming commercialized
>   B) Are _____ carvings
>   C) Are polished and _____
>   D) Animal and human subjects
>   E) Made of _____ but not wood

5. Complete the following summary with the words given below.

The Inuit are northern people who live in the Arctic areas of Canada, Alaska, Russia, and Greenland. Inuit art includes sculptures, paintings, and prints. Prior to the 1950s, (1)_____ _____ were small enough to hold inside one's fist. Today, the carvings have become bigger because the Inuit have settled into (2)_____ and are trying to satisfy market demand. So now, we have miniatures and larger sculptures. Also, since the 1980s, Inuit carvings have become more polished and (3)_____. The subjects of these carvings are usually animals and humans. The animals are bears, seals, whales, walruses, and (4)_____. Some themes are humorous while others are more serious. A (5)_____ of Inuit carvings is that they're never made of wood. The artists use whatever raw materials are (6)_____ and sea. The most common substance is a stone called serpentine. It's available in a range of colors from (7)_____. Other stones used include marble, quartz, and dolomite.

green to black	Inuit carvings	realistic
available from the land	unique characteristic	permanent settlements
sometimes birds		

201

B Listen to part of a lecture in a meteorology class. ⊙ 5-16

Meteorology

1. What can be inferred from the lecture?

  Ⓐ La Nina seems to be getting worse every year.
  Ⓑ There is still a lot that scientists do not understand about El Nino and La Nina.
  Ⓒ The Pacific Ocean causes more weather problems than the other oceans do.
  Ⓓ Peru and Bolivia receive bad weather year round.

2. According to the professor, what is a characteristic of La Nina?

  Ⓐ It brings warm water to the coast of South America.
  Ⓑ It originates in the northern hemisphere.
  Ⓒ In the winter, it tends to accentuate weather patterns.
  Ⓓ It essentially has the same impact as El Nino.

3. What kind of weather does El Nino cause?

  Ⓐ Both good and bad.
  Ⓑ Only bad.
  Ⓒ Only cold or rainy weather.
  Ⓓ Very dry, warm weather and some severe rainstorms.

• **accentuate (v)** to emphasize   • **desert (n)** very dry land   • **drastically (ad)** severely; seriously   • **drought (n)** an extended period of dry weather without rain   • **forecast (n)** a prediction   • **obliterate (v)** to destroy something completely   • **originate (v)** to start   • **meteorologist (n)** a person who studies climate   • **uncharacteristic (a)** unusual

4. Listen to the lecture, and fill in the blanks to complete the lecture notes.

1) Discusses _____

2) Mentions EL Nino
   A) Brings _____ to South America
   B) Occurs every _____ years
   C) Reduces _____ and _____ in area
   D) Can change weather worldwide

3) Mentions La Nina
   A) Brings _____ to South America
   B) Happens half as often as _____

4) Gives positive and negative effects of _____

5. Complete the following summary with the words given below.

El Nino and La Nina are weather phenomena that both originate in the southern hemisphere and occur in the (1)_____. Both cause major temperature changes in the surface waters of the Pacific Ocean, and eventually they trigger (2)_____ worldwide. El Nino brings warm water to the west coast of (3)_____, and La Nina brings cold water to the west coast of South America. The warm water El Nino brings to the coastal waters of Peru rises, replaces the cool nutrient-rich (4)_____ at the surface, and drastically reduces (5)_____ and fish in the area. El Nino causes unusual weather in many different areas, including droughts and severe rainstorms. La Nina contributes to (6)_____ _____ and in the winter accentuates climate in certain areas. For example, in the winter, it may cause Florida to be warmer and drier than usual.

Pacific Ocean	unusual weather phenomena	South America
water	the amount of plant life	hurricane development

C Listen to part of a lecture in a writing class.

1. **What can be inferred from the lecture?**

    Ⓐ *Angela's Ashes* is an autobiography.

    Ⓑ *Angela's Ashes* is a biography

    Ⓒ *Angela's Ashes* is a memoir.

    Ⓓ *Angela's Ashes* required a lot of research.

2. **According to the professor, which characteristic describes memoirs?**

    Ⓐ They require a lot of research.

    Ⓑ They are no longer written only by famous public officials.

    Ⓒ It is impossible to write one without doing some research on the Internet.

    Ⓓ Students do not have enough life experiences to write them.

3. **What will the students probably do after the lecture?**

    Ⓐ Go to the library to begin their research for their assignment.

    Ⓑ Contact their parents for details about their childhoods.

    Ⓒ Read an autobiography of a famous person.

    Ⓓ Go outside and start writing their assignment.

> • **chronological (a)** organized according to time • **conflict (n)** a fight, disagreement, argument, or war • **emotions (n)** feelings such as happiness, sadness, and anger • **essentially (ad)** mainly • **hardship (n)** a difficult time; a difficult experience • **interview (v)** to ask questions to get information • **flashback (n)** a quick memory from the past • **foreshadow (n)** a hint as to what might happen in the future • **in retrospect (ad)** looking back in time • **significant (a)** important

4. Listen to the lecture, and fill in the blanks to complete the lecture notes.

1) Professor gives assignment to _____
2) Explains _____
   A) Account of another person's life
   B) Autobiography describes _____
3) Describes memoir
   A) Does not need much research like _____
   B) Has narrow focus
   C) About important part of one's life
   D) Usually written by _____
   E) Is in _____ form

5. Complete the following summary with the words given below.

A biography is an account of another person's life rather than one's own. An autobiography is
(1)_____ of one's own life, usually from childhood to old age. It's a chronological,
detailed, (2)_____ that requires (3)_____ and interviews. It requires a lot
of work. A memoir is a type of autobiography which focuses on only (4)_____. The
writer merely needs to recall some events that have occurred in his life. No research is required.
It's usually shorter than an autobiography. It usually focuses on events that are significant to
the writer. If the person is (5)_____, then he writes his recollections and emotions
regarding some of the important public events of his life. Historically, they were written by world
leaders, politicians, (6)_____ and other famous people, but that's now changing.

| a lot of research | personal history | a public figure |
| a part of your life | a detailed story | military leaders |

D   Listen to part of a lecture in a geology class.

Geology

1.   What can be inferred from the lecture?

Ⓐ Tectonic plates have stopped moving.

Ⓑ The continents will soon stop moving.

Ⓒ Earthquakes are related to events in the lithosphere and asthenosphere.

Ⓓ Tectonic plates cause the asthenosphere to move.

2.   According to the lecture, how many plates are there?

Ⓐ 5

Ⓑ 19

Ⓒ 80

Ⓓ Thousands.

3.   Which of the following statements best describes what it is like below the Earth's surface?

Ⓐ The asthenosphere is at the core of the Earth.

Ⓑ The interior of the Earth is very hot.

Ⓒ The thickest part of the crust lies below the ocean floor.

Ⓓ The asthenosphere is rockier than the surface.

- **churn (v)** to move violently • **core (n)** the center part of object • **fluid (n)** a liquid • **generate (v)** to create movement of action • **glide (n)** a smooth, sliding motion • **inch (n)** 2.54 cm • **stabilize (v)** to stop moving; to stop changing

4. Listen to the lecture, and fill in the blanks to complete the lecture notes.

1) Describes _____
   A) Earth's exterior – _____
   B) Includes continents, rocks, and _____
   C) Like a giant puzzle

2) Describes asthenosphere
   A) Is semi-plastic _____
   B) Is fluid
   C) Causes _____ to move

3) Describes plate tectonics
   A) Causes _____
   B) Makes mountains
   C) _____ major and _____ minor plates

5. Complete the following summary with the words given below.

The lithosphere is the (1)_____. It's the crust, which includes the continents, the rocks, and the ocean floor. It also includes (2)_____ of the asthenosphere, which is located just below the crust. On the continents, the crust is about 80km deep, but below the ocean, it's only (3)_____. The exterior of the earth is like a puzzle broken up into giant plates that fit around Earth like a jigsaw puzzle. These giant pieces are called tectonic plates. The continents rest on these plates. They (4)_____ the upper part of the asthenosphere, which consists of a semi-plastic molten rock material, like silly putty. It is more fluid, and it moves as it responds to the churning motions of (5)_____of the Earth below. These movements inside the asthenosphere cause the tectonic plates to move as they glide or float on the moving asthenosphere. There are (6)_____ and twelve minor plates. Because the plates only move (7)_____ a year, it takes millions of years for the continents to move. But, at one time, the continents were mostly connected together.

Earth's exterior	slide along	seven major plates
the upper part	the extremely hot interior	a few inches
about 5km thick		

Integrated Listening & Speaking

Listen to a different version of the previous lecture, and say the answers out loud. 5-19

1) Professor discusses Inuit art
   A) Live in Arctic areas
   B) Mostly associated with Canada
   C) Have many kinds of artwork

2) Inuit sculptures
   A) Becoming commercialized
   B) Are miniature carvings
   C) Are polished and realistic
   D) Animal and human subjects
   E) Made of many raw materials but not wood

1. How would you describe traditional Inuit sculptures?

   _____

2. Where do most of the Inuit live?

   _____

3. What are Inuit carvings made of?

   _____

B Listen to a different version of the previous lecture, and say the answers out loud. 🔊 5-20

1) Professor gives assignment to write memoir

2) Explains biography
   A) Account of another person's life
   B) Autobiography describes writer's own life

3) Describes memoir
   A) Does not need much research like autobiography
   B) Has narrow focus
   C) About important part of one's life
   D) Usually written by important people
   E) Is in narrative form

1. What is the main difference between autobiographies and memoirs?

    _____

2. How much research is required to write a memoir?

    _____

3. Historically, what kind of people wrote memoirs?

    _____

TOEFL iBT Practice Test

Listen to part of a conversation between a student and a health club employee. 5-21

1. What is the woman's attitude toward the man?

   Ⓐ She is disinterested in his questions.
   Ⓑ She is somewhat aggressive.
   Ⓒ She is very patient with him.
   Ⓓ She is concerned about his welfare.

2. What did the man say happened to him at his previous school?

   Ⓐ He had to pay several hundred dollars to join the gym.
   Ⓑ He was allowed to use all the facilities for free.
   Ⓒ He could use the basketball court when the team was not there.
   Ⓓ He was robbed once while he was exercising.

3. Listen again to part of the conversation. Then answer the question.

   Why does the woman say this? 🎧

   Ⓐ To indicate that the man will not have to pay any money.
   Ⓑ To tell the man that he should consider the other gym.
   Ⓒ To warn the man that membership is expensive.
   Ⓓ To prove that she can answer the man's questions.

4. According to the woman, what is on the fifth floor of the building?

   Ⓐ The swimming pool.
   Ⓑ The locker room.
   Ⓒ The basketball courts.
   Ⓓ Peterson Gym.

5. What can be inferred about the man?

   Ⓐ He will visit the gym again.
   Ⓑ He will pay for a gym membership.
   Ⓒ He wants to continue speaking with the woman.
   Ⓓ He enjoys working out every day.

Listen to part of a lecture in a zoology class. 5-22

Zoology

1. What can be inferred from the lecture?

   (A) Arachnologists are predators.
   (B) Arachnologists are one species of spider.
   (C) Arachnologists believe that over 100,000 existing species of spiders have not yet been discovered.
   (D) The world's total spider population is growing.

2. According to the professor, where do spiders' webs come from?

   (A) They come from their feet and hands.
   (B) They come from their tongue.
   (C) They come from their spinnerets.
   (D) They make the webs by gathering silk.

3. Listen again to part of the lecture. Then answer the question.

   What is the professor talking about when she says this?

   (A) The development of spider webs.
   (B) The feeding habits of spiders.
   (C) The death of spiders.
   (D) The birth of spiders.

4. According to the professor, which of the following is a use of spider's silk? Choose 2 answers.

   (A) Poisoning their prey.
   (B) Raising their young.
   (C) Assisting in molting.
   (D) Climbing structures.

5. How does the professor organize the information about spider's silk that she presents to the class?

   (A) By explaining the process by which it is formed.
   (B) By making note of its numerous uses.
   (C) By listing the species that make use of it.
   (D) By refuting incorrect information students believe about it.

6. Why does the professor mention Spiderman?

   (A) To say that he does not resemble a real spider.
   (B) To compare his characteristics with actual spiders.
   (C) To make a joke about the student's answer.
   (D) To lead into a physical description of spiders.

Vocabulary Review

A Choose and write the correct word that matches each definition.

fluid	core	nomads	disposal	foreshadow
glide	derogatory	obliterate	orphanage	authentic
flourish	meteorologist	buck	tactic	obsolete

1. _____ a liquid
2. _____ to slide smoothly
3. _____ people that keep moving
4. _____ a plan or strategy
5. _____ to grow well
6. _____ insulting
7. _____ no longer useful or helpful; too old
8. _____ to destroy something completely
9. _____ to hint about what will happen in the future
10. _____ real and genuine
11. _____ a dollar
12. _____ a home for children with no parents
13. _____ the central part of an object
14. _____ a person who studies climate
15. _____ a place to put garbage

B Listen to the definitions, and fill in the blanks. Then choose the correct word. 🎧 ⊙ 6-01

lithosphere	Inuit	spiders	memoir	El Nino

1. This is _____ which describes only _____ of your life.

2. These people _____. They produce _____ including _____.

3. This weather phenomenon brings _____ to the west coast of _____ and causes _____ all over the world.

4. This is _____ in the world and it uses silk to _____ prey.

5. This _____ includes the crust, _____, ocean floor, tectonic plates and the _____ of the asthenosphere.

214

This part provides lists of important vocabulary words in each unit. They are essential words for understanding any academic texts. Many of the words are listed with their derivative forms so that students can expand their vocabulary in an effective way. These lists can be used as homework assignments.

Vocabulary Wrap-up

Unit 1 • Listening for Main Ideas

● Step A

☐ acidity	☐ albino	☐ anthropology	☐ anti-dumping
☐ aria	☐ bubonic	☐ buckwheat	☐ cavity
☐ cliché	☐ decimal	☐ deficiency	☐ discrepancy
☐ domestication	☐ extinction	☐ gingivitis	☐ habitat
☐ hereditary	☐ morbid	☐ pseudonym	☐ saliva
☐ scavenge	☐ soldiering	☐ speculate	☐ stipulation
☐ subspecies	☐ surmise	☐ traits	☐ trinity

● Step B

Noun	Verb	Adjective	Adverb
☐ intonation	☐ intonate	☐ intonational	☐ intonationally
☐ distribution	☐ distribute	☐ distributive	☐ distributively
☐ cultivation	☐ cultivate	☐ cultivatable	
☐ rigorousness		☐ rigorous	☐ rigorously
☐ deceiver	☐ deceive	☐ deceivable	☐ deceivingly
☐ poacher	☐ poach	☐ poachable	
☐ luxury		☐ luxurious	☐ luxuriously
☐ indication	☐ indicate	☐ indicative	☐ indicatively
☐ deferment	☐ defer	☐ deferrable	
☐ assistance	☐ assist	☐ assistive	
☐ recommendation	☐ recommend	☐ recommendable	
☐ registration	☐ register		
☐ absurdity		☐ absurd	☐ absurdly
☐ consideration	☐ consider	☐ considerate	☐ considerately
☐ stipulation	☐ stipulate	☐ stipulatory	

Unit 2 • Listening for Main Purpose

● Step A

☐ amplitude	☐ anatomy	☐ bizarre	☐ camouflage
☐ centigrade	☐ climatology	☐ cumulative	☐ custodian
☐ diameter	☐ disguise	☐ equatorial	☐ exterior
☐ fixture	☐ gaseous	☐ hydrogen	☐ ingredient
☐ magnificent	☐ porous	☐ predictor	☐ seismic
☐ sothic	☐ spectacular	☐ sophisticated	☐ trigonometry
☐ undue	☐ Uranus	☐ urban	☐ voyager

● Step B

Noun	Verb	Adjective	Adverb
☐ amplitude	☐ amplify		
☐ fixture	☐ fixate	☐ fixated	
☐ extension	☐ extend	☐ extended	☐ extendedly
☐ transparency		☐ transparent	☐ transparently
☐ withdrawal	☐ withdraw		
☐ revelation	☐ reveal	☐ revealing	☐ revealingly
☐ insulation	☐ insulate		
☐ initiation	☐ initiate	☐ initial	☐ initially
☐ response	☐ respond	☐ responsive	☐ responsively
☐ reiteration	☐ reiterate	☐ reiterative	☐ reiteratively
☐ catastrophe		☐ catastrophic	☐ catastrophically
☐ challenge	☐ challenge	☐ challenging	
☐ derivative	☐ derive	☐ derivative	☐ derivatively
☐ entirety		☐ entire	☐ entirely
☐ minimum	☐ minimize	☐ minimal	☐ minimally

Unit 3 • Listening for Major Details

◉ Step A

☐ amphitheater	☐ aqueduct	☐ candor	☐ cellulose
☐ considerate	☐ consonant	☐ convey	☐ defects
☐ drawback	☐ exterminate	☐ familiarize	☐ frustrate
☐ genetic	☐ hysterectomy	☐ impoverish	☐ invade
☐ keen	☐ moisture	☐ overdue	☐ pheromone
☐ Presbyterian	☐ rectangular	☐ regurgitate	☐ reminisce
☐ salvage	☐ termite	☐ thwart	☐ uterus

◉ Step B

Noun	Verb	Adjective	Adverb
☐ octagon		☐ octagonal	☐ octagonally
☐ endurance	☐ endure	☐ enduring	☐ enduringly
☐ exterminator	☐ exterminate	☐ exterminable	
☐ exception	☐ except	☐ exceptional	☐ exceptionally
☐ concept	☐ conceive	☐ conceivable	☐ conceivably
☐ distinction		☐ distinct	☐ distinctly
☐ improvisation	☐ improvise	☐ improvisational	☐ improvisationally
☐ inscription	☐ inscribe	☐ inscriptional	
☐ interpreter	☐ interpret	☐ interpretative	☐ interpretatively
☐ invasion	☐ invade	☐ invasive	☐ invasively
☐ moisture	☐ moisten	☐ moist	☐ moistly
☐ resonation	☐ resonate	☐ resonant	☐ resonantly
☐ regurgitation	☐ regurgitate	☐ regurgitative	
☐ reproduction	☐ reproduce	☐ reproductive	☐ reproductively

Unit 4 • Understanding the Function of What Is Said

● Step A

- [ ] aesthetic
- [ ] airline
- [ ] alluded
- [ ] anaconda
- [ ] aptitude
- [ ] arena
- [ ] ascend
- [ ] assimilate
- [ ] attire
- [ ] beech
- [ ] blight
- [ ] canopy
- [ ] diameter
- [ ] elaborate
- [ ] façade
- [ ] foyer
- [ ] fungus
- [ ] hybrid
- [ ] indigenous
- [ ] irrigation
- [ ] itinerary
- [ ] lenient
- [ ] majestic
- [ ] misconception
- [ ] otter
- [ ] piety
- [ ] progeny
- [ ] reminiscent
- [ ] satire
- [ ] sprout
- [ ] startle
- [ ] thwart

● Step B

Noun	Verb	Adjective	Adverb
☐ urgency	☐ urge	☐ urgent	☐ urgently
☐ orientation	☐ orient	☐ oriented	
☐ complication	☐ complicate	☐ complicated	☐ complicatedly
☐ purchase	☐ purchase		
☐ network	☐ network		
☐ benefit	☐ benefit	☐ beneficial	☐ beneficially
☐ gesture	☐ gesture		
☐ extension	☐ extend	☐ extensive	☐ extensively
☐ sustenance	☐ sustain	☐ sustainable	☐ sustainingly
☐ resistance	☐ resist	☐ resisting/resistant	
☐ retention	☐ retain	☐ retentive	☐ retentively
☐ imitation	☐ imitate	☐ imitational	
☐ assimilation	☐ assimilate	☐ assimilative	
☐ variety	☐ vary	☐ various	☐ variously
☐ electricity	☐ electrify	☐ electrifying	
☐ consideration	☐ consider	☐ considerable	☐ considerably
☐ typicality	☐ typify	☐ typical	☐ typically
☐ vividness		☐ vivid	☐ vividly
☐ chill	☐ chill	☐ chilling	☐ chillingly

Unit 5 • Understanding the Speaker's Attitude

● Step A

☐ aesthetic	☐ ameba	☐ artisan	☐ augment
☐ bachelor	☐ baffle	☐ cancerous	☐ chemotherapy
☐ choke	☐ cohabitate	☐ culminate	☐ drape
☐ enthusiasm	☐ exotic	☐ extraneous	☐ fabric
☐ fatal	☐ foster	☐ funnel	☐ garlic
☐ glial	☐ glioma	☐ herbaceous	☐ impromptu
☐ indecisive	☐ intolerable	☐ malignant	☐ merge
☐ mutualism	☐ parasite	☐ perennial	☐ pluck
☐ spiral			

● Step B

Noun	Verb	Adjective	Adverb
☐ aggression		☐ aggressive	☐ aggressively
☐ phenomenon		☐ phenomenal	☐ phenomenally
☐ sustenance	☐ sustain	☐ sustainable	☐ sustainingly
☐ proliferation	☐ proliferate	☐ proliferative	
☐ culmination	☐ culminate	☐ culminating	
☐ intimacy		☐ intimate	☐ intimately
☐ extraneousness		☐ extraneous	☐ extraneously
☐ disregard	☐ disregard		
		☐ prospective	☐ prospectively
☐ indefiniteness		☐ indefinite	☐ indefinitely
☐ predator	☐ predate	☐ predatory	
☐ prevalent	☐ prevail	☐ prevalent	☐ prevalently
☐ radiation	☐ radiate	☐ radiate	☐ radiately
☐ replication	☐ replicate	☐ replicative	
☐ resemblance	☐ resemble	☐ resembling	
☐ rotation	☐ rotate	☐ rotational	☐ rotationally

Unit 6 • Understanding Organization

Step A

- adornment
- aggravation
- ancient
- arousal
- dormancy
- durability
- excavate
- fascinate
- feat
- furor
- garment
- hibernate
- imminent
- impede
- incinerator
- irritation
- metabolism
- nitrate
- peril
- relic
- remnant
- reptile
- ridiculous
- sculpture
- talbot
- incinerate
- vacation
- waive

Step B

Noun	Verb	Adjective	Adverb
practicality	practice	practical	practically
urgency	urge	urgent	urgently
devotion	devote	devoted	devotedly
exposition	expose	exposed	
disability	disable	disabled	
frustration	frustrate	frustrated / -ting	frustratingly
jeopardy	jeopardize	jeopardized	
focus	focus	focused	
instant		instantaneous	instantaneously
modification	modify	modified	
erosion	erode	erosive	erosively
inevitability		inevitable	inevitably
emission	emit	emissive	emissively
horror	horrify	horrifying	horrifyingly
decoration	decorate	decorated	
furor	infuriate	furious	infuriatingly
impairment	impair	impaired	

Unit 7 • Connecting Content

Step A

- [ ] acclimate
- [ ] altitude
- [ ] archaic
- [ ] august
- [ ] commonplace
- [ ] communal
- [ ] connotation
- [ ] corruption
- [ ] detrimental
- [ ] dizzy
- [ ] frigate
- [ ] gratification
- [ ] hesitant
- [ ] infancy
- [ ] molecule
- [ ] monument
- [ ] nausea
- [ ] prey
- [ ] queasiness
- [ ] regurgitate
- [ ] replenish
- [ ] robe
- [ ] spiteful
- [ ] squid
- [ ] tablet
- [ ] tedious
- [ ] unison
- [ ] visage

Step B

Noun	Verb	Adjective	Adverb
[ ] strenuousness		[ ] strenuous	[ ] strenuously
[ ] ascension	[ ] ascend	[ ] ascendable	
[ ] consolation	[ ] console	[ ] consolable	[ ] consolingly
		[ ] crucial	[ ] crucially
[ ] desperateness	[ ] desperate	[ ] desperate	[ ] desperately
[ ] forfeit	[ ] forfeit	[ ] forfeit	
[ ] persuasion	[ ] persuade	[ ] persuadable	[ ] persuadably
[ ] interior		[ ] interior	[ ] interiorly
[ ] utilization	[ ] utilize	[ ] utilizable	
[ ] migration	[ ] migrate	[ ] migratory	
[ ] distinction	[ ] distinguish	[ ] distinct	[ ] distinctly
		[ ] brutal	[ ] brutally
[ ] tyranny	[ ] tyrannize	[ ] tyrannical	[ ] tyrannically
[ ] aspiration	[ ] aspire	[ ] aspirational	
[ ] distraction	[ ] distract	[ ] distractive	[ ] distractedly

Unit **8** • Making Inferences

◉ Step **A**

☐ abdomen	☐ accentuate	☐ appendage	☐ ash
☐ athletic	☐ churn	☐ collide	☐ crust
☐ derogatory	☐ dolomite	☐ foreshadow	☐ genuine
☐ hostility	☐ indigenous	☐ infirm	☐ intimate
☐ literally	☐ majestic	☐ marquis	☐ meteorologist
☐ miniature	☐ miscellaneous	☐ molten	☐ nomadic
☐ obliterate	☐ obsolete	☐ primitive	☐ retrospect
☐ rip	☐ susceptible	☐ tactic	☐ tectonic

◉ Step **B**

Noun	Verb	Adjective	Adverb
☐ authenticity	☐ authenticate	☐ authentic	☐ authentically
☐ rejection	☐ reject	☐ rejected	
☐ humor	☐ humor	☐ humorous	☐ humorously
☐ perception	☐ perceive	☐ perceived	☐ perceptively
☐ forecast	☐ forecast	☐ forecasted	
☐ frequency	☐ frequent	☐ frequent	☐ frequently
☐ significance	☐ signify	☐ significant	☐ significantly
☐ generation	☐ generate	☐ generational	
☐ glider	☐ glide		
☐ stability	☐ stabilize	☐ stable	☐ stably
☐ obligation	☐ obligate	☐ obligated / -tory	☐ obligatorily
☐ modification	☐ modify	☐ modified	
☐ scheme	☐ scheme	☐ schematic	☐ schematically
☐ magnification	☐ magnify	☐ magnificent	☐ magnificently
☐ bargain	☐ bargain		
☐ consideration	☐ consider	☐ considerate	☐ considerably
☐ adjustment	☐ adjust	☐ adjustive	☐ adjustively
☐ support	☐ support	☐ supportive	

Listening Section **Directions** ⊙ 6-02

This section measures your ability to understand conversations and lectures in English. The listening section is divided into 2 separately timed parts. In each part you will listen to 1 conversation and 2 lectures. You will hear each conversation or lecture only one time. After each conversation and lecture, you will answer questions about it. The questions typically ask about the main idea and supporting details. Some questions ask about a speaker's purpose or attitude. Answer the questions based on what is stated or implied by the speakers.

You may take notes while you listen. You may use your notes to help you answer the questions. Your notes will not be scored. If you need to change the volume while you listen, click on the Volume icon at the top of the screen.

For some questions, you will see this icon: 🎧 . This means that you will hear, but not see part of the question. Some of the questions have special directions. These directions appear in a gray box on the screen.

Most questions are worth one point. If a question is worth more than one point, it will have special directions that indicate how many points you can receive.

You must answer each question. After you answer, click on Next. Then click on OK to confirm your answer and go on to the next question. After you click on OK, you can not return to previous questions.

Actual Test 01

Conversation 1~5: Listen to part of a conversation between a student and a school official. `6-03`

1. What problem does the student have?

    (A) He cannot find his classroom.
    (B) He cannot find his girlfriend.
    (C) He does not have a key to a room.
    (D) He does not have a student ID card.

2. Why is the school official worried?

    (A) He is afraid he could lose his job.
    (B) He is afraid the student could hurt himself.
    (C) He does not want to see the student fail the class.
    (D) He does not want to be demoted.

3. According to the school official, what does the student need in order to get a lab key?

    (A) A registration signature.
    (B) A registration card.
    (C) A lab waiver.
    (D) The professor's written permission.

4. What can be inferred about the student?

    (A) He is not very diligent.
    (B) He lacks originality.
    (C) He is a genius.
    (D) He is very persistent.

5. Listen again to part of the conversation. Then answer the question.

    What is implied when the school official says this?

    (A) Something important is on the TV.
    (B) The school official is stating the obvious.
    (C) The student should watch the news more often.
    (D) The school official is aggravated with the student.

Actual Test 01

Lecture 6~11: 🎧 Listen to part of a lecture in an art class. ⊙ 6-04

6. What is the main topic of the lecture?

    (A) Monologues.
    (B) Casting calls.
    (C) Acting.
    (D) Auditions.

7. Why does the professor discuss sight reading?

    (A) To show how it has little to do with acting.
    (B) To show how memorization is a more effective method.
    (C) To show how good sight reading is often a barometer of ability.
    (D) To show the true quality of an actor's voice.

8. What does the professor say the audition is similar to?

    (A) A soliloquy.
    (B) A job interview.
    (C) An occupation.
    (D) An actual play.

9. According to the professor, what is a common practice in auditions?

    (A) Cold readings.
    (B) Producer and actor dialogue.
    (C) Impromptu speeches.
    (D) Length of rehearsal time.

10. What can be inferred about auditions?

    (A) There is usually just one audition per performance.
    (B) It is beneficial for an actor to speak to the casting director first.
    (C) Casting directors have little to do with the actors once they are hired.
    (D) Strong improvisation skills are crucial during them.

11. According to the lecture, which of the following are important factors in the later stages of the audition? Check the correct answers in the box below:

	Yes	No
(A) The actor's work ethic		
(B) Chemistry with other potential cast members		
(C) How well the actor gets along with the producer		
(D) The actor's ability to compromise		
(E) Getting along with the casting director		
(F) Getting a good review from a community theater		

Actual Test 01

Lecture 12~17: 🎧 Listen to part of a lecture in an ecology class. ⊙ 6-05

Ecology

12. What does the professor mainly discuss?

    (A) Different forms of pollution.
    (B) Different forms of water pollution.
    (C) Different forms of inbred water diseases.
    (D) Different forms of air pollution.

13. What is the professor's tone during the lecture?

    (A) He seems ambivalent.
    (B) He wants to motivate the students.
    (C) He seems lethargic.
    (D) He seems preoccupied.

14. How does the professor describe the worldwide pollution situation?

    (A) It is slowly but surely improving.
    (B) It is not as bad as it was ten years ago.
    (C) It is the leading cause of death.
    (D) It does not receive enough press.

15. Why does the professor talk about pollution's effect on fish?

    (A) To show how it can deplete an important food source.
    (B) To show how it can attack weaker species.
    (C) To show how it affects every step of the food chain.
    (D) To show how fish have built up immunity against it.

16. What is the students' general reaction to the professor's lecture?

    (A) They react apathetically.
    (B) Their reaction is one of concern.
    (C) They become enraged.
    (D) They disapprove of it.

17. According to the lecture, which of the following are some of the most important contributing factors that cause thermal pollution? Check the correct answers in the box below:

	True	False
(A) Sulfur dioxide emissions		
(B) Manatee waste products		
(C) Natural disasters like earthquakes and tornadoes		
(D) Sewage and other organic wastes		
(E) Methane gas emissions from power plants		
(F) Agricultural run-off		

Actual Test 01

Conversation 18~22: Listen to part of a conversation between a student and a professor. 6-06

18. What are the speakers mainly discussing?

    (A) Literary theory.
    (B) Faulkner.
    (C) Writing techniques.
    (D) An upcoming exam.

19. Why is the student anxious about speaking to the professor?

    (A) She fears she has done something wrong.
    (B) She fears she will be expelled from school.
    (C) She fears the professor.
    (D) She fears she is failing the class.

20. According to the professor, what will help the student most?

    (A) The use of more description.
    (B) The use of internal monologue.
    (C) The use of more metaphors.
    (D) The addition of more dialogue.

21. What is the professor's opinion of the student's ability?

    (A) She should not have taken the class.
    (B) She is an overachiever.
    (C) She has great potential.
    (D) She is too mechanical.

22. What does the professor explain as a common flaw of her students?

    (A) They are reluctant to trim their writing.
    (B) They are not very well organized.
    (C) They display too much confidence.
    (D) They lack creativity and freshness.

Actual Test 01

Lecture 23~28: Listen to part of a lecture in an archeology class. 6-07

Archeology

23. What is the main topic of the lecture?

  (A) The ancient Egyptians.
  (B) Archeology.
  (C) Radio carbon dating.
  (D) Willard Libby.

24. What is a half-life?

  (A) The time expected for the carbon to be depleted from the sample.
  (B) The time it takes for half the carbon to disappear from the sample.
  (C) The time it takes for the carbon to multiply in a given sample.
  (D) The time it takes for the carbon to thrive in a given sample.

25. What resulted from Libby's discovery?

  (A) It became easier to date specimens older than 70,000 years.
  (B) It created a lot of controversy among his colleagues.
  (C) It showed that Egyptian culture was much older than originally thought.
  (D) It allowed scientists to be more accurate in determining the age of objects.

26. What can be inferred about the professor's attitude during the lecture?

  (A) He is not confident in his lecture notes.
  (B) He is worried the lecture might be too difficult for his students.
  (C) He is excited about the student's expertise.
  (D) He wishes he had chosen a different topic.

27. How does the professor organize the lecture?

  (A) He reveals the main topic at the very beginning.
  (B) He begins the lecture with specific images and questions.
  (C) He fills the lecture with statistics.
  (D) He digresses confusingly throughout the lecture.

28. Why is carbon so helpful in the dating process?

  (A) It is a universal element of the life cycle.
  (B) Its atoms are easily identifiable.
  (C) It is found in dinosaurs.
  (D) Its half-life is more easily measurable than nitrogen.

Actual Test 01

Lecture 29~34: 🎧 Listen to part of a lecture in a dramatics class. ⊙ 6-08

29. What does the professor mainly cover in the lecture?

   Ⓐ Puritanism.
   Ⓑ A broad history of American theater.
   Ⓒ The rise of Broadway.
   Ⓓ Burlesque shows.

30. What can be inferred when the professor says "take a hike"?

   Ⓐ A student did not belong in her class.
   Ⓑ She likes hiking.
   Ⓒ She thinks the students need exercise.
   Ⓓ She thinks inflation is on the rise.

31. What is the initial general attitude of the students?

   Ⓐ Some students show disapproval.
   Ⓑ Some students disagree openly.
   Ⓒ Some students are uninterested.
   Ⓓ Some students display skepticism.

32. What does the professor mean by rudimentary theaters?

   Ⓐ Early theaters were not very popular.
   Ⓑ Early theaters were very basic.
   Ⓒ Early theaters were elaborate.
   Ⓓ Early theaters were not enclosed.

33. What was a minstrel show?

   Ⓐ A farcical comedy.
   Ⓑ An American version of Shakespeare.
   Ⓒ A play concerning racial stereotypes.
   Ⓓ The earliest version of the musical.

34. What can be inferred about Burlesque shows?

   Ⓐ They were ahead of their time.
   Ⓑ They were shunned by society.
   Ⓒ They were produced for the upper classes.
   Ⓓ They were popular among politicians.

Actual Test 02

Conversation 1~5: Listen to a conversation between a student and a financial counselor. 6-09

1. What problem does the student have?

   Ⓐ He got a bad grade.
   Ⓑ He needs a part-time job.
   Ⓒ He does not have enough money.
   Ⓓ He eats out too much.

2. Why does the student visit the financial counselor?

   Ⓐ He hopes to borrow some money from her.
   Ⓑ He wants her to ask his parents for more money.
   Ⓒ He wants to work for the university.
   Ⓓ He wants to solve his money problem.

3. According to the financial counselor, what is one way that the student can save money?

   Ⓐ He can get a full-time job.
   Ⓑ He can ask his parents for more money.
   Ⓒ He can stop eating breakfast.
   Ⓓ He can make food at home instead of eating out.

4. What can be inferred about the student?

   Ⓐ He is a hard worker.
   Ⓑ He is lazy.
   Ⓒ He does not need to save more money.
   Ⓓ He might fail in the field of microbiology.

5. What will the student probably do next?

   Ⓐ Get a part-time job.
   Ⓑ Try to save money.
   Ⓒ Ask the financial counselor for a loan.
   Ⓓ Go to the bank and borrow money.

Actual Test 02

Lecture 6~11: Listen to a lecture in a zoology class. 6-10

Zoology

6. What is the lecture mainly about?

   Ⓐ The reproductive cycles of the badger.
   Ⓑ Badgers and their coloring.
   Ⓒ The environments that badgers thrive in.
   Ⓓ Badger physiology.

7. Why does the professor explain about melanin pigmentation?

   Ⓐ To say that badgers eat melanin.
   Ⓑ To indicate how badgers build their homes.
   Ⓒ To state that it kills many badgers.
   Ⓓ To show what determines their coloring.

8. According to the professor, what is the purpose of the markings on a badger's head?

   Ⓐ They warn potential predators of danger.
   Ⓑ They attract a mate.
   Ⓒ They provide camouflage.
   Ⓓ They have no purpose.

9. What is the professor's attitude towards the female student's description of badger habits and habitats?

   Ⓐ He thinks she is absolutely correct.
   Ⓑ He thinks she is mostly correct.
   Ⓒ He thinks she is totally incorrect.
   Ⓓ He thinks she does not know anything.

10. How does the professor organize the information about badgers that he presents to the class?

   Ⓐ He only discusses general facts about badgers.
   Ⓑ He starts off by telling a story about hunter and a badger.
   Ⓒ He starts off discussing general facts and gets to specific details about coloring.
   Ⓓ He only discusses specific facts about badger coloration.

11. According to the lecture, which of the following are facts about the badger? Check the correct answers in the box below:

	Yes	No
(A) They are nocturnal.		
(B) Males are called bulls.		
(C) They are carnivorous.		
(D) Females are called sows.		
(E) They live in underground dwellings called homes.		
(F) They reproduce through delayed implantation.		

Actual Test 02

Lecture 12~17: Listen to a lecture in a psychology class. `6-11`

12. What is the main topic of the lecture?

    (A) Adolescent and adult life.

    (B) The basis of attachment theory.

    (C) John Bowlby.

    (D) The Harlow experiments.

13. Why does the professor explain Bowlby and Harlow's scientific work?

    (A) To explain their importance in establishing attachment theory.

    (B) To say that they were famous scientists.

    (C) To mention that they were the first to work on rhesus monkeys.

    (D) To show that deep-seeded attachments are important to understand.

14. According to the professor, what is true about rhesus monkeys?

    (A) They are capable of human emotions.

    (B) They are not subject to affectional bonds.

    (C) They are similar to humans in infantile stages.

    (D) They are not interested in their mother's warmth.

15. What is the professor's opinion of the Harlow experiments?

    (A) They were not as significant as the paper published by John Bowlby.

    (B) They were unethical because they mistreated rhesus monkeys.

    (C) They were important because they involved monkeys.

    (D) They were important because they were tests that could not be done on humans.

16. What can be inferred about rhesus monkeys?

    (A) They are kind creatures.

    (B) They will act abnormally if raised apart from their mothers.

    (C) They do not like being used in scientific experiments.

    (D) They are an endangered species.

17. According to the lecture, which of the following are features of an affectional bond? Check the correct answers in the box below:

	Yes	No
(A) It is persistent rather than transitory.		
(B) It involves three particular people.		
(C) It involves a relationship that is emotionally insignificant.		
(D) The individual who formed the bond wants to remain physically close to the person with whom he has bonded.		
(E) The individual will become happy if he is separated from the person with whom the bond was formed.		
(F) The person who formed the bond will always seek discomfort and emotional insecurity.		

Actual Test 02

Conversation 18~22: Listen to a conversation between a student and a professor. 6-12

18. What problem does the student have?

   (A) Her group failed to make any progress.
   (B) She is afraid she will get a poor grade.
   (C) She did poorly on a test.
   (D) She wants to drop the professor's class.

19. Why does the student visit the professor?

   (A) She wants to change groups.
   (B) She wants him to choose a leader.
   (C) She wants to get a higher grade than her partners.
   (D) She wants his advice.

20. According to the professor, how many benefits are there for Mary to become group leader?

   (A) One.
   (B) Two.
   (C) Three.
   (D) Four.

21. Listen again to part of the conversation. Then answer the question.

   What does the professor mean when he says this?

   (A) He thinks she has a long nose.
   (B) She dropped the solution on the floor.
   (C) The solution is obvious.
   (D) She should blow her nose.

22. What will the student probably do next?

   (A) She will probably join a new group.
   (B) She will probably become the leader of her group.
   (C) She will probably ask the professor for more help.
   (D) She will probably change classes.

Actual Test 02

Lecture 23~28: Listen to part of a lecture in a history class. 6-13

23. What is the main topic of the lecture?

  (A) The Peloponnesian War.
  (B) King Hammurabi's law.
  (C) The Epic of Gilgamesh.
  (D) The ancient Sumerian timber crisis.

24. Why does the professor explain the Epic of Gilgamesh?

  (A) To say it was the cause of the timber crisis.
  (B) To mention his favorite epic from that period.
  (C) To argue that it solved the timber crisis.
  (D) To say that it contains historical information about the timber crisis.

25. What resulted from the invention of the copper melting process?

  (A) The Bronze Age.
  (B) An increased need for wood.
  (C) A solution to the timber crisis.
  (D) The occupation of logging.

26. What can be inferred about the male student?

  (A) He has never studied Sumerian history before.
  (B) He is familiar with the work of Theodore Wertime.
  (C) He has never read the works of Theodore Wertime.
  (D) He is interested in the Sumerian timber crisis.

27. What can be inferred about the Sumerian timber crisis?

  (A) It was caused by King Gilgamesh.
  (B) It was a result of Egypt's need for wood.
  (C) It was the result of unsustainable logging practices.
  (D) It caused the Peloponnesian War.

28. According to the lecture, which of the following were uses for wood during the Bronze Age? Check the correct answers in the box below:

	Yes	No
(A) Mining		
(B) Smelting		
(C) Metalworking		
(D) Shipbuilding		
(E) Horse feed		
(F) Armor building		

Actual Test 02

Lecture 29~34: Listen to part of a lecture in a biology class. 6-14

29. What aspect of the eye does the professor mainly discuss?

    (A) The lens.
    (B) The choroid.
    (C) The hyaloid artery.
    (D) The zonules of Zinn.

30. Why does the professor explain the process of accommodation?

    (A) To say it is important to understand the way the lens ages.
    (B) To describe it as the most important part of the eye.
    (C) To mention that the zonules of Zinn are controlled by this process.
    (D) To state that the lens has too many organelles.

31. How does the index gradient affect the optical power of the lens?

    (A) It damages it.
    (B) It decreases it.
    (C) It does not affect it.
    (D) It enhances it.

32. According to the lecture, which of the following are layers of the crystalline lens? Check the correct answers in the box below:

	Yes	No
(A) Capsule		
(B) Zonule		
(C) Subcapsular epithelium		
(D) Cortex		
(E) Nucleus		
(F) Presbyopia		

33. How does the professor organize the information he presents to the class?

    (A) By beginning specifically with accommodation and moving to general information about the lens.
    (B) By focusing on general information about the crystalline lens.
    (C) By only discussing the lens specifically in regards to the process of accommodation.
    (D) By discussing general information about the crystalline lens and then moving towards specific information about accommodation.

34. Why does the professor feel it is important for the students fully to understand the process of accommodation?

    (A) Most of their future work in the field of optics will involve it.
    (B) It is the most sensitive part of the crystalline lens.
    (C) It is the most difficult part of the crystalline lens to understand.
    (D) It is the most commonly damaged part of the crystalline lens.

How to
Master Skills for the

TOEFL® iBT

Listening

Advanced

Answer Book

Unit 1 Listening for Main Ideas

Practice with Conversations

A   1. Ⓒ   2. Ⓑ   3. Ⓒ
   4. 1) the library
      2) Golden Retrievers
      3) a librarian
      4) the Dewey Decimal System
         A) 10, B) 000 to 999
      5) the card catalog
      6) call number
   5. ¹Dewey Decimal System ²ten broad areas
      ³Religions and Mythology ⁴card catalog ⁵broken
      down ⁶wrote down

🔊 1-02

W2: Excuse me. I was wondering if you could help me?

W1: Yes, of course! How can I be of assistance?

W2: Well, I'm writing a paper on how to train Golden
    Retrievers. A friend of mine recommended a book
    called *Golden Retrievers: Puppyhood and Beyond*.
    How would I go about finding this book?

W1: Golden Retrievers! Such lovely dogs! The first thing
    you need to know is that our library is set up on
    what is called the Dewey Decimal System. The
    Dewey Decimal System is split into 10 broad areas,
    with call numbers ranging from between 000 and
    999.

W2: That sounds complicated. I have to know and
    memorize the exact number of the book anywhere
    from between 000 and 999?

W1: Oh no, no. It's much more straightforward than
    that. You initially narrow your search by determining
    which of the ten broad areas your topic falls under.
    For instance, a Golden Retriever is a dog, an
    animal, and animals fall under the category Math
    and Science in the Dewey Decimal System. These
    categories are numbered 500-599.

W2: Okay, I think I see. So I need the Math and Science
    category for dogs, but what if I was researching
    something else? Can you tell me the other
    categories?

W1: Certainly. The ten areas are as follows, in order:
    General Knowledge, Psychology and Philosophy,
    Religions and Mythology, Social Sciences and
    Folklore, Languages and Grammar, Math and
    Science, Medicine and Technology, Arts and
    Recreation, Literature, and Geography and History.

W2: Wow! Okay, so I have narrowed my search to the
    Math and Science Section, and my book has a
    number that is somewhere between 500 and 599?

W1: Yes, that's right. Now, to find out the exact number,
    you go to our card catalog which is a filing system
    set up exactly as the books are arranged on the
    shelves.

W2: Okay, so I go to the file that has the cards
    500-599... Now what do I do?

W1: Now, each category is broken down into sub-
    categories. For instance, you see in this file that
    Math and Science has subheadings such as
    Biology, Chemistry, Dinosaurs, and so on. Find the
    category Animals.

W2: Okay, I see it!

W1: You notice how all the books relating to animals
    have 599 as part of their number?

W2: Oh! I get it! So I go through the cards that have 599
    as part of the number, and the book I am looking
    for should be listed there... Here it is!

W1: Exactly! What is the number?

W2: *Golden Retrievers: Puppyhood and Beyond* is listed
    as number 599.68.

W1: Good, so now you write down that number on a
    slip of paper, and you know exactly where to look
    for the book on the shelf.

W2: Wow! This is so helpful. And I love this system.
    Thank you!

W1: You're welcome. I'm glad I could be of assistance.

B   1. Ⓒ   2. Ⓑ   3. Ⓐ
   4. 1) calculus grade
      2) A) homework, B) has missed
      3) her personal problem
      5) higher grade
      6) A) to be more responsible
      7) apologizes
   5. ¹lagging ²quite a number of classes ³stress
      ⁴broken up with her boyfriend ⁵hard time staying
      focused ⁶special consideration ⁷not performing
      well ⁸unethical ⁹responsibility for her actions

🔊 1-03

W: Hi, Professor Smith. Do you have a minute?

M: Of course, Sally. What can I help you with?

W: Well, I wanted to talk to you about my grade in your
   calculus class.

M: Okay. Give me a second to find your information
   on this spreadsheet. Here it is. It looks like you're
   lagging behind on your homework assignments.
   Hmm, and you've also missed quite a number of

classes so far this semester. Is everything okay?

W: Well, I've been having a hard time this semester because I broke up with my boyfriend. We've been seeing each other for a bit, but he recently moved away from here. It's been hard trying to keep focused on school.

M: I'm sorry to hear that. It's certainly hard when someone important in our lives moves away. Coping with the end of a relationship can be difficult for anyone.

W: I know. It's been very difficult for me to deal with. I haven't been able to eat or sleep, and so when I'm in your class, I cannot concentrate because I am tired and hungry.

M: Well, that is not good. I suggest you try to get as much rest as possible and eat balanced meals. If not, your grades will not improve, and I'm afraid I'll be left with no choice but to fail you in my class.

W: Yes, I know, Professor Smith. I really don't want to fail, so that is why I am here.

M: I'm sorry, Sally. I guess I don't understand, as I have nothing to do with your relationships, and it is not I who is causing you not to eat or sleep. What can I do?

W: It is just that I was hoping you would take into consideration what I have been going through, and well, I thought maybe you could overlook my bad test scores and just give me a passing grade.

M: Sally, you cannot be serious. What you are asking me to do is favoritism. It is nothing more than cheating!

W: But Professor Smith! I've been under such stress!

M: That very well may be the case, Sally, but do you think you are the first person who has had to deal with personal issues while undertaking such serious matters as school or work? For instance, I am a married man with two children. Last year, when I was working on a very important paper for the university, my youngest child came down with a terrible case of the flu. My wife and I had to take turns staying up all night attending to her. I was tired, losing sleep, and worrying myself silly. But that did not stop me from coming to class every day, teaching, and seeing to my responsibilities. What you are asking me to do is not only unethical, but it also shows that you do not want to be an adult and take responsibility for your own actions.

W: Yes, you are right. I am sorry. It was silly of me to ask such an absurd question. I need to realize that my boyfriend has decided to move away and there is nothing I can do about it. I promise to do better

in your class. Can you forgive me for asking such a forward question?

M: Yes, Sally, of course. Let's just try to mend things and move on, shall we?

W: Yes, Professor Smith. And thank you for your time.

M: You're welcome, Sally. You can come and speak to me anytime.

C   1. Ⓒ   2. Ⓓ   3. Ⓐ

     4. 1) purchase book
        2) book card
        3) personal information
        4) B) old books first
        6) she didn't pay for the book yet
        7) Apologizes

     5. [1] would like to purchase a book [2] asked to make a deferred payment [3] have enough [4] was not responsible [5] had forgotten [6] enough money to pay

1-04

W: Hi. I would like to purchase this book.

M: Can I have your card please?

W: Card? Oh... the book card. I don't have it with me right now. I left it at home. But I think you can identify me with my phone number, right? My phone number is 683-8585 and my name is registered as Julie.

M: Very good, Miss. If you would just bear with me a moment, I will pull up your records.

W: Thank you.

M: Um, I'm sorry, Julie, but my computer indicates that the last time you were in our store, you asked to make a deferred payment, due... two weeks ago. I am sorry to tell you this. But it seems like you have still not made the payment.

W: What? Are you certain? I find that highly dubious. I am sure I made that payment. What was it for?

M: Let's see. Our records show that we allowed you to take two textbooks that were required for your biology class under the condition that we would send you a bill through the mail and that you would pay it by the due date. You have missed that due date, and until you pay the arrears, I cannot let you purchase another item.

W: Oh, my God. There must have been something wrong. I need this book right now! It is for my English class, and we are having a lecture on the text tomorrow, but I only have enough money to buy this book!

M: Well, I am sorry, Julie, but either you find more

money, or you return the book to the shelf and pay only for the two textbooks which are already in your possession.

W: Well, I don't believe this! I have never heard of such treatment! I could have sworn I received the bill and put a check in the mail. I blame the school post office!

M: I am sorry again, Julie, but one of the stipulations on the deferment slip is that we are not responsible if the school post office happens to misplace your check should you decide to put it through the mail, which it appears you did.

W: Well, I refuse to pay another dime for the bo... Oh! Oh, wait one moment! Silly me! The payment I put in the mail was for another store for a set of folders I bought for my accounting class. Excuse my rudeness! And you are right. I received the bill for the textbooks, but I stuck it on my dresser and forgot all about it! Here is what I will do. Allow me just to put this book back on the rack. I can borrow my friend's book until I have enough money to come back and purchase my own. That way, I will have enough money to pay for the two textbooks I received last week.

M: That sounds like a good plan.

W: Thank you for your patience and for being so kind.

M: You are welcome, Julie. It is not a problem.

D 1. Ⓑ 2. Ⓓ 3. Ⓐ
    4. 1) her appointment
        2) sign up for
        3) A) when student would like to graduate,
           B) four years, C) 15 credit hours
        4) B) take science class
    5. ¹scheduling classes ²graduate on time ³could not afford ⁴major she was choosing ⁵prerequisite ⁶interest in geology

🔊 1-05

W1: Hi, Professor. I am here for my 9:00 appointment.

W2: Good morning. So you're here to register for next semester's classes?

W1: Yes, that's right. I want to make sure that I am signing up for the courses that I need for my journalism major.

W2: Let me get out the journalism requirements checklist so we can make sure that you're taking the classes you need. Here we go. Okay, now, how many course hours do you want to have next semester?

W1: As few as possible. I really don't want to get burned out!

W2: Well, I can understand that. I was a student once, too, but remember that you need 126 credit hours to graduate, and I suspect you want to graduate in the usual four years?

W1: Oh, yes, I really can't afford to stay longer than four years!

W2: Okay, so keeping that in consideration, I would recommend that you take at least 15 to 18 hours each semester.

W1: Well, okay. I took 15 credit hours each for the last two semesters. And I'm signed up for six credit hours of summer school. Fifteen hours hasn't been so bad, so maybe I'll continue with that. But can we try to schedule my classes so that I get to sleep in a little bit in the mornings?

W2: Sure, absolutely. And the fact that you took so many credits last semester means you've gotten off to a good start! Have you taken all the required courses for first-year journalism students?

W1: Yes, I have. Oh, wait a minute! I actually took a biology class instead of a mass communication class. Is that a problem?

W2: No, it's not a problem. Actually, you need to take two science classes before you graduate, so now you have filled one of those two requirements. But you definitely need to take the mass communication class this next semester because it is a prerequisite for other classes that you need.

W1: Oh, that's good to know. Well, I'll write down that course to take next semester. Should I take my other science class in the fall semester also?

W2: It would be a good idea to take that class in one of the next two semesters so you can focus on the classes in your major. Is there a science class offered next semester that interests you?

W1: There is a geology class that looks interesting, and I've heard good things about the professor. It's offered at three different times, so I should be able to work that in around my other classes.

W2: Great. So I will sign this for you now. Do you have any other questions while you're here?

W1: Not that I can think of at the moment. Thank you very much for helping me, Professor.

W2: No problem. That's what I'm here for. Good luck next semester!

Practice with Lectures

A 1. Ⓑ 2. Ⓐ 3. Ⓒ

4. 1) operas

2) boring, B) wrong ideas

3) A) the ancient Greeks, B) the Renaissance

4) A) a singer's abilities, B) emotions

6) A) dramatic opera, B) comical opera, C) short, comical opera

5. ¹music ²dancing ³ancient Greeks ⁴during the Renaissance ⁵Italy ⁶Germans ⁷Russia ⁸*comique* ⁹very short opera ¹⁰complex musical passage

🔊 **1-06**

M1: Today, class, we are going to be talking about opera.

M2: Opera! Oh no. I know what that is. Operas are so boring.

M1: Boring? Not at all! Operas are dramas that employ the use of music.

M2: They are dramas? I thought an opera was when performers dressed up in costumes and then sang in foreign languages on the stage.

M1: Well, I am sure an opera appears that way if you don't know what is happening. Why don't we look at the history of opera to find out exactly what an opera is and how this form of drama evolved? We have the ancient Greeks to thank for inspiring this form of expression. The ancient Greeks performed dramas that incorporated music and singing and sometimes even dancing.

M2: The ancient Greeks? But when I think of opera, I think of a large woman wearing a horned helmet, and she is singing in… I don't know… German? Italian?

M1: Either one would be correct, as both the Germans and Italians embraced operatic performances. Modern opera began in Italy during the Renaissance. One of the very first modern operas was composed during the late sixteenth century by Jacopo Peri. It was called *Dafne* and was an opera based on a Greek myth.

M2: It is hard enough to follow a play. Why must they add such complicated songs? Sometimes it sounds like the singers are screaming!

M1: Those "complicated songs," as you refer to them, are known as arias. An aria is a complex musical passage created to showcase a singer's vocal range. But can you think of another reason why a wide range in vocal sound might be important?

M2: To show… when someone is angry?

M1: Close. An aria allows the performer to express a varied range of emotions through the tone of his singing. It can be compared to how babies cry using differing intonations depending on their need, say, hunger or tiredness.

M2: Are Italy and Germany the only places where operas are performed?

M1: Not at all. The art form of opera is very popular all over the world but especially in Europe. Venice, Italy, was where the first opera house was created, but there are opera houses in England, France, Portugal, Spain, and Russia. Still, because opera is thought of as an Italian art form, composers from other countries, such as Germany's Handel and Austria's Mozart, still wrote their works in Italian. It wasn't until later that composers felt confident enough to write operas in their own language.

M2: It seems that everyone ends up dying in an opera. Are all operas so morbid?

M1: Again, you are thinking of opera in its clichéd form. Just as a play can be a comedy or a tragedy, so too can operas. The most popular is the one you mentioned, the *opera seria*, which has a dramatic plot that may involve death, but there is also the *opera comique*, which is a comical opera. Operettas are shorter versions of operas that often have comical plots.

M2: Can you recommend an opera to us? They don't appear so boring after all!

M1: Certainly. There is, of course, Puccini's *Madame Butterfly*, Mozart's *The Marriage of Figaro*, George Bizet's *Carmen*, or Wagner's *Der Ring des Nibelungen*. These are all examples of dramas that utilize music, singing, or dancing.

B **1.** Ⓒ **2.** Ⓑ **3.** Ⓓ

4. 1) origins of rice

2) A) naturally, B) 16,000, C) in Asia in China

3) A) Chinese culture, B) traits

4) myths, A) *The Sky Flood*

5. ¹rice ²wild ³nearly impossible ⁴ancestors were harvesting ⁵Australia ⁶China ⁷rice paddies ⁸occurs naturally ⁹to yield desired traits

🔊 **1-07**

W: We've been talking a lot about how rice is prepared, but what is the actual origin of rice?

M: An excellent question, but one that is complicated.

W: Complicated?

M: Yes, because it all depends on which way you approach the question. Do you mean the origin of wild rice or domestic rice? Are you interested in the scientific origin of rice, or are you interested in the mythological stories surrounding it?

Let's assume you are interested in all the possibilities and begin with wild rice. Now, because wild rice occurs naturally, it is very hard to pin down a precise date in history when it first developed. What is known, however, is that the earliest evidence of rice dates back more than 16,000 years ago, when the Great Ice Age was coming to an end. Early humans, who were once mainly hunters, now cultivated the land, gathering, among other things, wild rice. Scientists know this because microscopic rice cells have been discovered near the sites of these ancient civilizations. What is also known, through a process called electrophoresis, is that cultivated rice from areas as widespread as Australia, Asia, Africa, and North America all stem from one common type of rice that existed when the continents were connected. Despite the widespread distribution of rice – there are 20 wild species spread across four continents – experts believe the likely location of its origin is Asia due to a 1920s finding of rice imprints from the Yang-shao site in Northern China (c. 3200–2500 B.C.) in the 1920s.

W: That is wild rice, but what about the rice that we eat today?

M: Domestic rice originates back to the early days of Chinese culture. Various archeological sites revealed deep rice paddies in Hunan Province. The oldest paddy sites date from nearly 12,000 years ago in an area just south of the Three Gorges Dam on the middle Yangtze River.

W: But what do you mean by domestic? Does domestic just mean that it is collected by people?

M: No. People can harvest wild rice, but that doesn't make it domestic. Domestication happens when people plant seeds to form a new generation of rice that carries certain desired traits. For example, early humans would have tried to grow heartier crops or crops that yielded more volume, so they would have sown only seeds from crops that exhibited those positive traits.

W: That is the science behind the origin of rice, but I want to hear the myths!

M: Well, I am certain there's more than one myth behind the origin of rice, but I will briefly summarize one such legend, called *The Gift of the Sky Flood*. The Chinese story states that a long time ago, a girl named Shuhwa lived with her family cultivating buckwheat along the bank of the Yangtze River. One year, however, powerful rains flooded the area, and so Shuhwa and her family were driven to higher

ground. During the flood, Shuhwa spied a wild dog clinging to a floating log. Shuhwa saved the dog, and, later, as she was running her fingers through the dog's fur, Shuhwa found a small seedling. The very next day, Shuhwa planted the seedling on the higher, yet still marshy ground, and year after year the plant thrived, yielding the grains which were later to be known as rice. So you see, there are three different ways to look at the origin of rice.

C   **1.** Ⓒ   **2.** Ⓐ   **3.** Ⓐ
   4. 1) oral plaque
      A) sugar, B) bacteria, C) periodontis, gingivitis
      2) A) substance, B) red, swollen, C) gingivitis
      3) A) regularly, C) Saliva
   5. ¹yellowish, sticky film of bacteria ²hard substance ³gingivitis ⁴natural defense ⁵actively neutralizing ⁶remove

🔊 **1-08**

M1: Yesterday we ended our lecture with a discussion of cavities. Today, we will be discussing oral plaque. Does anyone know the definition of oral plaque?

W: Is oral plaque a build-up of sugar on your teeth?

M1: That is a good guess. Plaque can build up on your teeth due to the ingestion of too much sugar, but oral plaque is actually a yellowish, sticky film of bacteria. It is not so much the presence of this particular bacteria that is bad for your teeth. After all, it occurs naturally within our mouths. It is the failure properly to clean the plaque from our teeth on a day-to-day basis that leads to what we discussed yesterday – dental cavities or even more serious diseases such as periodontis or gingivitis.

M2: But if the bacteria that makes up plaque occurs naturally, then it must be good for us. And if it is good for us, why would it lead to cavities or diseases?

M1: Good question. It is because if the plaque is not removed regularly, it hardens into what is known as tartar. Tartar is a very hard substance that irritates our gums, causing them to grow red and swollen. And once tartar starts collecting near the gum line, it becomes very difficult to clean your teeth properly. Your gums may even start to bleed, leading to one of the diseases I named earlier, gingivitis.

M2: Eww! That sounds disgusting!

M1: It is very disgusting and a serious problem if a person fails to take proper care of his teeth. The good news is that the body has a natural defense against plaque, and so with regular brushing and regular visits to the dentist, you can help protect your teeth from the build-up of plaque.

W: Would diligent brushing be good enough? I just hate going to the dentist!

M1: I wish I could say yes, but it is imperative that you see a dentist at least twice a year so that he or she can clean plaque not only from your teeth but also from below the gum line. Once the dentist has cleaned your teeth thoroughly, it takes three to four months for the plaque to return. In the meantime, your own saliva is doing its utmost to help you keep plaque at bay by actively neutralizing the acidic environment caused by the bacteria. Eventually, however, the plaque builds up to such a level that your saliva is no longer able to penetrate and neutralize the acidity. When that happens, the microorganisms in the plaque release their acids, which attack your tooth enamel and cause it to break down.

W: I guess I never considered the serious consequences of not brushing my teeth regularly!

M1: Well, don't worry too much. The practice of good oral hygiene – daily brushing and flossing – is the best way to prevent the build-up of plaque. This, combined with regular visits to the dentist, should keep you in good oral health.

D 1. C 2. D 3. A

4. 1) the tiger, B) orange, black, C) white markings
   2) A) skin pigmentation, B) stripes
   3) A) – 13, 200~700
   4) eight
   5) A) 2,500 – 5,000, D) Asia

5. [1]mammal [2]black [3]chest [4]largest [5]Siberian tiger [6]thirteen [7] 200 [8]eight different subspecies [9]extinct [10]Javan tigers [11]endangered species [12]Turkey [13]poached

🔊 1-09

M1: Today we are going to be discussing the beautiful and yet intimidating animal, the tiger. First of all, I am assuming everyone knows what animal I'm talking about when I mention the word tiger?

M2: I do! A tiger is a mammal with orange and black striped fur. It also has white markings on its face, chest, and underside.

M1: Good. And did you also know that no two tigers share the same stripe pattern?

M2: So their stripes are like our fingerprints. Each has their own unique print!

M1: Yes, an excellent analogy.

M2: Professor, but one time I was at a zoo, and I saw an all white tiger. Was it sick?

M1: Oh no, not sick. What you saw was something very rare – an albino tiger.

M2: An albino tiger? What is that?

M1: An albino tiger is a tiger with a marked deficiency in skin pigmentation, for example, white fur, pinkish eyes, and no stripes, due to a hereditary defect.

M2: The tiger I saw was enormous! When you see tigers on television or in a magazine or book, they never appear that big.

M1: A tiger's size can be very deceiving. Did you know that they are the largest of all the cats?

M2: No way! Lions are the largest cat!

M1: One would think so. But a lion's mane can actually add to the illusion that it is bigger than a tiger. It is, however, the tiger that can grow up to thirteen feet in length and weigh as much as 700 pounds or as little as 200 pounds. And yet some tigers are as small as four feet.

M2: That's a pretty big discrepancy in the range of tigers' length and weight. There must be a lot of different types of tigers.

M1: Good observation. Most people may think that all tigers are the same. Besides the size differences that occur between males and females, there are also eight subspecies of tiger that scientists have identified. The biggest tiger is the Siberian tiger.

M2: With eight different subspecies, you'd think we would see lots of tigers, but aren't tigers on the endangered species list?

M1: Unfortunately, yes. About 100 years ago, there were an estimated 100,000 tigers in the wild. Today, estimates are anywhere from 2,500 to 5,000, both in the wild and in wildlife preserves and zoos. And not all of the subspecies of tigers are still in existence. The Bali tiger, for example, became extinct in the 1940s. The Caspian and Javan tigers are also extinct. Of the remaining subspecies, all are endangered. These include the Siberian, Bengal, Indochinese, Sumatran, and South China tigers.

M2: Where are all of these tigers? Are they in North America? Australia?

M1: In the past, tigers ranged anywhere between eastern Turkey and Asia. Now, sadly, most tigers are found only in parts of Asia.

M2: But why are tigers endangered? They seem too beautiful and majestic to kill!

M1: It is for this precise reason that tigers are becoming

extinct. Poachers hunt them for their skins mainly. And many hunters consider them valuable as big game trophies. Also, as humans move into tiger habitats, people increasingly see the tigers as a threat to humans and their livestock and crops.

Integrated Listening & Speaking

A

1. An opera is a drama that incorporates music or dancing or a combination of both.
2. The Italians were the first to develop modern opera, but the ancient Greeks first developed the art form.
3. It is a complex musical passage exhibiting a singer's vocal range.

1-10

Last week we defined an opera as a form of drama that incorporates music or dancing or both. Modern opera developed in Italy during the Renaissance, but the origin of operas goes further back, to the days of the ancient Greeks. The operatic movement quickly spread throughout Europe and into Russia during and after the Renaissance. Such widespread interest in the composition and production of operas naturally led to the art form acquiring many different elements. One such development was the operetta, a short opera often comical in nature. *Opera seria* is a dramatic opera, often involving death, and the *opera comique* is an opera comical in nature. However, one of the most famous elements of opera is the aria, a complex musical passage that exhibits a singer's amazing vocal range.

B

1. Oral plaque is a yellowish, sticky bacteria that occurs naturally in the mouth and forms on our teeth.
2. If not properly removed, plaque can build up into tartar.
3. Brush and floss daily, and make regular visits to your dentist.

1-11

I hope everyone is brushing their teeth, as yesterday we discussed oral plaque and defined it as a yellowish, sticky film of bacteria that forms naturally on our teeth. If the plaque is not properly removed, it may build up into the hard substance known as tartar. If the tartar is not removed, it can lead to such oral diseases as gingivitis or periodontis. Our saliva does its best to combat the build-up of oral plaque by helping to break down the

bacteria by actively neutralizing the acidic environment. The best way to prevent oral plaque is to brush and floss daily and to visit your dentist regularly.

TOEFL iBT Practice Test

A   1. Ⓒ   2. Ⓐ   3. Ⓓ   4. Ⓑ   5. Ⓒ

1-12

M: Hi, Susan. How are you?

W: Oh, hello, Mike. It's great to see you! Things are going well. Thanks. Actually, I'm moving this weekend.

M: Moving? You mean from the dormitory? You live in East Hall now, on campus, right?

W: Yes, I do. I've been there for more than two years now.

M: Where are you moving? Is your new place off campus?

W: Yes, it is off campus! I am moving into an apartment complex. It's only four blocks from campus, over off Stevens Street and Adams Road, so it's not too far away!

M: That's not bad at all. I actually just moved myself, and my place isn't too far from yours. I'm in a different apartment complex, over off Stevens Street and Garfield Road. It's just one street away from you, actually. I usually walk or ride my bike to class, and it usually takes me about 10 minutes to get to campus.

W: Wow, I had no idea that you'd even moved. So how do you like living off campus? Do you find that it's difficult to make it to your classes, especially the ones early in the morning?

M: I love off-campus life! Even though I've been there only a month now, I find that there are plenty of things to do. There are a lot of other college students living in my apartment building, so not only are there fun people there to hang out with, but we also help each other study.

W: I never thought of it that way! I know more and more people are moving off campus now that the college is accepting more freshmen. Some of my friends are already living in my apartment building, so we're planning on meeting to walk to the library together in the evenings so we can study there. And a lot of us have classes at the same times, so we're going to go to class together in the mornings.

M: That's wonderful.

W: So how did you choose your new apartment? It seems like there are so many around here to choose from!

M: You're right. There are a lot of places nearby. My friend Karl and I wanted to rent a place together, so we just sat down and tried to determine what was important to us. First, we wanted it to be affordable. We also wanted to be relatively close to campus. And we wanted it to be in a pretty safe neighborhood.

W: Those sound pretty much like the same reasons my friend Cindy and I thought of. We are renting together. She saw a bunch of places before we finally decided on the one we got. We also wanted to be able to have a dog though, so that limited the options too.

M: Our place allows cats, so we've been thinking about getting one. Being able to have pets is definitely one of the benefits of off-campus living!

W: Yes, it certainly is! Our place also has an exercise room and a swimming pool.

M: So does ours! I used to live on campus near the student recreation center, and I used it all the time. Since I'm not that close to it anymore, it was great to be able to rent an apartment in a building with an exercise room. I use ours all the time!

W: We're excited about having one in our building, too. And since our exercise room is open 24 hours a day, we'll have more options as far as the times that we work out.

M: Hey, it's been great talking with you, Susan, but my psychology class is starting in two minutes, so I need to get going.

W: My anthropology class is getting ready to start as well, so I should go, too.

M: It was good seeing you! Take care!

W: It was good to see you too! Bye!

B 1. Ⓑ 2. Ⓒ 3. Ⓒ 4. Ⓑ 5. Ⓓ
6. Ⓐ 1599-1608 Ⓑ 1599-1608
Ⓒ 1589-1594 Ⓓ 1599-1608

🔊 1-13

W: I really loved reading *Hamlet, Prince of Denmark*. Who was William Shakespeare that he could write such an amazing play?

M: Ah, Shakespeare, truly an amazing man, and such an enigma!

W: An enigma? But why?

M: Well, it is because there are many conflicting historical reports of the great English bard. For instance, no one knows exactly on which date Shakespeare was born. All that is known is that he was most likely born at one of his father's two houses on Henley Street in Stratford-Upon-Avon, England. The earliest record of Shakespeare was recorded on April 26, 1564, in Holy Trinity Church in Stratford, but only because it was custom to baptize a child three days after his birth. So Shakespeare's birthday is recognized as April 23 which, coincidentally enough, was the same day as his burial fifty-two years later.

W: Wow! That is a coincidence. But did he learn to write plays when he was at school? How did he become such a great writer?

M: Actually, there is no record of Shakespeare having gone to school although there is no record against it either. Things were not recorded as meticulously as they are today. What is known is that William Shakespeare married Anne Hathaway in 1582, when Shakespeare was just eighteen years old and Anne Hathaway was twenty-six years old. Soon after, they had three children. From 1585 through 1592, there is no official record as to what William Shakespeare was up to. It is speculated, based on the range of knowledge revealed in his plays, that William could have been doing as many things as money lending, gardening, sailing, scavenging, soldiering, printing, or even working as a school master in those "lost" years. Whatever the case, Shakespeare moved to London in 1592, and that is when Shakespeare's name first started showing up in records, most of them surrounding the realm of theater.

From 1589-94 William was working hard, writing the plays, *Henry VI*, *Titus Andronicus*, and *The Comedy of Errors*. It was also during that time that the dreaded bubonic plague hit England, closing down the London theaters, and so Shakespeare spent most of his time writing poetry. For the next two years, he would be busy writing both plays and poetry, and in 1597 he purchased New Place, the second largest house in Stratford-Upon-Avon, where his wife and his children lived, making frequent trips between there and London, balancing work and family life. In 1599, he became one of the prime shareholders in the popular playhouse The Globe in London, and he had a hand in all aspects of play production.

The following nine years would prove to be Shakespeare's most productive. In that time, he wrote the great plays, *Twelfth Night*, *Troilus and Cressida*, *Hamlet*, *Othello*, *Measure for Measure*, *King Lear*, *Macbeth*, and more.

W: So many plays in one lifetime!

M: Indeed. He continued writing plays until 1613, moving permanently out of London around the year 1611 to live out the rest of his days in Stratford. On April 23, 1616, the great English bard, William Shakespeare, breathed his last and died.

Vocabulary Review

A

1. absurd
2. prerequisite
3. assistance
4. arrears
5. valiant
6. essential
7. deceive
8. diligent
9. yield
10. evolve
11. swollen
12. unique
13. cliché
14. embrace
15. paddy

B

1-14

1. This is a build-up of yellowish, sticky bacteria that occurs naturally on our teeth. (oral plaque)
2. This is a naturally occurring grain that is generally grown in Asia. (rice)
3. This is a form of drama that incorporates music and dancing. (opera)
4. This is a system of organization found in a library. (Dewey Decimal System)
5. This is a form of visual art that became popular during the Renaissance. (portraiture)

Unit 2 Listening for Main Purpose

Practice with Conversations

A   **1.** Ⓒ   **2.** Ⓐ   **3.** Ⓒ

4. 2) long, drop
   3) late
   4) fine
   5) law or graduate school
   6) tutoring program A) HIT, C) free
5. ¹withdrawing ²too much material ³she wasn't worried ⁴it would be too difficult ⁵summarizing the textbook ⁶became excited

1-16

M: It's great to see you. Please have a seat.

W: Thank you.

M: How can I help you?

W: Well, in our last lecture, you mentioned that the final exam would be a cumulative test and that it would cover the entire textbook and at least one other history book. I think the textbook is too big! It has over 800 pages! So, I'm thinking of withdrawing from your history course.

M: Oh, that's a shame!

W: I really don't want to drop the course, so I thought I'd consult you in case you had any helpful advice.

M: Well, first of all, it's unusual for students to withdraw this late in the semester. We've already completed five weeks of the course.

W: Yes, I know, but the deadline for withdrawal isn't until next week. I enjoy your class, and I love history, but there's too much information to study. Also, I have a part-time job here on campus, so I don't have much time to study.

M: Well let me take a quick look at your record... Hmm... I see... Uh huh! It looks good. You're doing fine! I don't think there is any danger of you failing the course.

W: No, there isn't.

M: It appears to me that you're working quite hard. Uh, so far, you have done well on the quiz and on the book report. Your participation is good, too. So, I think it would be a real shame to see you withdraw after having done so much work.

W: Yeah, I know. To be honest, I'm not worried about passing the course. The problem is that I need high grades so I can get into law school or graduate school. I don't want to risk getting a low grade, and there's too little time to study the entire textbook. What do you think I should do?

M: Well, are you familiar with HIT? It's our history tutoring program.

W: No, I'm not. I've heard about math tutors and ESL tutors, but I've never heard anything about tutors for history classes.

M: Let me tell you about it. It's not a well-known program because we just started it this semester. Graduate students can provide you with free tutoring three times a week. Some of the HIT tutors reported to me that they spend a lot of time summarizing the textbook and providing advice for exams and assignments.

W: Yes, but unfortunately, most of these university services are offered only in the day- time, and that's when I have to work. I usually work until the early evening.

M: Oh, no problem! The tutoring sessions usually don't start until after 8:00 p.m.

W: Wow! Can anyone use HIT?

M: Yes, it's available free of charge for all undergraduate students.

W: That's good. Where can I get more information?

M: Visit our homepage. Click on the HIT icon, and you should be well on your way.

W: Okay, now I'm excited. I'm going to check this out as soon as I get back to my computer.

M: Let me know if you have more questions.

W: Thanks for your help.

M: My pleasure.

B 1. Ⓒ 2. Ⓐ, Ⓒ 3. Ⓐ

4. 2) extend hours, B) far, convenience store
   3) A) cleaning, C) union
   4) only packaged goods
   5) exam week

5. 1cafeteria manager 2disappointed 3allow the custodians 4were not allowed 5suggested 6packaged goods 7the manager agreed

◉ 1-17

M: Are you the cafeteria manager?

W: Yes.

M: Oh, you're just the person I want to see.

W: Yes, I heard you wanted to talk to me about the snack bar.

M: That's right. I live in the dormitory next door, and for the past month, some of my friends and I have tried to buy things from your snack bar late in the evening, but it usually closes at 10:00. We want it to stay open much later.

W: Well, we've already extended the snack bar hours to 10:00 p.m. Last year, we closed at 9:00.

M: I know, and I appreciate the extended hours. But, you're unaware that many students, especially those from the dormitory, like to hang out in the cafeteria in the evening to take a break, do homework, work

on group projects, or to study. There's usually a steady flow of traffic there until late in the evening, especially during exam week. It would be very convenient if you stayed open until midnight. Late at night, students don't always feel like walking ten minutes to the nearest convenience store. And during exam week, we're too busy to go for a walk late at night.

W: Well, I understand your situation. But we need to close by ten o'clock so that the cleaning staff can come in and clean the snack bar and surrounding area. Our custodians finish work at 10:30, and therefore, there's nobody to clean the snack bar after 10:30. If the students working at the snack bar leave at 11:00 or later, there's nobody to clean up after them. It takes about 30 minutes to clean the grill and cookers.

M: Well, why don't you ask the snack bar staff to clean up?

W: I'd like to, but we usually only employ them to serve in the snack bar rather than to do cleaning work. Also, the custodians are unionized, and there's a clause in the collective bargaining agreement that prevents other people from doing their work.

M: Well, why don't you just extend the hours until 12:00 but not allow any cooking after 10:00? Just sell packaged goods after 10:00.

W: Well... I don't know. Hmm... I don't really know what to say.

M: Well, I started a petition. Let me show it to you... Here it is... I've already got over 100 signatures from students. Many of them live in the dormitory, and I think I can get more.

W: Oh my goodness! Well, in that case, I don't think we need to have a big debate over this. When are the midterm exams?

M: They start on October 22.

W: All right, I'll ask the snack bar staff to keep it open until 12:00 from October 22 to October 27.

M: That would be good, but we'd appreciate if you could start doing it on Sunday, October 21, the evening before the exams begin.

W: Okay, we'll keep it open until 12:00 for a full week. If everything goes well, or, uh, rather, I should say, if there are no complaints, we can do it again during exam week.

M: We would appreciate that.

C 1. Ⓑ 2. Ⓓ 3. Ⓒ

4. 1) their midterm exams

2) part-time, A) 30, B) basic math, C) challenging, enjoyable

3) tutoring, A) in math, B) first-year math

5) not tutor

5. ¹typical part-time jobs ²first-year students ³it might be difficult ⁴expected ⁵statistics ⁶he suddenly realized

🔘 **1-18**

W: Hey, Mark. I haven't seen you in a while. How are you doing?

M: Hi, Julie. I'm fine. Did you eat lunch yet?

W: Yes, I just ate. I had a slice of pizza.

M: Why don't you sit with me for a while? I'm almost finished eating.

W: Sure.

M: Would you like some of my juice?

W: No, thank you. I just had a coke. How were your exams?

M: They were okay. I just finished my last midterm examination an hour ago. Now it's all over. It's such a real relief! I didn't sleep much in the last few days.

W: I know how you feel. Fortunately, I finished my last midterm exam a few days ago, so I have been off for the last few days.

M: Why are you on campus then? I'd be at home resting.

W: Oh, I have a part-time job here today.

M: Really! How's the pay?

W: It's great! It's the best part-time job I've ever had. I'm getting $30 an hour.

M: $30! That's great! What are you doing?

W: I'm tutoring math.

M: That sounds good! Is it difficult work?

W: Not really. I guess you could say it's a little difficult but challenging and enjoyable.

M: What kind of math are you teaching?

W: Mostly it's basic math. Many of the students are freshmen or high school students.

M: It sounds like a great idea! I had a part-time job, but it only paid minimum wage or close to it. I'd rather do tutoring work.

W: Yes, the pay is much better, and it's more interesting.

M: Is it easy to find students?

W: Well, if you do a good job, the number of students will gradually build up. I get most of my students by word of mouth.

M: That sounds great! Do you think I could do that?

W: Maybe, but you have to be good at math. You're majoring in history or psychology, aren't you?

M: Yes, I'm majoring in psychology. I used to major in

history.

W: I've studied a lot of math, so I'm capable of teaching it well.

M: Well, I haven't studied much math, but I've already studied first-year university math, and I passed the course without much difficulty.

W: Hmm. I think most people prefer to learn from someone that has taken a lot of math.

M: Yes, I know, but I think I could do it.

W: Perhaps, but you should think it over. You know a little more than the students, but in my opinion, you should be at least twice as knowledgeable as the person you are tutoring.

M: Perhaps you're right.

W: And you need to be familiar with all areas of math, including algebra, trigonometry, calculus, statistics, and so on.

M: Did you say calculus?

W: Yes.

M: You know, on second thought, you might be right. I'm not very familiar with calculus. It's very difficult.

W: Well, perhaps you could teach some other subjects. If I hear anything, I'll let you know.

M: Sure. Thank you.

D **1.** Ⓒ **2.** Ⓑ **3.** Ⓒ

4. 1) A) called and e-mailed, B) responded

2) out of town

4) Student Employment Center

5) A) outdated

6) B) minimal

5. ¹set up an employment conference ²good idea ³unsuccessful ⁴do much work ⁵insufficient experience ⁶pleasantly surprised

🔘 **1-19**

W1: Professor Smith, can I speak with you for a minute?

W2: Sure.

W1: I tried to call you three times this week, and I sent you three e-mails in the last few days, but you never responded.

W2: Oh! Jennifer, I'm very sorry. I have been out of town for the last few days. I didn't have time to open all of my e-mails yet. In fact, yesterday, I didn't get home until well past midnight. And I couldn't receive any phone calls while I was out of town.

W1: That's okay. I understand.

W2: What can I do for you?

W1: I want to know if you can help us set up an employment conference for November 20 and 21.

W2: Oh, Jennifer, conferences are a lot of work, and

I already have a lot on my plate. Conferences can be better accomplished through the Student Employment Center. That's what the center is there for.

W1: The Student Employment Center indicated that it won't set up an employment conference exclusively for nursing majors.

W2: Well, maybe you don't need an employment conference because the center has a lot of connections and it can introduce you to a number of employers. Isn't that enough?

W1: No, not at all. The center isn't necessarily the best way to find a nursing job. Most of their contacts are outdated.

W2: That's too bad! But, Jennifer, I'm already overworked as it is. More importantly, we've tried this a few times before, and the conferences were a huge failure. The students were unwilling to do any work. They expected the faculty to do everything, so very little was accomplished. Part of the problem is that the students had no experience arranging conferences. Meanwhile, the faculty didn't have quality time to make it a success.

W1: Well, don't worry about that. I have lots of experience arranging conferences. I used to work for the Nursing Association and helped organize numerous nursing conferences. So, I already have a lot of names and key contacts, and I know a lot of people in the industry.

W2: Good for you. I didn't know that about you.

W1: But most of my contacts are regional. You've worked abroad and in other states, so you have a lot of contacts in areas where I don't. All we need you to do is make a few phone calls to see who is interested in participating and who's looking for nurses next year. I think that with your contacts and mine, that should be enough. Other than making phone calls, your participation will be very limited. The students will take care of the logistics and do most of the work.

W2: It sounds like you've really thought this out and you know what you're doing. I wish you were here the last time we had a conference. It was quite embarrassing. I'd love to help you, so go ahead, and start organizing.

W1: Thanks a lot!

W2: But don't expect me to do all the work!

W1: No, I won't.

Practice with Lectures

 A 1. B 2. C 3. C
4. 1) polar bears, A) temperature, D) enemies
2) A) brown, black, B) 1,600lbs, C) thick, white
3) B) less
5. 1Arctic 2harsh environment 3roams 4floats 5seals 6coat 7paws 8species 9ice 10population is decreasing

🔊 **1-20**

The next kind of bear I'd like to discuss with you today is the polar bear. As I already mentioned on Tuesday, polar bears only live in the Arctic, primarily in northern Canada, northern Russia, and Alaska. If, for example, you are in southern Canada, you won't see any of these bears.

Now, you're probably aware that the Arctic is an extremely harsh environment and one of the coldest places on Earth. But let me remind you of what it's really like in the Arctic, especially in late December or early January. The temperature frequently drops below minus 40 degrees centigrade and sometimes gets even colder! Combine that with strong winds, little or no sunlight, and very little vegetation, and what you get is an environment in which very few species are capable of surviving. The polar bear, however, thrives in this kind of environment. The polar bear spends his time roaming throughout the Arctic, walking on land and ice, swimming in freezing sea water and floating on sheets of ice while looking for seals, fish, and other food. Their favorite food is seals, which they find along the edges of the ice, in holes in the ice, and under cracks in the ice. They have no natural enemies in this environment, which is perfectly suited for them.

Now, what you see behind me is a photo of a polar bear. As you can see, it's very beautiful. But what's not apparent in this and other similar photos is the bear's actual size! Polar bears are much bigger than the brown and black bears we discussed earlier. In fact, they're huge! They weigh up to 1,600lbs, or 720kg. And they're designed to survive in their environment. They have very thick, white fur, which camouflages them from the snow and ice and insulates them from the extreme cold. It's much thicker than the fur of bears that we discussed earlier. Polar bears are also strong swimmers. They have large front paws that amazingly allow them to swim a few hundred kilometers from land.

Despite their impressiveness, polar bears, unlike black bears, are an endangered species. This is a result of global warming, which will be topic of our next film.

The Arctic is becoming too warm for the bears. That ice I just mentioned to you is now disappearing! It breaks up much earlier in the spring, and now it's a lot further from land! Ice thickness in the Arctic has decreased by 40 percent in the last 30 years, and some scientists predict that the Arctic basin might not have any ice in another 50 years. For polar bears, this is terrible! Ice is essential to their existence! Less ice means fewer seals and less food.

Polar bears do their hunting in the winter, but because the winter is getting shorter and because the ice is disappearing earlier, they have less time to restore their fat. In the summer, they're forced to remain on land for longer periods of time, and during that time, they live off the fat stored in their bodies. Thirty years ago, they spent just over three months on land. Now it's almost four months! The shorter the winter and the earlier the ice breaks up, the less time they have to restore their fat. This reduces their strength and energy. With less ice, polar bears must swim further to reach it. This further reduces their strength and energy. These circumstances have steadily decreased the bear population over the last 30 years.

B   **1.** Ⓓ   **2.** Ⓒ, Ⓓ   **3.** Ⓑ

     4. 1) earthquakes B) catastrophic results
         2) A) sound, light, B) reflect, refract
         3) A) Body waves, B) Surface waves
     5. 1major explosions 2during an earthquake 3first kinds of waves 4deep inside 5hear them 6damage 7lower frequency 8duration 9moving up and down 10cars

🔊 1-21

Uhhh… okay now, um… I don't have anything further to say about volcanoes. Unless there are any more questions. Uh, are there any questions? Uh, okay, good then. I shall continue our discussion on waves, but this time, I'd like to focus more on earthquakes. As you know, some earthquakes are not powerful enough to be felt on the Earth's surface while in others, people can, indeed, feel the earth shaking. And of course, there might be violent movement, often with catastrophic results. What we feel during an earthquake or huge explosion are a series of waves called seismic waves. These waves are similar to sound waves and light waves. For example, they reflect and refract. And they change speed and direction as they travel through different densities of rocks.

In an earthquake, you might initially feel some minor trembling, then perhaps violent shaking, and then some

more tremors. The reason why you feel these different types of movement is because there are different kinds of seismic waves. Some of them may easily be felt at the Earth's surface while others are not. The reason for this is that not all waves travel at the Earth's surface or with equal amplitude. There are two major types of seismic waves: body waves and surface waves. The waves that you feel first are body waves. These mainly travel deep through the Earth's interior rather than at the surface. Some of them travel very fast, and that's why you feel them first. But because they travel deep inside the Earth, they're felt only as tremors. There are two types of body waves. The first type of body wave is the P wave or primary wave. It's the fastest kind of seismic wave. These waves can move through any type of material, including rock and fluids. Because of this and because of their speed, these waves are the first to reach the Earth's surface. You likely won't even hear or feel these waves, but animals may hear them. They're not strong enough to cause significant damage. The other type of body wave is the S wave or secondary wave. Because S waves travel at half the speed of P waves, you won't feel them in the beginning. This kind of wave moves rocks from side to side or up and down. Their amplitude is several times higher than P waves and they are more destructive than P waves. The second major category of wave is the surface wave. Unlike body waves, surface waves move at or near the Earth's surface. These waves are similar to ripples on water. They are usually the most destructive type of seismic wave because of their lower frequency, larger amplitude, and longer duration. There are two types of surface waves. The first kind of surface wave is called a love wave. It's the fastest surface wave. These make the ground move from side to side. The other kind of surface wave is the Rayleigh wave. It rolls along the ground just like a wave rolls across a lake or an ocean. As a result, it moves the ground up and down and side to side in the same direction that the wave is moving. Most of the shaking felt from an earthquake is due to the Rayleigh wave, which can be much larger than the other waves. They are slower than body waves, and sometimes cars might appear to be moving up and down with these waves.

C   **1.** Ⓓ   **2.** Ⓒ, Ⓓ   **3.** Ⓑ
     4. 1) Jovian planets B) Earth, Mars, C) gases, liquids
         2) A) gaseous
         3) A) rings, moons
         4) A) storms, B) clouds

5. ¹rocky core ²exterior ³landing on ⁴number of rings ⁵twice as massive ⁶at least ⁷a layer of clouds

Your textbook uses the terms Jovian planets and gas giants interchangeably. And I'm going to do the same. There are four of these planets: Neptune, Uranus, Saturn, and Jupiter. The biggest of these is Jupiter, and that's the planet I'll be focusing on. Jupiter and the Jovian planets are very different than Earth, Mars, and even our moon. These gas giants have a rocky or solid core, but they're composed mostly of various gases such as hydrogen, helium, methane, and others. They're also composed of liquids.

One huge difference between the Jovian planets and the rocky planets is that the Jovian planets do not have a solid surface. Their exteriors are gaseous, and these gases blend with their atmospheres. Therefore, you wouldn't be able to land a spacecraft on Jupiter nor on any of the other gaseous planets, nor would you be able to walk on them. Possibly you could float through them, but if you tried that on Jupiter, you would eventually burn up because Jupiter is extremely hot.

Now here are some more facts about the Jovian planets. These planets have a number of rings and moons. Saturn has the most spectacular rings and Jupiter, with 63 moons, has the most moons. Neptune has some faint rings and 13 moons. Uranus has 13 faint rings and 27 moons. Jovian planets are also the largest planets, much larger than the rocky planets. Jupiter is the biggest planet in the solar system, and it's huge. It's several times bigger than any of the other planets in the solar system. In fact, it's twice as massive as all of the other planets combined! By comparison, it's about 318 times more massive than Earth, with a diameter 11 times greater than Earth. Now, believe it or not, despite its magnificent size, Jupiter is not the largest planet in the universe. Larger planets have recently been discovered outside the solar system, and I'm sure more will be discovered in the future.

Weather patterns on the Jovian planets are much different than the rocky planets. For example, they don't have any oceans or landmasses, which greatly influence weather conditions on Earth. Jupiter has the Great Red Spot, a storm which is at least 340 years old and seems to be a permanent fixture on the planet. The storm is bigger than Earth. Wind speeds on Jupiter often reach up to 600km/hr. Neptune has a similar phenomena, the Great Dark Spot, a cyclonic storm about the same size as Europe and Asia combined. This type of phenomenon does not exist on the rocky planets. Again, I reiterate, the Jovian planets are much different than Earth.

The rings that surround Jupiter are composed of smoke-like particles that are sprayed about when its moons are bombarded by energetic meteor impacts. The halo, which is the innermost ring, is 22,000km wide! And Jupiter is always covered by a layer of clouds. The rings surrounding the other Jovian planets are composed of similar particles.

Spacecraft have taken numerous close-up photos of the Jovian planets. Some of these photos appear in your textbook. The word close-up has to be taken with a grain of salt. The photo I'm showing you now, uh, just a minute… would someone turn off the light please…? Okay, there it is! This breathtaking view was obtained by Voyager 1 when the spacecraft was 9.2 million km from Jupiter… Oh, and here's another. This is Neptune. I think it's the most beautiful planet. I love the blue color. It looks like one gigantic ocean, but it's not ocean.

Is there life on the Jovian planets? Is that possible? Well, scientists seem to agree that there probably wouldn't be any Earth-like life on these planets because there's little water in their atmospheres and any possible solid surface deep inside these planets, for example, in Jupiter, would be under too much pressure.

D 1. Ⓒ 2. Ⓐ, Ⓑ 3. Ⓓ
   4. 1) monsoons, C) various
      2) A) 90, B) crops
      3) A) flooding
      4) predict
   5. ¹annual ²primarily in Asia ³over the ocean ⁴causing flooding ⁵these rains ⁶impossible

The last thing I want to discuss with you today are monsoons. Because we don't have much time remaining in today's lecture and because the next class will be our physical geography midterm examination, I'm not going to go into a lot of detail. Your textbook provides you with more than ample information on this topic, so please refer to it before next Monday's examination. Needless to say, I can guarantee there will be at least a few examination questions on this topic.

Very briefly though, I'd like to tell you that monsoons are an annual weather phenomenon. In fact, the word monsoon derives from an old Arabic word which means season because these rainstorms occur every year. More specifically, they're very heavy rains which originate from moist air masses that move inland from the ocean. What actually happens is that air masses move from cool air to warm air or from a high pressure system above the Indian Ocean to a low pressure system over the continent, causing it to rain in South Asia. And as your textbook indicates, most monsoons happen in continental Asia. Smaller ones occur in northern Australia, equatorial Africa, and, to a much lesser extent, right here in the southwestern U.S.

Now, unlike earthquakes, volcanoes, flash floods, ice storms, droughts, and most of the other natural phenomenon that we discussed during the last few weeks, monsoons, surprisingly, have a very beneficial impact. Although the heavy rains might be unwanted in some places, monsoon rains supply about 90 percent of India's total water supply. So right there, you have a billion people benefiting and relying on this rain. This rain is essential for crops. Imagine the hardship a billion people would endure if there were no monsoons! In fact, Asia, where most of the monsoons occur, contains half of the world's population. In other words, three billion people live in areas affected by the monsoons. Many of these people are poor, subsistence farmers, totally reliant on monsoons for their livelihoods. Too little rain would result in famine.

By the same token, these same people can suffer undue hardship if there's too much rain, resulting in disastrous floods. Flooding leads to severe damage and famine. Monsoons are also less appreciated in the urban areas, where many people, both poor and wealthy, would be greatly inconvenienced by too much rain. Again, imagine the millions of poor people in third world cities, living in porous, shabby homes, drenched by extensive leakage.

I mentioned that monsoons occur annually. But the precise date, duration, and quantity are impossible to predict. Also, monsoons are more common in the northern hemisphere, where there are more large landmasses than in the southern hemisphere, which is mostly comprised of sea water.

So to reiterate, monsoons have positive and negative impacts. I'd like to continue this discussion on monsoons, but, unfortunately, we've run out of time today, and our examination will be during the next class. So I urge you to read more about this in your textbook.

Integrated Listening & Speaking

A

1. They are huge, white bears covered by thick, white fur, and they have large front paws.

2. They eat meat, especially seals.

3. The Arctic climate is perfectly suited for polar bears, but now it's getting too warm for them. There are less ice and fewer seals.

2-01

Last week we talked about polar bears. I told you they lived in the Arctic, a very harsh environment. In late December and early January, the temperature falls below minus 40 degrees, and there is little or no sunlight. Very few species can survive in this environment. But, as I mentioned to you, this environment is perfect for polar bears. They cannot live without it. They are huge, white animals, weighing up to 740kg. They have thick, white fur and are camouflaged from the environment. They have large front paws, allowing them to swim a few hundred kilometers from land. These meat eaters spend most of their waking hours hunting seals under or near the ice. Unfortunately, these beautiful animals are now an endangered species. This is because the Arctic is becoming too warm for the bears. There is less ice and fewer seals to feed on. They have to swim further to reach the ice, and this reduces their condition. Most importantly, the polar bear population is now decreasing and expected to decline even more.

B

1. Cool, moist air above the ocean collides with dry, warm air above India.

2. Monsoons provide farmers with water for their crops.

3. The northern hemisphere is where most of the large landmasses are located.

2-02

Now, just as a brief review, monsoons are an annual weather phenomenon that usually occur in Asia. Typically, what happens is that cool, moist air above the ocean collides with dry, warm air above India. When this happens, it turns into heavy rain. The rainfall can impact all areas of Asia, especially India. Unlike other natural phenomenon, monsoons can be extremely beneficial. For example, they supply India with 90 percent of its water supply and water for subsistence farmers throughout Asia, who use it for their crops. Unfortunately, too much rain can result in disaster, such as flooding and famine. The precise dates and duration of monsoons are impossible to predict. Monsoons are more common in the northern hemisphere, where there are more large landmasses, than in the southern hemisphere, which is mostly comprised of sea water.

TOEFL iBT Practice Test

A   1. Ⓒ   2. Ⓐ   3. Ⓐ   4. Ⓒ   5. Ⓑ

Ⓞ 2-03

M: Excuse me. I was here last week for a few interviews. I'm just checking if you've heard from any of the employers yet?

W: Yes, we've started to hear from a few. I have a list here…

M: Oh! That's me… right there…! What job is that?

W: This is the media assistant position. It's a three-month contract, and it starts soon.

M: Media assistant? I didn't even have an interview for that job. How did I get it?

W: Well, I guess they received your application and then hired you based on your experience and qualifications. Or perhaps they contacted your references.

M: That's great! I mean, I hope it's a good job… I don't know anything about it. Do you know exactly what it's about? Is it a good job?

W: Well, first of all, the job is with Bestviews. They're a local company that produces a lot of educational films, documentaries, news clips, and sometimes special events. Also, many of the professors from this university work on those films. But, to answer your question, I think it is a good job. It's not dirty or dangerous or anything like that. A lot of the students here had that job, and they liked it. It's very interesting, and it's a lot better than most of the work students end up getting.

M: Well, what exactly does a media assistant do?

W: A number of things. It's not really an office job or a sedentary job. You have to travel a lot.

M: Really? That's good. I don't mind traveling. Which cities would I have to travel to?

W: Well, I didn't mean road trips, but you have to travel a lot around the city or near the city. You have to pick up and deliver any movies, videos, and films that are being edited. So, perhaps the filming might take place at an event just outside of the city. You'd take the film back to the Bestviews Media Center, which is located just across the street from campus and then return any edited films to other destinations throughout the city. You have a driver's license, right?

M: Yes, sure. I used to have a part-time job as a taxi driver. I drove full-time last summer.

W: I see! Well, maybe that's why they hired you. This job is going to require a lot of driving, and you'll be driving their vans. They have nice vans.

M: Okay. When does the job start?

W: You'll have to get all of the details directly from the employer. But most of these jobs are supposed to begin early next month. Here's a phone number. Just call this person. Her name is Emily. I've met her a few times. She's very nice. She should be able to answer all of your questions. I think she might be your supervisor.

M: I'll do that. Thanks a lot.

W: No problem. I hope it all works out for you.

B   1. Ⓐ   2. Ⓑ   3. Ⓓ   4. Ⓑ   5. Ⓑ
      6. Ⓑ

Ⓞ 2-04

M1: Are there any more questions about the Chinese calendar…? No…? Okay, so to continue… The ancient Chinese were not the only ones who had a calendar. Other ancient cultures, including the Romans, the Assyrians, and the Babylonians, all had calendars, and, of course, so did the Egyptians. Many of the ancient calendars were relatively useless. In Egypt, there were different kinds of calendars.

M2: What do you mean different kinds of calendars?

M1: Well, for example, they had a civil calendar for the government and another one for agriculture.

M2: Wait…! You mean they had two calendars at the same time?

M1: Yes. In fact, for 2,000 years, they had three! Three concurrent calendars!

M2: That sounds so confusing! Why did they have so many different calendars?

M1: Well, different calendars developed for different reasons or different purposes. And, yes, it probably was confusing because these calendars varied in length. One was a little shorter than another, and you'd have to wait forever before they were in sync again.

M2: Ha ha ha! It sounds bizarre.

M1: Well, lets not forget, these were ancient times.

W: Were these calendars any good?

M1: Yes, in fact, the first usable calendar started in Egypt, a very long time ago… in 4236 B.C. This was originally a lunar calendar, but over time, they started to use the stars rather than the moon for making more accurate predictions. It was a useful calendar because it predicted precisely when the

Nile would flood. At that time, farmers depended heavily on the Nile and its flooding to supply water for their crops. The floods also deposited rich soil throughout the plains. Because of this rich soil, they were able to develop a sophisticated agricultural system which helped sustain a large population. So the calendar was useful and important for planting and harvesting crops.

The year was divided into three seasons, each with four months. There were 30 days in a month. They added five days at the end of the year to make it 365 days. The civil calendar regulated the government and its administrators.

One problem was the discrepancy between these two calendars. Months in the lunar calendar occurred at the same time every year. But this was not the case for the civil calendar. It was a few hours shorter than the lunar year, and, therefore, its months occurred at a different time every year. In fact, it took 1,460 years for the two calendars to agree or be in sync with one another. This 1,460 year period is referred to as uh… a Sothic cycle. Therefore, a second lunar calendar was created based upon the civil year. Its purpose was to regulate religious affairs, and it was designed to agree with the civil calendar. However, the original lunar calendar was never abandoned and was continued to be used because of its usefulness for agricultural purposes. Thus, three different calendars coexisted, each with a different purpose. The years were counted according to the duration of the reign of a king. For example, they'd have "the eighth year of King A" and "the second year of King B." Also, of note, the Egyptians started their day at sunrise rather than at sundown, and so a month would begin at sunrise as well.

Vocabulary Review

A

1. camouflage
2. drenched
3. blend
4. initiate
5. respond
6. transparent
7. reveal
8. capable
9. insulate
10. extend
11. ripples
12. gradually
13. petition
14. steady
15. anatomy

B

 2-05

1. This weather phenomenon is a heavy rain that occurs when cool, moist air over the ocean reaches dry, warm air above the Asian continent. (monsoon)
2. Neptune, Uranus, Saturn, and Jupiter are examples of these planets. Their exteriors are gaseous. (Jovian planets)
3. These waves move through the Earth whenever there is an earthquake or major explosion. (seismic waves)
4. These large creatures are very comfortable living in the harsh Arctic environment. (polar bears)
5. This is the largest planet in the solar system. (Jupiter)

Unit 3   Listening for Major Details

Practice with Conversations

A   1. Ⓒ   2. Ⓑ   3. Ⓓ
4. 1) A) roommate - loud music
   2) impossible
   3) new roommate
   4) A) low, B) library
   5) allow
5. ¹living situation ²plays loud music ³poorly ⁴halfway through the semester ⁵chemistry class ⁶signatures

 2-07

M2: Hi, Mr. Jones. I was wondering if I could speak to you for a moment.

M1: Certainly, Bobby. What seems to be the trouble?

M2: Well, I really like my classes and everything, but I am having some trouble with my roommate. The problem is that we have completely different schedules. I like to go to bed early and then get up in the morning to do my studying. My roommate likes to stay up late and then sleep through the morning. This wouldn't be too much of a problem

269

if he were quiet when I am trying to sleep, but at night he likes to play loud music and talk on the telephone. I try to be as patient as possible with him, but when the shoe is on the other foot, he is not as understanding. For example, one night I invited a few of my friends over so we could work on a project. My roommate got upset when they wouldn't leave by eleven in the evening, but then the very next night, he invited his friends over, and they stayed up talking until two a.m.! I just want to live with someone who keeps the same schedule as me.

M1: That certainly does sound like a bit of a problem, Bobby, but I'm afraid I cannot allow you to switch roommates, as it's the middle of a semester.

M2: But Mr. Jones, I have already found another roommate! I met him in my chemistry class. His name is David, and he is in the same situation I am in. His roommate stays up late and is loud when David is trying to sleep. David's roommate is also not very considerate of David's situation when he wants to have his friends over. I told him that we would be a lot happier if we were able to live together, and likewise my roommate and his roommate would be a lot happier if they were able to live together.

M1: Yes, I understand that you would like to change roommates, Bobby, but again, the rule states that students cannot switch roommates in the middle of a semester. It causes too much upheaval, especially when students are in the middle of their studies.

M2: But that is just the thing, Mr. Jones. My studies are suffering already because my sleep keeps getting interrupted, and then I am too tired to study in the morning. There would be less interruption of my studies if you allowed me to switch roommates.

M1: Well, have you tried talking to your roommate first? How about studying in the library instead of studying in your room?

M2: I did try talking to my roommate, but he said that the only way he can study is if he stays up late and plays music. And I would go study at the library, but it's all the way across campus. It's more than an hour's walk!

M1: Okay, well, in this case, I am going to make an exception, as I don't want to see you slipping in your studies. However, I do want to have signed proof from your friend David attesting that he agrees to change roommates mid-semester. I also want to have signed proof that your roommate

and his roommate are willing to do this also. If you return with the signatures, then I will allow you to switch. Is that understood?

M2: Yes! Thank you, Mr. Jones. I will be sure to bring the signatures to you as soon as possible. Now we all will be able to study without being so distracted. Again, thank you!

M1: You're welcome, Bobby. And also remember that although I am allowing you to switch roommates, sometimes having the experience of living with a difficult person teaches us valuable lessons about how to compromise. It sounds like in this case you did all that you could.

M2: I certainly did, Mr. Jones. I tried my best!

B 1. Ⓒ 2. Ⓐ 3. Ⓒ
4. 2) theater history
3) next semester
4) audit, B) credit
5) A) discussion, B) major classes
5. ¹theater history class ²eighteen credits ³theater history major ⁴will not be able ⁵following semester

🔊 2-08

W: Hi, Professor Williams. I just have a quick question regarding your theater history class.

M: Hello, Julie. Yes, what is your question?

W: Well, I am currently taking eighteen credits, which is a full load for a semester, but I really would like to take your theater history class as well.

M: I would love to have you in class, Julie, but it sounds as though you are taking enough classes as it is. Why don't you just take my class next semester?

W: I would take it next semester, but I am going to be majoring in theater history, and I just feel as though I should be taking it right now, as there are other classes I will need to take in the future to secure my major.

M: I am sorry, Julie, but I just don't see how it would be possible. If you were to take my class on top of another eighteen credits, you would be studying all the time and would have no time for anything else.

W: Yes, I have considered this, which is why I've come up with an idea. What if I were to audit your class and be like an audience member? That way I am taking notes on all of your lectures and learning the material, but I don't have to take the class for credit.

M: Well, that is certainly an idea, Julie. You could audit the class for no credit, according to the policy at this school, but then you will not be able to join in on the class discussions. What if you have a question concerning a lecture I am giving? Are you going to feel okay about not participating?

W: Wow, I guess I never considered that. I would have to say that I would be frustrated if I weren't able to ask questions in class or add my own comments to a discussion.

M: You also have to consider how not having theater history credits is going to affect your theater major. Ideally, we would like you to have credit for all of your major classes. And if you decide to do something in the theater world later on, then it would also be a good idea to get credit for all of those classes. Do not worry, Julie. You are a great student, and putting off my class for one semester is not going to set you back at all. Take your eighteen credits this semester, and I will for sure get you into my theater history class next semester, okay?

W: You are right, Professor Williams. I guess I just got worried that I would not have time to fit in all of my theater history classes. But it is more important to me that I have full credit for my major courses and that I am able to participate in the discussions. I look forward to taking your class next semester though. Thanks very much for talking to me.

M: That is no problem, Julie. It's always a pleasure talking to you, and I will pencil you in for next semester's class right now. Have a good afternoon.

C 1. ⒟ 2. ⒝ 3. ⒞
4. 1) A) online registration
   2) library fine
   3) A) payment
   5) the fine
   6) home
5. ¹complete his registration ²he has not paid a library fine ³get a receipt ⁴must hurry ⁵ends at 4:00 p.m. ⁶ends at 10:00 p.m. ⁷register online

🔊 2-09

M1: Good afternoon. How can I help you?

M2: Good afternoon. My name is Daniel. I seem to be having some trouble registering for classes.

M1: Okay, can you specify what kind of trouble you're having? Are you having trouble choosing the classes or deciding which professor you would like to have?

M2: Oh no, nothing like that. I find I am only having trouble when I am trying to register for next semester's classes online. Whenever I press the "Complete Registration" button, I get a notice that

reads, "Sorry, we cannot complete this registration. Please see a clerk for details." I am not sure what the problem could be. I am a very good student and always make sure that I am choosing classes to complete my major.

M1: Well, let me take a look on my computer here. Ah! It seems that your problem has nothing to do with your classes at all. My computer screen shows that you have an overdue fee at the library. It says you owe the library ten dollars for a book entitled *Psychology and the Universe*. Do you remember checking this book out?

M2: What? But I paid that fee just last week! I remember that book very well because it was a book I checked out for a psychology paper. It is true. I did forget to return the book on time, but I received a library notice last week and went in and paid the fine.

M1: Hmm. Well, there is the possibility that you did pay the fine but the library clerk forgot to log the information into the main computer. If that is the case, then my computer wouldn't be updated with that information. You are sure you paid the fine, right? You are certain you didn't pay a fine for a different book you checked out?

M2: I am positive. I haven't checked out any other books at the library in a long time. In fact, I distinctly remember paying the fine because when I was in the library, the clerk who took my money was someone I knew when I was a child. We started reminiscing and talked for forty-five minutes. Hey! Perhaps she got sidetracked by our conversation, and that was why she forgot to update the computer.

M1: Well, I am sure it's happened before, and it could very well be the situation again. However, the only way we can resolve this is if you can go across campus and get a receipt from the library. But you must hurry as today is the last day you can register for classes, and it is already well past noon.

M2: Today is the last day I can register? I had no idea. I thought registration ended next week!

M1: No, I'm afraid today is the last day. Well, if you hurry you may be able to get to the library and get back here by 4:00 p.m. when our office closes. If, however, you cannot make it back in time, our online registration is open until 10:00 p.m..

M2: I very much doubt that I can get to the library and then back here by 4:00 p.m.. I think I will just go to the library after dinner and then make sure I go home directly after that and register for my classes online.

M1: Wonderful. Just make sure that the library enters the receipt into the system. That way, your name will be cleared, and you can register online. However, please bring me the receipt tomorrow so that we have a paper trail in case there is a problem.

M2: Yes, I will make sure to let them know. Thank you very much for your help.

M1: You're welcome. Good luck with your registration!

D 1. Ⓑ 2. Ⓒ 3. Ⓐ
   4. 2) physics, A) a tutor
      3) lab partners
      4) changing lab partners
   5. [1]concerned about her grades [2]learning the new concepts [3]part-time tutor [4]lab partners [5]become upset [6]upcoming physics project

 2-10

M: Hello, Sarah. Thank you for answering my e-mail and setting up a meeting with me. You are probably wondering why I've asked you to make an appointment.

W: I guess I am a little bit curious. Is it about the upcoming physics project?

M: Well, yes and no. You see, I am very worried about your grade in my class. You've failed the last two tests, and you've not been handing in your homework. Is there something going on outside of class that would cause your work to suffer like this? I looked into your records and see that you did fine in your entry level physics class.

W: Yes, I guess I have done pretty poorly lately, haven't I? It's a mixture of things, really. First off, to answer your question, I am finding the new things we are covering in your physics class to be very challenging. Before the last test, I stayed up and studied most of the night, but I was still having trouble understanding the concepts.

M: Well, we can definitely try to help remedy this particular part of the problem. In fact, I have just hired a part-time tutor. Perhaps you would be interested in meeting with the tutor for a few sessions until you can get caught up with the material.

W: That would be very helpful. Thank you.

M: Is there anything else that is affecting your performance in this class?

W: Well, I am also having some trouble with my lab partners. You see, we can never agree on a time to do our lab together because of our schedules, and so often we are left to do parts of the lab on our own. This causes some trouble for me, especially when I am left to do harder parts of the lab or equations that I am not familiar with. When we do finally get together to exchange information, instead of helping me, they get angry at me for not doing the work right and then complete it themselves without sharing the correct answers with me or showing me how to do it. I know you put the lab groups together, but do you think it's possible that I could change to a different group?

M: Certainly, Sarah. I would be happy to move you into a different group. In fact, before you leave here today, if you could give me a copy of your schedule, then I can try to match it with some other students in the class who have similar schedules, so that you are all able to do the lab work together. Do you think meeting with a tutor and switching lab groups will help you get back on track again?

W: I think so. I will at least give it my best effort. Thank you for being so understanding, Professor Miller.

M: You are welcome, Sarah. I just wish you'd come to me sooner so that we could have sorted this out. You are going to have to work really hard now to salvage your grade this semester.

W: I know. I guess I was so embarrassed by how badly I was doing that I didn't want to say anything.

M: That is nonsense. You are always welcome in my office. I just want you to do the best that you can. In fact, I am going to extend the deadline for the upcoming project I assigned today in class just to give you enough time to try to catch up with the tutor.

W: Thank you, Professor Miller. I really appreciate it.

Practice with Lectures

A 1. Ⓑ 2. Ⓐ 3. Ⓓ
   4. 1) development of theater
      2) ancient Greece
      3) amphitheaters, A) hillside, C) Attic Theater, D) bad
      4) A) amphitheaters
   5. [1]Theater architecture [2]ancient Greeks [3]amphitheaters [4]round [5]hillsides [6]Athens [7]props [8]open air [9]octagonal [10]pit [11]trapdoors [12]London

W: We have been talking a lot about different kinds of plays, but when did the idea of having theater develop?

M: That is a very excellent question. We can find the first theaters in the same place that Western drama was first developed – ancient Greece.

W: So the ancient Greeks had theaters like we have today... with a big curtain and comfortable seats and sometimes balconies?

M: Well, not exactly. You see, the first theaters were called amphitheaters. The word amphitheater comes from the Greek work *theatron*, which referred to the large wooden stands that the Greeks erected on hillsides so that an audience could watch the unfolding drama. By having spectators sit on the hillsides with the action taking place down slope from themselves in a hollowed out part of the hill, sounds such as actors' voices or music resonated better throughout the space so that the audience was able to hear clearly. Another key feature of the amphitheater was that they were round in shape, again, so as to harness sounds better. The orchestra was situated on a raised platform near the actors that was also round in shape. Two of the earliest theaters were the theater at Delphi, also known as the Attic Theater, and the Theater of Dionysus in Athens.

W: But did the ancient Greeks have any props or a set?

M: Most of the early plays were done in the open air during the daytime with few or no props. Later, however, scene buildings were used, not only for the purpose of a set but also as a changing room for actors and a sounding board. Initially, the building was only temporary, put up and taken down each time a play was completed. Eventually, however, the building was left standing and served as a stage for all plays, like what we have today.

W: But we don't watch plays in amphitheaters now. Why did things change?

M: Well, just like other things in life, theaters evolved over time and through technology. For example, one of the drawbacks to performing plays in amphitheaters was that a play could not be performed in bad weather. Now, however, we can see a play any time of year regardless of the weather. What was not lost during the changes was that the most important thing about putting on a play is that you must make sure your audience can hear the performance. It's not like going to watch a movie, where the sound can be turned up to accommodate the crowd. A play is a living thing. It is not a recording. Actors are speaking, and musicians are playing live.

One of the most famous theaters in the world is William Shakespeare's Globe Theater. The Globe was built in London sometime around the year 1598. Just like the Greek amphitheaters, it is open-aired, though octagonal in shape. It is three stories high with enough seating for 3,000 people and a pit, or floor, for people to stand in. The stage itself is rectangular and has such features as trapdoors and other riggings for special effects.

W: Does the Globe Theater still exist?

M: Sadly, the original Globe Theater burned down in a fire in 1613; however a new one was built, an exact replica of the original, in the mid 1990s.

B 1. Ⓓ 2. Ⓑ 3. Ⓐ

4. 1) Pearl S. Buck, A) China, B) forty
   3) *The Good Earth,* A) two million
   4) Nobel Prize

5. [1]Presbyterian missionaries [2]Three months [3]China [4]English [5]year 1910 [6]Virginia [7]Anhwei Province [8]teacher [9]was adopted [10]publisher [11]Pulitzer Prize

Today we are going to be discussing the life and work of the American literary figure Pearl S. Buck. Pearl was born in West Virginia in the year 1892 to Absalom and Caroline Sydenstricker. Pearls' parents were Presbyterian missionaries, and when Pearl was only three months old, they moved to China, where Pearl spent the better part of the first forty years of her life. From early childhood, Pearl was able to speak both English and Chinese, being taught by both her mother and a Chinese tutor, Mr. Kung. In 1910, Pearl enrolled in Randolph-Macon Women's College in Virginia. After graduation in 1914, Pearl returned to China for a short time, as her mother was seriously ill. The following year, Pearl met an agricultural biologist, Mr. John Lossing Buck, and the two married in 1917 and settled in the rural Chinese province Anhwei. Pearl worked as a teacher and also as an interpreter for her husband, whose job required that he travel around China. In the early 1920s, Pearl and her husband moved to Nanking, China, where Pearl took up a position teaching English and American literature at a university.

It was during these years in Nanking that Pearl gave birth to a daughter, Carol, who had a rare genetic disorder that left her mentally handicapped. During delivery, it was also discovered that Pearl had a tumor, and so she underwent a hysterectomy. In 1925, Pearl and her husband adopted a second daughter, Janice, but that did little to ease the strain of the stressful marriage between them. In 1926, Pearl returned to the United States with her first daughter, Carol, to seek medical attention for her condition, and it was during this time also that Pearl studied for and achieved a Master's degree in literature from Cornell University. The Bucks returned to China in the year 1927 only to be evacuated to Japan during the Chinese Civil War. Pearl was never to return to China again. In 1935, she divorced her husband and married her publisher, Richard Walsh, with whom she moved to Pennsylvania, and it was there that Pearl S. Buck penned her most famous novel, namely *The Good Earth*, which was published in 1931.

The Good Earth follows the life of Wang Lung, an impoverished man who eventually becomes a rich landowner. *The Good Earth* gained a worldwide audience, sold nearly two million copies in its first year of publication, earned her the Pulitzer Prize, and was eventually made into a motion picture. Many books were to follow, for example, *The Patriot* (1939) and *The Child Who Never Grew* (1950), with many stories and essays in between. In 1936, she was made a member of the National Institute of Arts and Letters, and, in the year 1938, she won the Nobel Prize for literature.

After the death of her second husband, Richard Walsh, she began a relationship with a young dance instructor, Ted Harris, who was forty years younger. She died at the age of eighty in Vermont on March 6, 1973. She is remembered for her work in literature but also her humanitarian work, for her candor, and for her faith in her fellow peers. In 1939, she said, "I feel no need for any other faith than my faith in human beings." Pearl's work spanned forty years, during which she published over eighty works of literature.

C   **1.** Ⓑ   **2.** Ⓒ   **3.** Ⓒ
   4. 1) the Latin alphabet
      A) Roman alphabet, C) twenty-six - consonants
      3) pronunciation
      4) rules, exceptions
   5. ¹Roman alphabet ²twenty-three ³twenty-six
      ⁴smallest unit ⁵five ⁶act as vowels ⁷long or short

🔊 2-13

W: We've been working really hard on spelling Latin words, but Latin pronunciation seems so hard to understand!

M: Well, first, before you get too frustrated, let's back up and talk a little bit about the alphabet in general. Can anyone tell me what alphabet we use?

W: The Roman alphabet?

M: Very good. But did you also know that the Roman alphabet is also known as the Latin alphabet?

W: Is it?

M: Yes. And the Latin alphabet was based upon the Etruscan alphabet, which had only twenty-three letters. Latin is the most widely used alphabet, its earliest known inscriptions starting somewhere around the 7th or 6th century B.C. While classical Latin only had twenty-three letters, the language later developed into the twenty-six letter alphabet system we have today. Now, each of the twenty-six letters represents a phoneme. A phoneme is the smallest unit in a language that conveys a distinct meaning. Can anyone give me an example of a phoneme, in terms of our alphabet?

W: Like the B sound in the word bat?

M: Yes, that is an excellent example. Now each of the twenty-six letters is made up of two types: consonants and vowels. There are five vowels (A, E, I, O, and U) and twenty-one consonants, with the letters Y and W – normally considered consonants – sometimes acting as vowels.

W: But each of the letters can have more than one sound, right? For instance, the letter A has a different sound in the word fate than it does in the word car. And the letter P has a different sound in the word happy than it does in the word photograph.

M: This is a very good observation. Traditionally, long and short vowels were not distinguished in Latin, meaning that the pronunciation was often the same despite the spelling of words or despite the coupling of one vowel with another. Today, however, each vowel's pronunciation can be termed long or short. Let us look at the letter I, for instance. In the word vine, the I has a long sound. In the word pin, the I makes a short sound.

W: But how are we supposed to know which sound it is making?

M: In the word vine, we know that the I makes a long sound because there is an E at the end of the word. When there is an E at the end of a word, it more often than not makes the vowel before it have a long sound.

W: Oh! And because the word pin does not have an E at the end of it, this means that the I makes a short sound?

M: Exactly. Now, of course, there are exceptions to the rule, just like there are in any language.

W: Can you give us an example?

M: Yes, and this time why don't we use a consonant as an example? How about the letter P? Now, the letter P starts all of these words: poke, photograph, and psychology, however, in each of these three words, the P makes a different sound. Regarding the word poke, the P makes its traditional phonetic sound. However, in the word photograph, the letter P coupled with the letter H makes the traditional F sound. And finally, in the word psychology, the P next to the letters S and Y makes the P totally silent.

W: Wow! So I guess that for one to master the Latin language, one must memorize both the exceptions and the rules.

D   **1.** Ⓑ   **2.** Ⓒ   **3.** Ⓓ

    4. 1) white ant, A) termite, B) cockroach
        2) A) termites, B) – eggs, protect
        3) exterminate
    5. ¹termite ²cellulose ³in damp timber
        ⁴reproduction of young ⁵grooming and feeding
        ⁶digestive bacteria ⁷damage ⁸exterminator

2-14

Today, class, we are going to be taking a look at the insect known as a white ant. Actually, a white ant isn't an ant at all, but a termite, and in our case, we will be focusing specifically on the subterranean form. These termites are called white ants because, for the most part, they resemble ants, although they are more closely related to cockroaches. Now, before we look at their genetic make-up, let's talk about the living systems of these termites. White ants live in colonies and work in highly organized units. Within each colony there is a king and queen termite, soldiers, swarmers or alates, nymphs, and thousands of worker termites. White ants are mainly found in parts of Australia and can cause considerable damage to timber, homes, and commercial buildings because they feed on cellulose, which is a form of a plant tissue. These little creatures require contact with soil and with moisture, so they tend to make their nests in the ground, which stand out as visible mounds, or sometimes they build their nest in a damp and rotting tree. They have soft bodies and are relatively small, roughly half the size of a matchstick. It is only the worker white ants that can digest the cellulose due to a certain bacteria in their gut. Therefore, the workers are also responsible for feeding the other white ants by partly digesting the cellulose and then regurgitating it for the other ants. Imagine having to regurgitate your food to feed your brothers and sisters! It is also the responsibility of the worker ants to maintain the nest, to make subterranean tunnels from the nest to nearby food sources, to gather and distribute food, to groom themselves and all the other white ants, and to care for the young nymphs until they are adults. Now, compared to the worker white ant, the queen white ant has a much lazier lifestyle. Her sole responsibility is to lay eggs. She can live for more than twenty-five years, everyday laying up to 2,000 eggs, which are then tended to by the worker ants. Along with the worker white ants and queen ant, there are soldier white ants, who look slightly different from their worker counterparts, with an orange-colored head and pinchers to crush their enemies. Some of the solider white ants even have a pointed nose, which emits a sticky substance that helps to hold their prey. It is the job of the solider termites to protect the nest and all the other termites from other invading insects. The final type of white ant found in a colony is called a swarmer or alates. These white ants have wings and become the future king and queen termites of different colonies, as they are equipped with reproductive organs. Once a colony is well established, the swarmers fly in groups of thousands, land, shed their wings, and attract a mate by emitting chemical pheromones. It is the sight of these swarmers flying in large groups that signals that a white ant colony is well established. If this is the case in a house, the owners should call an exterminator as soon as possible! In their relationship with human beings, white ants cause considerable damage to homeowners and business owners in Australia. Millions of dollars are spent each year trying to keep these little timber-eaters from causing too much damage, especially structural damage. Professionals instruct people that if they find a white ant nest, they should refrain from disturbing it. White ants have very keen survival instincts and, if their colony is disturbed, they are likely to move on and cause further damage to a different part of the tree or building. If a white ant nest is found in rural or non-residential areas, the best thing to do is to stay away from it. If the colony is found in a residential or business area, the best thing to do is to contact a professional exterminator.

Integrated Listening & Speaking

A

1. They are termites, so white ants eat away at the structural timber in homes and buildings.
2. White ants are small insects with soft, off-white bodies.
3. Soldier white ants are responsible for protecting the nest from enemies.

◉ 2-15

Last week we looked at the insect known as the white ant, otherwise known as a termite. White ants are mainly found in Australia. Each year these little creatures cause considerable damage to homes and commercial buildings due to their appetite for wood. White ants are small insects with soft, off-white bodies. They live in colonies, either in old, damp trees or mounded earth, with different white ants performing different duties. The king and queen white ants are solely responsible for reproduction while soldier ants protect the nest. Swarmer white ants, otherwise known as alates, are future king and queen white ants of other colonies, as they are born with reproductive organs. And finally, the worker white ants are responsible for a number of tasks within the colony, such as building and maintaining the nest, finding food, feeding and grooming, and caring for the young.

B

1. The round shape of theaters helps with the sound so that the audience members can hear the performers better.
2. London, England
3. The audience was seated on high wooden seats on the hillside.

◉ 2-16

The other day I gave a lecture concerning the history of theater architecture. Initially, we identified ancient Greece as the origin of drama and then went on to discuss the architecture of Greek amphitheaters. We listed the qualities of amphitheater design, for example, that an amphitheater is round in shape and open-aired. There was a round platform for the orchestra, and the audience was seated on high wooden stands that were built into the hillside. The seating arrangement allowed for better sound and sight quality during the performance. We then skipped ahead in time and saw that theater architecture had evolved. The modern theater we used as an example was Shakespeare's

Globe Theater in London, England. The Globe Theater was octagonal in shape with wooden seating three stories high and a pit in the middle, in front of the stage, which was for standing room only. On stage, there were various trapdoors and riggings to aid with props and special effects during the performance.

TOEFL iBT Practice Test

A   1. Ⓑ   2. Ⓑ   3. Ⓓ   4. Ⓐ   5. Ⓓ

◉ 2-17

W1: Hello, Professor Adams. I was wondering if you could help me for a minute.

W2: Certainly, Heather. Come on in. What can I help you with?

W1: Well, I have chosen to write about Shakespeare's play *A Midsummer Night's Dream* for the literature project you assigned, but I am having a little trouble finding sources for my essay.

W2: Ah! *A Midsummer Night's Dream*, my favorite Shakespeare comedy! I am glad you have chosen that play. Before we talk about sources, why don't you tell me what aspect of the drama you are going to write about? That may help us in our search for source material.

W1: Well, I especially like *A Midsummer Night's Dream*, as it is a wedding play. I also like many of the characters in the play, especially the weaver, Bottom, and how he convinces his friends to put on their own play in the enchanted woods. I guess I just don't know how to combine these elements into one idea.

W2: One idea would be not only to read the play, as you have done, but also to look at it through another medium. I suggest you go to see a production of the play and also see it on film. There was a film version of *A Midsummer's Night Dream* done in 1999 by the director Michael Hoffman. I would suggest you familiarize yourself with both the written and visual material of the play before you begin. Now, after you have done that, you can decide how you wish to narrow your focus. You mentioned the aspect of marriage in the play.

W1: Yes, I was thinking that maybe I could talk about the treatment of women during those times in relationship to the marriages in the play, as marriages were decided by the father, and if the daughter did not obey and marry her father's choice of husband, then she could be put to death or sent to a nunnery under Athenian Law.

W2: That sounds like an excellent avenue to follow in terms of an essay. One book that I would highly recommend is called *A Midsummer Night's Dream Manual/Study Guide*. This book is full of information, not only about the play but also about Shakespeare. It has a timeline and many cross-references. What it also contains, which would be of considerable help to you, is a bibliography, which will list even more sources regarding the play.

W1: That sounds like the perfect reference book for my essay!

W2: Another thing I would suggest is to look online and in the encyclopedia, even, regarding the issue of marriage and the treatment of women during Elizabethan times. This way you will have some factual information about marriage tradition to compare to the themes of marriage and the treatment of women in the play.

W1: Thank you so much, Professor Adams! Now I not only have the play to take information from, but I also have a film to watch, a new book to order, and ideas on how to look up more information online and in the encyclopedia.

W2: You are very welcome, Heather. And good luck on your essay. I look forward to reading it!

B 1. Ⓒ 2. Ⓑ 3. Ⓓ 4. Ⓒ 5. Ⓐ
6. Ⓓ

 2-18

W: Now, class, we have been discussing the Great Lakes in North America, and no lecture on this subject would be complete without mentioning the Erie Canal. Has anyone here heard of the Erie Canal or know where it is located?

M: The Erie Canal is a system of waterways, correct? Running through New York State?

W: Yes, that is correct. There are four main waterways that run through New York State – the Erie, the Champlain, the Oswego, and the Cayuga-Seneca – which are connected by a five-hundred-and-twenty-four-mile system of canals. What is most important about the Erie Canal, however, is that it allows boats to pass from the Hudson River into Lake Erie, one of the five Great Lakes.

M: When was the canal built and why?

W: Well, let's take your second question first. Can anyone tell me why it would be advantageous to have the Hudson River connect to the Great Lakes?

M: Well, it would be important for shipping because the Hudson River empties into the Atlantic Ocean, so it would mean that imports and exports could be transported through the waterways all the way from the East Coast of America to the Midwest.

W: Excellent. That is one of the main reasons that the canal was built. Another reason was that it was another method of transportation for the migration of American settlers westward. To address your first question, the Erie Canal was proposed by the governor of New York, Dewitt Clinton, around 1818. The idea was dismissed at first and dubbed "Clinton's Folly" because the project seemed impossible. What Clinton was proposing was to build a canal that would cut through three hundred and sixty-three miles of wilderness. When finished some seven years later in 1825, the Erie Canal had eighteen aqueducts and eighty-three locks.

M: What exactly is a lock?

W: A lock is a piece of engineering in a canal system that allows for a boat to go either uphill or downhill. This is why there are so many locks in the Erie Canal system – eighty-three – because Lake Erie sits five hundred and sixty-eight feet higher in elevation than the Hudson River.

M: Five hundred and sixty-eight feet higher! You mean a big ship can go that far uphill or downhill?

W: There are some length and height restrictions. A vessel up to three hundred feet long and forty feet wide can pass through the canal system; however, there are bridge clearance restrictions of fifteen and a half to twenty feet in height. Still, this allows for just about any boat or barge to go through the Erie Canal.

M: Is the system still used for imports and exports?

W: Well, transportation has come a long way in the last one hundred and fifty-some years. We can now transport goods by truck or plane, even by railroad. The Erie Canal is now mainly used for pleasure and recreation. It is a tourist hotspot, with many neat sites along the way. There are quaint inns and waterway restaurants along the way as well as canal museums and beautiful scenery to take in as you travel through the canal system.

Vocabulary Review

A

1. salvage

2. reminisce

3. impoverished

4. hysterectomy

5. slope

6. harness

7. nymph

8. upheaval

9. unique

10. remedy

11. brilliance

12. drawback

13. invade

14. tutor

15. gather

B

 2-19

1. This is one of twenty-one characters in the Latin alphabet. (consonant)

2. This was built in an octagonal shape with three stories. It was first built in London. (Globe Theater)

3. This term means living underground and is a characteristic of the white ant. (subterranean)

4. This was a structure first created by the ancient Greeks. (amphitheater)

5. This woman won the Pulitzer Prize for her work in literature. (Pearl S. Buck)

Unit 4 Understanding the Function of What Is Said

Practice with Conversations

A 1. Ⓑ 2. Ⓑ 3. Ⓐ

4. 1) business card design
   2) car magazine cover
   3) wrong assignment
   4) useless
   5) A) networking, B) important

5. ¹another project ²car magazine ³designing business cards ⁴an important marketing tool ⁵networking ⁶a project of his choice

 2-21

M1: Pardeep, how is your design going? May I see it?

M2: Oh, sure… Here you are.

M1: What's this…? I don't understand… What are these photographs for? I just want to see the business card you designed. That's what this assignment is all about.

M2: Oh, uh… sorry… I, I, I changed my mind. I decided to do something more elaborate. I want to design a cover page for a car magazine. So that's why I… I have all these photos of classic cars. I love old cars and I think they'd make a very nice cover page. But… I'm just not sure which ones to choose.

M1: Pardeep, I think you misunderstood what this assignment is all about. And it looks like you're already doing too much work. All you have to do is design a simple, basic business card.

M2: Yes, I know, but I decided to do something different and more beneficial even if that means doing extra work.

M1: Well, save that for another assignment. You'll get plenty of opportunity later on to choose your own project. You're getting too far ahead of yourself.

M2: Maybe, but anyone can make a business card, and they all look the same. Also, a business card isn't much of a marketing tool.

M1: Oh, I disagree with you. They're very valuable marketing tools… and… uh, businesspeople need them for networking and establishing contacts. You might have a customer that insists on a specific design, and it would be embarrassing if you couldn't design a card according to the purchaser's requirements. Business cards are very basic, but they're also very important, so that's why we're doing this for our first assignment.

M2: Oh, I didn't think about that. I had the impression business cards were not too important.

M1: You're not looking at the whole picture. Business cards are not just there for marketing. They're essential for conducting business. You might be busy during a meeting or conference, perhaps simultaneously talking to several people, many of whom are potential customers, and you'll want to maintain contact with them. There might not be enough time to exchange names and phone numbers, but if you have some business cards, you'll at least be able to maintain your contacts and develop further business relationships. Also, business cards need a variety of designs so that when people collect several cards, yours will be easy to identify. So that's why it's important for you to develop a unique design.

M2: Okay, I didn't think about that… So after we design

278

a business card, may I work on a magazine cover?

M1: No, not yet. Our second assignment will be another business card assignment. For now, I just want you to keep things simple and think of ways to design basic business cards. But next month, I'll give everyone an opportunity to design their own product, and, of course, for your final project, you can do whatever you want.

M2: Okay. So you just want us to design a basic business card. Is that it?

M1: Yes, and next time, we'll do a more elaborate design.

M2: Okay, no problem.

 B 1. Ⓐ 2. Ⓐ 3. Ⓐ

4. 1) A) schedule, course outline
   2) orientation, B) trip planned
   3) familiar

5. ¹including a name tag ²orientation ³booked a vacation ⁴around campus ⁵gather ⁶upcoming semester

W1: Hi. I'm just checking to see if my schedule and course outlines are available.

W2: Your name, please?

W1: Yes, I'm Nancy.

W2: Oh! Nancy, I have a package for you. This package has everything you'll need: your schedule, your psychology syllabus, a campus map, a coupon book, your name tag for the orientation program, your orientation itinerary, and…

W1: Oh, I won't be here for the orientation.

W2: Sure, you will. Orientation day is the most enjoyable day on campus. You'll meet a lot of people, get a tour of the facilities, meet some of your professors, and receive valuable information about life here at the university. By the way, there's a variety of festivities… the free dinner, followed by the orientation night party.

W1: I know. But I won't be going.

W2: Why not? You don't have to worry about the costs. They're already included in your student activity fees.

W1: Yes, but the orientation festivities are during the final week of summer vacation. I worked all summer, so orientation week is my only chance to go on vacation. I've already paid for my airline ticket. I'm going to Quebec City and Niagara Falls.

W2: Aw… that's too bad. The program has a lot to offer. It's great that you get to go to Canada, but I'm

worried that perhaps you'll have some difficulty adjusting to life on campus.

W1: Well, I think I'll be okay. My older brother graduated from this university, so I'm already familiar with the campus here. Uh, when I return from my trip, my brother can show me around if necessary. And another thing… I'm a transfer student. I've already completed two years of university, so I don't need the orientation as much as the freshmen do.

W2: Well, you should take this package just in case. I think some of it will be of use.

W1: Thanks.

W2: I really hope you have a good trip. I envy you. I've never been to Canada … Anyway, since you won't be attending orientation, is there anything I can do for you?

W1: Yes, this package only has my psychology syllabus. Could you find out what textbooks I'll need and who my professors are?

W2: Okay. I'll try to gather whatever information I can. When are you leaving for your vacation?

W1: Two weeks from today.

W2: Okay. Maybe I can even arrange for you to meet some of your professors before you leave for Canada.

W1: That would be great.

W2: Also, you'll have to get a library card. That's usually done on orientation day. If you'd like, I'll arrange for you to come and get your photo before you leave, and then you won't have to do it when you return from Canada.

W1: Okay, I think I'll be back here next week. So I'll talk to you then.

W2: Sure, you have a nice day.

W1: Thanks. You, too!

 C 1. Ⓐ 2. Ⓐ 3. Ⓐ

4. 2) France, C) bank
   3) any bankers
   4) businessman, B) an introduction

5. ¹A student told her professor ²he lived in France as a teenager ³banking jobs ⁴a commerce major ⁵she could find a job ⁶arrange

 2-23

W: Hi. Can… can I come in?

M: Most certainly! Come on in… I wasn't expecting anyone this early… Just a minute, and I'll clear my sofa so you can sit down… Okay, there we are. Please have a seat.

W: Thank you.

M: Can I get you anything?

W: No, I'm quite okay.

M: Now forgive me. I recognize your face, and I know you're in my Psych 420 class, but I don't remember your name.

W: I'm Michelle.

M: Yes! I'm sorry, Michelle.

W: It's no problem.

M: So, how are your classes going?

W: Everything is fine. I just thought I'd let you know that I'm looking for a job in France.

M: France! That's wonderful! I spent two years there when I was in high school.

W: Yes, you've said that a few times in class, so that's why I am mentioning it to you.

M: Can you speak French?

W: Oh, yeah! In fact, I've already been to France. I loved it. I fell in love with every element of French society.

M: What kind of job are you looking for?

W: Well, I'm mostly interested in working at a bank.

M: A bank. Wow! Are you sure you want to do that? Banking is a very complicated business, especially in Europe. The last time I was there, I met a few people who really complained about the complexities of it all. Have you studied banking?

W: Yes. In fact, psychology is not my major. My major is commerce. Prior to this semester, I hadn't taken any banking courses, but right now I'm taking a course in European banking.

M: Well, that's good. I'm sorry, but I don't really know anyone in the industry. If I did, I'd hook you up with them. Most of the people I know in Europe are in the social sciences.

W: Oh, I understand. But I'm wondering... I've never lived in France. Well, not really. I was in Paris for six weeks, but I stayed in a dormitory. I'm thinking of maybe moving there and then looking for a job. Do you have any suggestions as to where I could stay? And I'm also wondering if you have any advice on getting a banking job there.

M: Well, those are very good questions. But, unfortunately, I haven't lived in France for twenty-five years. When I lived there, I was still a teen and didn't have to worry about finding a place... Oh, hold on! I have an idea. I have a friend. I actually met him when I lived there, and his major was the same as yours, and now he's a businessman. He still has family living in France, and he spends most of his time there. His daughter is your age, and she's living there. He also does a lot of business there. I think he

would be glad to help you out. And I'm sure if you talk to him, he can give you some good ideas and hook you up with some people. Maybe you can meet his daughter.

W: Oh, sure that would be great.

M: Here's his business card. His name is Frank.

W: Thanks.

M: But you don't have to call him. I'll talk to him, and then the next time we meet, I'll let you know the best way for you to contact him.

W: Okay, I'll talk to you about it next week.

D 1. Ⓓ 2. Ⓒ 3. Ⓑ

4. 1) ID card
   2) purse
   3) an urgent file
   4) driver's license, passport
   5) her friend

5. [1]retrieve an important file [2]The student told him [3]her driver's license [4]in her purse [5]the dormitory [6]Eventually [7]another person

3-01

M: Excuse me, Miss. I can't let you in. This is a high security building, and nobody is allowed in without an ID card.

W: I know, but I lost my purse, and I have no idea where it is. My ID card was in my purse.

M: I'm sorry. There's nothing I can do about...

W: But I traveled a long way to get here, and I really need to go in.

M: I'm sorry. I can't let you in without your ID card.

W: I know. I know, but I lost my purse, and my ID card was in my purse, and I traveled a long way to get here. Look! I really need to retrieve an important file inside the building, and I'm in a big hurry. This is very urgent! I have to attend a real important meeting.

M: Sorry. I just can't let you in.

W: Look! Don't you recognize me? I've already been in here many times.

M: Yes, but I have strict orders not to let anybody in without proper identification!

W: Please!

M: Sorry. I can't do that.

W: Well, what is proper identification?

M: If you don't have your ID, you at least need to show me your driver's license. Then I could let you go into the main foyer and arrange for you to make a temporary ID card... until you get a new one.

W: Oh, come on! I can't do that! My ID card is in my stupid purse, and I have no idea where it is. Maybe someone stole it.

M: Well, then, get your passport!

W: I can't!

M: Why not?

W: Because my passport is in the dormitory!

M: Well, then just go to the dormitory, and get your passport!

W: I can't. I can't get into the dormitory without my ID card!

M: Then I can't help you.

W: Oh, please don't say that! You have to help me!

M: There's nothing I can do. I know you. I've seen you here many times, but I'm simply not allowed to let you in without proper identification.

W: Okay, wait! I have an idea. I just remembered something. Can I just give you my ID number?

M: Hmm... I don't know.

W: Look! My friend will be picking me up in a minute. How about you let her in with her ID card and let me go in with her. I'll give you my ID number. Is that okay?

M: Where's your friend. I don't see her?

W: She's going to pick me up. She'll be here in a minute.

M: Okay. Uh, if she has proper identification, I'll let you do that.

W: Oh, thank you! I really appreciate this.

Practice with Lectures

A   **1.** Ⓓ   **2.** Ⓒ   **3.** Ⓓ

4. 1) poem, B) rainbows
2) A) satire, B) Romanticism
3) A) Back-to-nature

5. ¹romanticist ²it describes nature ³emotional ⁴contradicted ⁵truth and reason ⁶adulthood

🔊 3-02

M: All right... Uh, what I'm displaying now, uh, on the screen is, uh, as you can see, yet another poem. Please follow along as I read it to you:

My heart leaps up when I behold
A rainbow in the sky:
So was it when my life began;
So is it now I am a man;
So be it when I shall grow old;
Or let me die!
A child is father of the Man!
I could wish my days to be
Bound each to each by natural piety.

W1: Wow! That's a beautiful poem.

W2: Wonderful!

M: What's it about?

W1: It's about rainbows... how much he loves rainbows and how his love for rainbows and nature transcends time.

M: Okay. Now tell me... who wrote it?

W2: Well, it doesn't sound like Dryden or Pope.

M: Really?

W2: Yes, the first three poems we discussed were satires, but this one is something different. It's more about feelings and nature. It's more emotional.

M: Good observation. That's because it was written by William Wordsworth. Prior to Wordsworth, the major poets were busy writing, uh, satirical verses. But this poem is different than the other ones we just looked at because by the time Wordsworth came along at the end of the 18th century, poetry in England had entered a new phase and, uh, a new genre: romanticism.

W1: But what exactly is romanticism?

M: It was a back-to-nature movement. Poets such as Wordsworth described nature as a healing and spiritual force and they wrote very vividly about it. Their themes included walking along the sea, rowing across a lake, ascending a mountain, and admiring a rainbow.

W2: What's the name of that poem?

M: Should I tell you, or can you guess?

W2: Beautiful rainbows?

M: Not quite. But you're close! It's merely called *Rainbow*.

W2: Oh, very simple.

M: The romanticists typically wrote about the joy they derived from nature and its beauty. A perfect example is *Rainbow*.

W1: I like it.

M: And why is that?

W1: Because I love nature. And a rainbow is one of those things that everyone admires and gets excited about. It's pure. It's a symbol of sunshine and hope. And Wordsworth's attitude seems down to Earth. Did he write many poems?

M: Sure. In fact, I encourage you to read some. You should read *On the Banks of a Rocky Stream* and *To the Cuckoo*, and in a moment, we'll look at *To a Butterfly*. All of these poems typify the genre. They stress emotion, aesthetic experience, and the awe of nature. Prior to the romanticists, the emphasis was more on truth and reason. The romanticists became tired of that. So they, uh, they dismissed reason and embraced beauty, describing how it made them feel more peaceful. Wordsworth himself lived in a lake area where he spent most of his adulthood enjoying nature. His love for nature undoubtedly influenced his writing style.

B 1. Ⓒ 2. Ⓑ 3. Ⓑ
   4. 1) Nile, Amazon, B) Encourages
      2) A) a rain forest, B) diversity, C) ecosystem
      3) B) over six-feet
      4) vegetation
   5. ¹the second longest river ²tropical rain forest ³surrounded ⁴immense vegetation ⁵creatures ⁶canopy ⁷undiscovered species

🔊 3-03

You probably learned in middle school that the Nile River is the longest river in the world and it's the cradle of civilization. But, more impressive, is the Amazon River, the second longest river in the world. As you know, I have spent a lot of time working along both of these rivers, doing research, filming, and sometimes just relaxing. If you ever get a chance to visit one of these rivers, go for it. However, if you have to choose between visiting the Amazon or visiting the Nile, then you should definitely visit the Amazon. In my opinion, it's way more interesting than the Nile! In fact, it's the most interesting place I've been to, and I've been everywhere, including all seven continents. In my opinion, it's more interesting than regular tourist destinations such as the Swiss Alps and the Himalayas.

The main reason why I think it's so interesting is that the Amazon delta is the largest tropical rain forest in the world. And where there's a rain forest, there's life. Plenty of it! The Nile flows mostly through dry desert, where there's little wildlife or plant life. Meanwhile, there's more life in the Amazon than in any other place in the world. For example, there are 500 species of mammals, one third of the world's bird population, hundreds of reptiles, 175 different kinds of lizards, up to 300 million types of insects, and immense vegetation. The trees are so dense that they form a canopy. The basin contains the Earth's richest and most varied ecosystem. It will startle your senses… your sight, your hearing, and your sense of smell.

Let me briefly describe for you some of the impressive creatures you'll see on the video next week. The first is the jaguar. It is the largest and most powerful cat in the western hemisphere. It measures up to six feet in length and weighs up to 350 pounds. Their powerful jaws can crush a turtle shell. I heard three of them roar one night as I was paddling in a stream a few hundred meters away. The sound was electrifying, though chilling. As you'll learn, they prefer to do their hunting at night, near the river and its streams. In the river, there are giant otters over six feet long, twenty species of piranha, and 300-pound dolphins. And not far away is the world's largest snake, the anaconda.

As I alluded to a moment ago, the Amazon basin is thick with vegetation, including a very dense forest of tall trees. By far the most amazing thing in the basin is the treetop world. The canopy, as scientists call it, is nine times bigger than Texas and home to millions of undiscovered species. It consists of trees, shrubs, vines, and other plants and covers much of the forest. 80% of the forest's food is found in the canopy. Most of the plants and animals live on the trees' branches. Many of the trees are 150 feet tall, with canopies exceeding 80 feet. The trees have narrow trunks and, therefore, can be described as top-heavy. Some scientists believe this canopy alone may contain half of the world's species!

Among these species is the harpy eagle, which has a six or seven-foot wingspan and is perhaps the most powerful bird in the world. It's big enough to carry a full-grown monkey and then eat it. There is the Macaw parrot, considered by many to be the largest and most beautiful of its species. The video will illustrate what I'm talking about.

C 1. Ⓓ 2. Ⓑ 3. Ⓒ
   4. 1) Native American culture
      2) powwows, B) singing, dancing, C) dances, D) half a day, one week, E) formal
   5. ¹mainstream culture ²Canadians ³indigenous ⁴the owl dance ⁵drum music ⁶organized by committees

🔊 3-04

M: I'm surprised by how little my students know about native culture. Although it's the oldest culture in North America, most people know very little about it.

W1: Well, isn't that because the native culture that existed prior to 1900, the type you see in the movies, has disappeared? Didn't these people give up their old ways and become totally assimilated into mainstream culture?

M: No, not at all! That's a popular misconception.

W2: Well, I once visited a native community, and it looked the same as any other community. The housing, schools, and buildings were the same.

And the people were dressed the same.

M: You're not looking close enough.

W2: What do you mean?

M: They've retained a lot of their old culture.

W1: Well, they don't have long hair, and they don't wear deerskins anymore. They don't use bows and arrows... And they don't have powwows anymore.

M: You're half correct and half wrong. They don't use bows and arrows, and they don't wear deerskins, but many of them still have long hair, and they still have powwows.

W2: What exactly is a powwow?

M: A very good question, and I'm glad you asked it. Take a look at these photos. I'm going to pass a few photos out. You guys just pass them around. These are photos from a powwow. Basically, a powwow is a gathering of Native Americans or native Canadians, usually from the same tribe. Some of them are only for community leaders while others are for a variety of participants. These photos are from one of the bigger powwows. In many of the photos, you can see native people having a good time. These are often major socializing events with singing and traditional dancing, and in one photo, you can see a man playing a drum. Often the powwows have booths where you can buy food, supplies, arts, and crafts. Some of the food is indigenous.

W1: Do they still do the rain dance like you've seen them in some Westerns?

M: No, not a rain dance. But there are many others, such as the round dance, the crow hop, the gourd dance, the owl dance, and the snake and buffalo dance. In the snake and buffalo dance, the dancers imitate the motions of a snake and then later, the movements of a herd of buffalo. Most of these dances, such as the horse stealing song, are played with drum music. There are also various dance competitions where dancers are dressed in traditional attire, similar to what you see in the photos. Most of these dances originate from the glory days of the plains Indians in Canada and the U.S., when people lived at one with nature. It also explains the theme behind most of these songs.

W2: How long do they last?

M: Powwows vary in duration, from half a day to a week.

W2: How big are these events?

M: Again, the total varies, but it's possible that you could have up to a thousand people in attendance. Some of these are very formal events, organized by committees a year in advance and have sponsors, promoters, masters of ceremonies, arena directors, judges and so on... Have I answered your question?

W2: Yes, thank you. In fact, I want to learn more about native food. I didn't know they had special food.

M: Oh, that's good. And I'm happy you asked about powwows. They're a good example of how the native people still retain a lot of their culture, and in fact, it's a way of continuing their culture.

D 1. Ⓓ 2. Ⓓ 3. Ⓒ
   4. 1) chestnut tree, A) eastern U.S., southern Canada, B) beech, oak
      2) 1940s
      4) A) hybrid trees, B) disease-resistant
   5. ₁Some of these trees ₂a wonderful supply ₃swept across ₄American chestnut trees ₅a breeding program ₆The process is repeated ₇fully resistant

🔊 3-05

Until about 100 years ago, the American chestnut tree was an important tree spread throughout the forests of the eastern United States and in southern Canada. It was a majestic hardwood, belonging to the beech and oak tree family. Some of these trees reached up to 150 feet tall and were three meters in diameter. They were a valuable source of timber. Also, they were a wonderful supply of nuts, which fell to the ground in the fall, providing plenty of food for deer, bears, and other animals. At one time, these trees numbered in the hundreds of millions.

But, by the 1940s, these trees were virtually extinct! This was the result of a disease that had accidentally been imported to North America between 1900 and 1908. After that, it quickly spread through the forests, wiping out the American chestnut trees... By the way, when people sell roasted chestnuts in the United States, those chestnuts are not from the U.S.. They're imported.

Anyway, getting back to the disease... It is called the chestnut blight, a fungal disease that affects the bark of the chestnut trees. Sometimes it's called chestnut bark disease. Normally, the fungus will enter a wound in the tree and then get under the bark and grow. Gradually, it goes around the trunk, branch, or twig and kills the cambium. Now, cambium is the tissue that divides the bark from the wood. It also forms those rings you're all familiar with. I mean the annual rings that go around the tree's wood, making it possible for you determine the age of the tree. The fungal infection causes the tree trunk to split. Once the cambium is cut, the tree will die. However, the tree's root system is quite resistant to the blight. Sprouts will develop at the base of the tree, and, therefore, several small American chestnut trees still exist. But they are only shoots from existing bases. That's because before they can reproduce, the disease will eventually attack and infect the tree again. It dies, and then the process starts again. Are there any questions?

No questions? Okay then, I'll continue. Although the American chestnut tree is all but extinct, it's not totally extinct. Efforts are now being made not only to thwart its extinction but also to revive the tree. One is a breeding plan conducted by the American Chestnut Foundation. It is known that Japanese trees and some Chinese trees are resistant to the fungus. Even when they're infected, they rarely die. This is because they have two genes that are resistant to chestnut blight. The foundation made simple hybrids of susceptible American trees with Asian trees. The results showed that the hybrids carried at least two genes resistant to chestnut blight. Then they started back-crossing, where the partially resistant hybrid trees were then crossed with the susceptible American trees. One fourth of the progeny inherited both of the resistant genes and was therefore resistant. These are then crossed with the American trees. This back-crossing process will be repeated over and over so that the percentage of American genes in the hybrids increases and insures passage of the resistance genes. Eventually, a final cross will be made between a pair of trees carrying two resistant genes. One out of sixteen of these trees will have four resistance genes, making them fully resistant to the blight fungus. In short, the foundation is breeding the trees for resistance to blight. Its goal is to reintroduce, within the next few decades the blight-resistant American chestnut tree to the forests of eastern North America.

Integrated Listening & Speaking

A

1. The Amazon River is the second longest river in the world. It has the largest river basin in the world and is home to the largest tropical rain forest in the world. It's rich with life.
2. In the canopy (the treetops).
3. About 50 percent.

Last week, we talked about the Amazon River. I indicated to you that, although it isn't the largest river in the world, its basin is the largest one in the world, and it's also home to the world's largest tropical rain forest. Also, it's very rich with life, containing more life than any other place on Earth. The Amazon is home to 500 species of mammals, one third of the world's bird population, hundreds of reptiles, 175 different kinds of lizards, up to 300 million types of insects, and immense vegetation. The trees are so dense that their tops form a canopy. The Amazon is home to such creatures as the jaguar, the most powerful cat in the western hemisphere, 20 species of piranha, 300-pound dolphins, and the anaconda. The treetop canopy is nine times bigger than Texas and home to millions of undiscovered species. Some scientists believe this canopy alone may contain half of the world's species!

B

1. It had a big emphasis on nature. It very vividly described the beauty of nature.
2. *Rainbow*.
3. He enjoyed nature and the outdoors.

Okay, during our last class, we began to discuss a new form of poetry, romanticism. And we also read a beautiful poem, *Rainbow*, by William Wordsworth, who ushered in the romanticist movement in the late 18th century. The emphasis among these poets was on nature. The romanticists were a back-to-nature movement. Their poems were not concerned about politics, current events, or with truth and reason. They wrote about the mountains, the rivers, and the sea. They tried to capture nature's beauty and did it very vividly. Wordsworth himself really enjoyed the outdoors and spending his time in natural surroundings rather than in a big city.

TOEFL iBT Practice Test

A   1. Ⓒ   2. Ⓑ   3. Ⓑ   4. Ⓒ   5. Ⓓ

3-08

M1: Professor Robertson!
M2: Barry, what are you doing on this bus?
M1: I'm going home.
M2: Me too. But first I have to get off at the subway station. How are you doing?

M1: I'm fine. Tomorrow, I'm going to a job interview.

M2: A job interview? What for?

M1: So I can get a job after I graduate.

M2: What kind of job?

M1: I'm looking for a teaching job.

M2: Oh, Barry, are you sure want to do that? Your writing is so good. You have too much potential. I'm sure you can get into any graduate school if you want to.

M1: I'm not sure I can afford to go to graduate school. It's too expensive.

M2: Too expensive! What are you talking about? You can get a full scholarship! It won't cost you a dime!

M1: What do you mean?

M2: Barry, Barry, Barry! I've been teaching at this university for twelve years. In those twelve years, I've only met one student that could write better than you, and now he's a bestselling author.

M1: You really think I'm that good?

M2: Sure! Why don't you enter some of your poems or essays in a competition? In about six weeks from now, there'll be a writing conference right here in town. It'll have two writing competitions... one for students and one for everyone else. And as I said before, you're one of the best I've ever seen. I think the first prize for students is a full scholarship to a top university. Second prize might be a full scholarship to a mid-level university, and the third prize is probably a partial scholarship. Furthermore, the conference will get you a lot of exposure, and it will be a great way to meet a lot of the top writers in this community and some other influential people. I think the mayor is going to be there too, so it'll be a wonderful opportunity for you.

M1: So how do I get into one of these conferences?

M2: Well, first you need a sponsor.

M1: A sponsor? How do I get a sponsor?

M2: Don't worry about that. If necessary, I'll sponsor you myself.

M1: You will?

M2: No, I won't have to. If you don't mind, I'd like to show some people your last essay. Is that okay?

M1: Sure.

M2: Okay, well, in that case, send it to me by e-mail. As soon as I start showing your essay to people, there'll quickly be a lot interest in sponsoring you.

M1: If I can afford to go to graduate school, what should I study?

M2: Anything... just so long as you to keep writing. It could be English, journalism, history, or even political science... but keep on writing! You have a gift, so make the most of it.

M1: Okay, here's your stop. I'll send you my essay just as soon as I get home.

M2: You do that. Take care.

M1: Thanks.

B 1. Ⓒ 2. Ⓑ 3. Ⓑ 4. Ⓐ 5. Ⓐ
6. Ⓑ, Ⓓ

🔊 3-09

During the 1930s, America was in the middle of the Great Depression. If one of us were to take a time machine back to the United Sates of the 1930s, it would have looked like a third world nation compared to what it is today. Despite the harshness of the era, it was also a time of gigantic architectural and engineering accomplishments. The Empire State Building, the Hoover Dam, and the Golden Gate Bridge were all erected during this period. These achievements were impressive, even by today's standards. We don't have much time left today, so I'll begin by talking about one of these, the Hoover Dam, and then next week we can discuss some of the other architectural accomplishments of the 1930s.

What I'm showing you on the screen now is a series of photos of the Hoover Dam. Some were taken before the dam was completed and then some others after its completion... The creators of the Hoover Dam wanted to build a modern façade, and they wanted to make the whole thing aesthetically pleasing. The dam's original design was very functional, but it was unbalanced with massive eagles. It had been designed by engineers, and, therefore, it wasn't modern or good-looking. To acquire a more modern and pleasant look, Gordon Kaufman, an architect from Los Angeles, was hired, and most of his suggestions were subsequently implemented. He simplified the design, giving it the modern and pleasing appearance that had been sought. He replaced the four unequal towers and the overhanging balcony with a series of observation niches and towers that were very balanced. You can see them in this photo I'm showing to you now, rising from the wall as they continue upward with no interference.

Now if you look to where I'm pointing, you can see that the new design emphasized a series of small vertical shadows and larger shadows from the elevator and utility towers. Kaufman treated this as part of the dam's face. Also, the four large towers, which you see, uh... up here, are reminiscent of a building we just looked at last week, the Los Angeles Times Building, with its cutback corners. But in this case, the corners and the towers have a simpler look. More modern! The two inner towers were public entrances to the dam, and the outer ones were for utilities and public washrooms.

By the way, the two inner towers contained an ornament… Here it is… This was the only ornament on the dam. It's a large, concrete panel depicting various subjects, including irrigation, flood control, and some of the history of the area. The sculpture was a semi-classical cubist work. As you might have already guessed, this is an Art Deco sculpture, the modern style of art and architecture popular throughout the 1920s and 30s. Putting small ornaments on buildings was typical of the Art Deco style.

Now, as I think I mentioned earlier, the Hoover Dam was no minor undertaking. First, in 1930 or 1931, they had to install a town of houses and the infrastructure to support the four or five thousand workers that would to be needed to work on the dam. A railway was set up nearby to supply the town and the project. And a year or two before they started to pour any cement, tunnels had to be carved through the walls of the canyon so that water could be diverted away from the project. This took time. The employees worked different shifts so that the project continued twenty-four hours a day. The first bucket of cement was not poured until 1933. This continued for two years until the last bucket was poured in May of 1936. It was finally completed a year later. And, like the Empire State Building, it was completed ahead of time, two years ahead of schedule!

Vocabulary Review

A

1. infant
2. purchaser
3. simultaneously
4. indigenous
5. essential
6. thwart
7. beneficial
8. retain
9. gesture
10. retrieve
11. perhaps
12. arrange
13. mention
14. complain
15. exchange

B

🔊 3-10

1. William Wordsworth wrote this type of poetry that vividly described the beauty of nature. (romanticist)
2. This is the second longest river in the world and home to the world's largest tropical rain forest. (the Amazon River)
3. This is a gathering of North American Native people. (Powwow)
4. In the early 1900s, this disease spread throughout the forests of eastern North America, killing almost all of the American chestnut trees. (chestnut blight)
5. This is a form of communication through body movements. (gestures)

Unit 5 Understanding the Speaker's Attitude

Practice with Conversations

A 1. Ⓑ 2. Ⓐ 3. Ⓑ

4. 1) housing fine, B) quiet, clean
   2) halogen lamp
   4) fire hazards
   5) new lamp today
5. ₁inquires about a fine ₂halogen lamp ₃pose a fire danger ₄buy a new lamp ₅stands by the school rules ₆brings the secretary

🔊 3-12

W1: Hello. My name is Rebecca. I was wondering if you could help me clear up a question.

W2: Yes, Rebecca. What can I do for you?

W1: Well, you see, I picked up my mail this morning to find that I've received some sort of housing fine. I keep a very clean dorm room and am generally quiet, so I have no idea what this fine is regarding. I was wondering if you could tell me what it is about.

W2: Okay. Please just bear with me one moment while I check my computer. Ah, it appears as though you are being fined for having a halogen lamp in your room. Is this true? Do you have a halogen lamp in your room?

W1: Yes, I do, but, are you saying I am being fined for having a lamp? Every student in my dormitory has a lamp in their room. How can it be that my lamp is more dangerous than the others? It doesn't make any sense at all!

W2: Well, you see, you are not being fined for having just any lamp. You happen to have a halogen lamp, and the school does not allow these because they are a hazard. If left on too long, they can reach very high temperatures and may cause a fire if they come into contact with curtains or papers or something of that nature.

W1: But it is only a little desk lamp that I use when I am studying late at night. It's tiny, and I make sure to place it as far away from any books or drapes as possible.

W2: I am sure that you are a very responsible young lady and try to be cautious, but I am afraid the school is very firm on this issue. A few years ago, a student disregarded this rule and unfortunately fell asleep with the halogen lamp on. The lamp was sitting very close to a pile of papers and ignited them. Two rooms in that dormitory burned down, and one student was taken to the hospital to be treated for minor burns. Did you not read the rules when you signed the dorm contract?

W1: There were so many rules, and I read it so fast... I must have missed the clause about the halogen lamps.

W2: The only thing I can suggest is that you stop using your halogen lamp immediately and buy a new desk lamp.

W1: But what about my fine? Fifty dollars seems like a lot for a fine!

W2: I'll make a deal with you, Rebecca. If you go out today and buy a new lamp and bring me the receipt as proof of your purchase, then I will waive your fine. Does that sound fair?

W1: Oh, yes! That sounds very fair. I will go out right now and buy a new desk lamp and then bring you the receipt. Thank you so much for being so understanding!

W2: You are very welcome, Rebecca.

B   1. Ⓑ   2. Ⓑ   3. Ⓐ
   4. 1) volunteering, A) visiting students
      2) A) around campus, C) courteous, enthusiastic
      4) 10-15
   5. ₁host visiting students ₂on a tour ₃have the option ₄not obligatory ₅one of two mandatory ₆Monday ₇Thursday

3-13

M: Hello, Professor Harris. I am here to inquire about how I can volunteer to become a host for visiting students. My roommate said he did it last semester and had a great time meeting and helping new students.

W: Well, hello, David! I'm so glad you are willing to volunteer for this job. We are always looking for new students to help us with this, and you seem like a great candidate.

M: That is very kind of you to say, Professor Harris. But before I commit, can you tell me exactly what the job entails?

W: I would be happy to. Your main responsibility is to lead a group of prospective students around campus, show them all of the facilities, and answer any questions they might have along the way. You should be courteous and show enthusiasm when the students ask questions about our school.

M: I will show plenty of enthusiasm because I love our school! But would I be showing them not only dorms but also classrooms?

W: Oh, yes. We want visiting students to see as much of the campus as possible. We want the students to see everything from dorms and the cafeteria to classrooms and the recreation center. This way, the students can get a feel for the entire operation of our campus. It gives them an idea of how things are run.

M: That sounds like something I could do although I am not very good with big crowds. How many students are coming?

W: We have 200 prospective students scheduled to visit this coming week.

M: 200 students! I could never speak in front of that many people! I would be too nervous!

W: Oh, no, David, that is how many students are coming in total. We break the students down into smaller groups. Could you handle ten or fifteen in a group?

M: Oh, yes! That sounds much better! I thought you were asking me to lead a group of 200. That is about the same number of people who come to watch our dramatic performances, and I am no actor!

W: Wonderful. Now students also have another option, which is to sit in on any classes that interest them. So, say a student comes and says he is interested in chemistry and would like to sit in on a class. Then you would lead him to the appropriate lecture hall and retrieve him when the lecture is finished. This is optional, however, and not mandatory. You may have a lot of students who wish to sit in on a class in your group or you may have none at all. It just depends.

M: That sounds fair. I think I would like to do this.

Is there anything else I need to know? What are the logistics of this particular group of 200 that is arriving?

W: There are two orientations scheduled during the week. One is on Monday afternoon, and one is on Thursday evening. These orientations are mandatory, so make sure everyone in your group goes to one or the other.

M: I will, Professor Harris, and thank you for considering me for this job!

W: You are welcome, David. I am sure you will do great!

C 1. Ⓑ 2. Ⓓ 3. Ⓐ
  4. 1) campus post office, A) a semester, B) receiving mail
     2) B) three months
     4) B) student newspaper subscription
  5. 1leaving the country 2concerned 3forwarded to Spain 4up to three months 5school newspaper 6cancel her subscription

🔊 3-14

M: Yes, Miss, how can I help you?

W: Hello. My name is Cindy Anderson. I am going to study in Spain for three months next semester, and I am a little worried about my mail situation. I just don't want any of my mail to be misplaced while I am gone. What are my options for how my mail will be handled when I am away?

M: Well, Cindy, you have one of two choices. First, you can give us the address you will be living at in Spain, and we can have your mail forwarded there, or you can choose to have your mail held here at the post office.

W: You will hold my mail here indefinitely?

M: No, not indefinitely. We will only hold mail for an individual for three months, but that seems to be the exact time you will be gone. For three months, right?

W: Yes, I suppose that is an option. I guess I really don't know what to do. What would you decide to do if you were in my position?

M: Well, I guess that depends on if you have anything of value coming through the mail that you would urgently need within the next three months. If the answer to that question is yes, then I would suggest you have us forward your mail to Spain. If you are only receiving a few items in the mail as it is, and they are not very urgent, then I would suggest you just have us hold your mail, as it will take a while for your forwarded mail to arrive in Spain. I traveled to Italy when I was in college, and I chose to have my

mail held until I returned.

W: I really don't have anything of urgency coming through the mail in the next three months, so I guess I will go ahead and have you hold my mail for me.

M: Okay, that sounds fine. If you could just fill out this form for me, that would be wonderful. Oh! I almost forgot. If you choose to have your mail held here, I must tell you that if you currently receive the school newspaper, I am afraid we cannot hold it, as it would take up too much room in our storage area.

W: Oh, that is okay. I will just go ahead and cancel my school newspaper subscription right now, as I don't read it regularly anyway. I would also like to cancel my subscription to any school event fliers, as I won't be here to go to the events anyway!

M: Excellent. That sounds good. You are all set. When you get back from Spain, just pop into the office, and we will have a tub of mail waiting for you.

W: Thank you very much. I appreciate your time.

M: You are very welcome, Cindy. And have a great trip!

D 1. Ⓑ 2. Ⓑ 3. Ⓐ
  4. 1) biology grade, A) low-score
     2) A) good, B) very bad
     3) importance of attendance
     4) important, C) hands-on experience
  5. 1confused 2very good test scores 3a third of her classes 4problem 5learning all of the material 6lively discussions

🔊 3-15

W: Hello, John. I see you made an appointment with me today. What can I help you with?

M: Hello, Professor Higgins. Yes, I did make an appointment with you, and it is because I am slightly baffled by my final grade in your biology class, especially since I did so well on the last few tests. I felt like I understood all of the concepts this year and cannot understand why you marked me so poorly.

W: Well, let me just go into my computer, John, and check my records. You never know. I have been known to make mistakes in my grade book in the past! Let's see... yes, it looks like you had some outstanding scores on the last few tests, the last two in particular, when we were studying microorganisms.

M: Exactly! I really enjoyed learning about amoebas. Do you think it could be some kind of scoring error?

W: Possibly, but... Oops! Look here! When I view your attendance record for this semester, it shows that you were missing for more than a third of my classes. This is the reason that your grade is so low.

M: But, Professor Higgins, why does attendance matter? Isn't the important thing that I earned good test scores? It proves that I am learning the material!

W: Yes, John, you are learning the material that can be found in the textbooks I provide, but when you do not attend class, you are still missing out on the lively discussions we have that add to your overall knowledge of the material. For example, during one of the classes in which you were absent, a student brought in an interesting article about microbes that happened to be in the newspaper. We were then able to apply the concepts we learned through the lecture and out of the textbook to a current-events article that dealt with cutting-edge research. What good are all of the things I am teaching if they are never applied to the thoughts and research of today?

M: I guess I never thought that I'd miss too much from the discussions, but it's apparent that I did.

W: It also appears as though quite a few of the classes you missed were classes in which we conducted labs. These are a vital part to my course, as they provide hands-on experience. The fact that you missed them would be comparable to the analogy of getting 100% on a written driving exam but never having actually driven an automobile. Would I trust you to drive me around town? I don't think so!

M: I see your point, Professor Higgins. I am sorry I missed so many of your classes, and I now realize why my grade was lower than what I had anticipated.

W: It is okay, John. I just hope that our conversation has made you realize the importance of attending your classes.

Practice with Lectures

A 1. C 2. B 3. D

　4. 1) gliomas, A) tumors, B) central nervous system,
　　　C)- neurons, support, nutrition
　　2) A) aggressive
　　3) malignant
　　4) B) eighteen months

　5. 1glial cells 2central nervous system 3affect ependymal cells 4very aggressive 5less aggressive 6numbness in the extremities 7radiation

3-16

M1: Continuing our discussions regarding the human brain, recall that yesterday we finished our lecture talking about neurons. Carrying on from that, today we are going to be discussing gliomas. Does anyone here know the definition of a glioma?

W: Isn't a glioma a kind of tumor that affects the central nervous system?

M1: That is a very good start. More specifically, a glioma is a primary type of tumor that affects the central nervous system, as you stated, but gliomas arise only from glial cells. Now, before we go on to discuss gliomas, can someone also enlighten us as to what a glial cell is?

M2: Glial cells are cells found in the central nervous system which are not neurons but are cells that provide support and nutrition to the neurons.

M1: Excellent. So gliomas are tumors found in the central nervous system, arising out of glial cells. This, of course, is a very serious matter. No one wants to discover that they have a tumor in any part of their body, let alone their central nervous system.

M2: But some gliomas are different than others, right? Some are more aggressive while others are slower growing, right?

M1: This is also very true. Gliomas are classified by grade. For instance, a low grade glioma is less aggressive, and therefore the patient may be granted a better prognosis for recovery. On the other hand, a patient may undergo a pathologic evaluation on his tumor and find that he has a high-grade glioma, which means the glioma is more aggressive and therefore the prognosis for recovery is not as good.

W: My uncle underwent aggressive therapy for his glioma because the doctors said it was malignant. What does malignant mean?

M1: Malignant tumors are cancerous, which means that they can invade neighboring cells and organs other than the ones they first originated in. If a patient is found to have a malignant glioma then the doctors would classify it as high-grade.

W: Yes, that's right. They did classify it as has high grade. High-grade and a number four, but I never understood what the number four meant. I guess I was too worried about him to listen very closely to the doctors.

M: Your uncle must have had an astrocytoma, which is a form of glioma, as the number system that you speak of refers to high-grade astrocytomas. You see, there are different types of gliomas, depending on the type of cells they resemble. For example, ependymomas is a glioma of the ependymal cells. Astrocytoma is a glioma of the astrocytes. Your uncle's diagnosis was the most serious of all astrocytomas. I do not mean to be insensitive, but how did your uncle manage the prognosis?

W: Oh, he was very frightened when he learned of his condition. The doctors gave him only a twelve-month period to live. We were all very worried for him. He responded very well to the treatment initially, however, he succumbed to the disease eighteen months later.

M1: I am very sorry for your loss. If it is not too painful for you, do you think you can share with the class the kind of treatment your uncle underwent for his glioma?

W: Yes, I believe so. My uncle underwent a combination of radiation therapy and chemotherapy.

M1: Let us clarify that radiation therapy utilizes the use of x-rays while chemotherapy utilizes the use of chemicals to help combat the tumor. Can you also tell the class what his symptoms were that prompted him to visit his doctor?

W: Initially, my uncle was experiencing headaches, which he initially disregarded, as he'd experienced minor headaches in the past. However, they eventually grew worse, and when he started vomiting, he knew it was time to go to the hospital.

M1: Thank you very much for sharing this with us. In summary, a glioma is a tumor found in the central nervous system that affects non-neuron cells called glial cells.

B   **1.** Ⓒ   **2.** Ⓐ   **3.** Ⓑ

    4. 1) Martian Dust Devils, B) a tornado, C) cooler air, D) Australia
       2) B) rotates, swirling, C) funnel
       4) satellite

    5. 1very hot air 2forms an updraft 3creates a swirling motion 4air speed and friction 5ten times higher 6cleaned the solar panels

🔊 **3-17**

W1: Today we are going to take our discussion about weather phenomenon to the planet Mars by discussing a Martian Dust Devil.

M: A Martian Dust Devil! That sounds like a cartoon character!

W1: It does, doesn't it? However, a Martian Dust Devil is far from an animated character. First, before we talk about this phenomenon as it appears on Mars, let's first discuss dust devils as they appear on Earth. Does anyone know what a dust devil is?

W2: Is a dust devil a tornado?

W1: Well, not exactly, or at least not on such a grand scale. A tornado forms a downdraft from a thundercloud while a dust devil forms an updraft when hot air from the surface of the Earth rises quickly into a pocket of cooler, low pressure air. And for the most part, dust devils are relatively harmless, but I doubt anyone here would call a tornado harmless!

M: I think I've seen a dust devil before! We were on a trip in Australia, and I saw this swirling cloud of dust moving over the ground!

W1: Yes, from your description, what you saw was a dust devil. In fact, they are very prevalent in Australia.

M: I still don't understand what you mean when you describe a dust devil as an updraft of hot air. I cannot visualize this.

W1: Let me elaborate further so that we are clear. A dust devil forms when very hot air rises quickly and passes through cooler air. This causes the air to rotate, thus creating the swirling effect. The air swirls in a column, and the dust devil stays intact as more hot air rushes toward the vortex to replace the moving air.

W2: So it ends up looking like a sort of funnel?

W1: Exactly. Think of a fully formed dust devil looking sort of like a funnel-shaped chimney.

W2: But what causes it to move over the ground?

W1: The fast spinning or swirling gives the dust devil momentum, and that is what causes it to appear as though it is gliding over the ground. Most dust devils are only a few meters in height, but the dust devils that were filmed on Mars were much larger.

M: But how did scientists get pictures of dust devils on Mars? I didn't think Mars could sustain human life as it is now.

W1: It can't. The images were taken by a satellite on several space missions. What was crucial for astronauts and space engineers to discover was that because dust devils on Mars can be up to fifty times wider and up to ten times higher than dust devils on Earth, Martian Dust Devils posed a serious threat to terrestrial technology sent to Mars. However, on one occasion, a Martian Dust Devil actually helped clean the solar panels of the robot, Spirit Rover.

W2: So the dust devil actually helped the space mission?

W1: It did indeed, and it also gave scientists valuable

information about how dust devils on Mars compare to dust devils on Earth.

C 1. Ⓑ 2. Ⓒ 3. Ⓓ

4. 1) Industrial Revolution, A) late eighteenth century, C) manufacturing, capitalism, D) machine power

2) A) faster, C) steam engines

3) A) manufacturing, C) cotton mill

4) A) protect

5. [1]socioeconomic [2]Britain [3]man or horsepower [4]allowing machinery [5]protect the working class [6]steam engine locomotive [7]Industrial Revolution

🔊 3-18

Today, class, I am going to be speaking to you about the Industrial Revolution. The term "industrial revolution" refers to the technological, social, economic, and cultural changes that occurred in England in the late eighteenth century. This change eventually spread around the world, creating many big cities based upon the ideals of manufacturing and capitalism. Prior to the Industrial Revolution, the production and harvesting of products was completed through manual labor. The Industrial Revolution replaced this manpower with machine power.

One of the initial, and perhaps most important, developments of the Industrial Revolution was the steam engine. This advance in transportation allowed for the faster delivery of manufactured goods. However, the steam engine wasn't only used for transportation but instead for the construction of machine engines that enabled faster production. For example, before the Industrial Revolution, most tasks were undertaken by either wind or water power or by the sheer strength of man or horse. But, in 1698, a man by the name of Thomas Savery constructed the first steam-powered engine in London. His idea was to create a machine that would pump water from mines. Different types of steam engines were created over the following hundred years, culminating with a Cornish blacksmith's (Richard Trevithick) work on steam boilers, which eventually led to the production of locomotive steam engines.

The development of the steam engine sparked a host of other changes technologically, socially, and economically within British culture. Steam engine technology led to the development of factories, where products were turned out in the hundreds or even thousands. The first manufacturing change involved the production of textiles in the English city of Manchester. Before the revolution, British textile manufacturing

was handled by individual artisans who did spinning and weaving in their own homes. This meant that the process of making a pair of pants or a shirt could take days or even weeks depending on how fast the artisan was at his trade. Imagine having to wait weeks for a new pair of pants, when the only pair of pants you owned was suddenly un-wearable! In the mid-eighteenth century, two Englishmen from Birmingham, Lewis Paul and John Wyatt, advanced the process slightly by developing a roller spinning machine and the fly-and-bobbin system of making clothes; however it wasn't until Richard Awkright created the cotton mill, which ultimately utilized steam power for its production, that cotton production became a mechanized industry.

The factory industry eventually gave rise to what we now know as the modern city. Manchester, for example, due to its cotton mills, became known as Cottonopolis because there were so many factories producing textiles. However, these early cities were not as clean or well kept as the ones we are familiar with today. Along with the growth of industry came the proliferation of sometimes harsh or dirty living conditions. Children were forced to work long hours in factories until the Factory Act of 1833 came into effect, which stated that children under nine were not allowed to work and children over nine were not to work at night or for more than twelve-hour shifts. Trade unions were also born out of the Industrial Revolution, giving workers rights and freedoms that they had not had in the past.

Prior to the Industrial Revolution, working conditions for British workers was not favorable. Men, women, and children worked long hours for little money. The poor conditions of the working class prompted many educated British historians and authors to write Marxist and communist manifestos lamenting the state of the working class. And even those that were not British, such as Friedrich Engels, a German political philosopher, used England as a model for change when he wrote *The Condition of the Working Class in England* in 1844. Within this text, Engels spoke of the Industrial Revolution and how it was to change the whole fabric of society.

D 1. Ⓑ 2. Ⓐ, Ⓑ 3. Ⓐ

4. 1) symbiosis A) dissimilar, C) symbiont

2) A) – fish, shrimp

3) beneficial

5. [1]form of symbiosis [2]benefit [3]eats the parasites [4]potentially fatal parasites [5]merge into parasitism [6]will draw blood

M1: Carrying on with our discussion of symbiosis, today we are going to be talking about one of the forms of symbiosis, mutualism. However, before we begin, can someone please define symbiosis for us again?

W: Symbiosis is when two dissimilar organisms interact either in a very intimate living situation or when they merge together and live as one unit.

M1: Very good. And if the two organisms happen to merge, what were the terms used to describe this situation?

M2: The larger, or macro, organism is called the host and the smaller, or micro, organism is called the symbiont.

M1: Excellent. So give me an example of this relationship as it was discussed yesterday.

W: Well, yesterday we talked about parasites and how, when we contract a virus, we are the host, and the virus is the symbiont.

M1: This is a wonderful example. And so today we are going to move on with our discussion of symbiosis and talk about the form, mutualism. Mutual symbiosis, or mutualism, is a relationship between two differing organisms in which both organisms profit from the relationship. A very famous incidence of mutual symbiosis is the relationship between the Egyptian Plover bird and a crocodile. One would think that a relationship between these two organisms would be impossible. Surely the crocodile would eat the Egyptian Plover if it got too close to its jaws! However, this is not the case. The Egyptian Plover bird depends on certain parasites for food, which in turn feed upon crocodiles. Because the parasites are potentially lethal to the crocodile, the crocodile allows the Egyptian Plover to search its body for these parasites, even opening its jaws and letting the bird pluck parasites from its mouth. Now, going back to the definition of mutualism, someone tell me what both of these organisms are gaining from their relationship to one another.

M2: The crocodile is benefiting because the Egyptian Plover bird is eliminating the harmful parasites from its body, and the Egyptian Plover is benefiting because he is getting an easy meal.

M1: Yes. Another example is the relationship between the goby fish and shrimp. The shrimp is responsible for digging out a burrow in the sand for both the goby fish and the shrimp to cohabitate. In return, because the shrimp has such poor vision, the goby fish keeps a lookout for predators, and when under threat, the goby fish touches the tail of the shrimp to warn it of the impending danger.

W: Does their relationship ever change? For example, what if food was scarce for the crocodile and the crocodile decided to start eating the Egyptian Plovers?

M1: This is a great question. The scenario you provide is highly unlikely. However forms of symbiosis are not always exclusive but are often fluid with each other. For example, it was often thought that the relationship between the Oxpecker bird of Africa and certain African mammals, such as the buffalo or zebra, shared a relationship based on mutualism. The Oxpecker would eat the parasites off of the buffalo or zebra and, in turn, the Oxpecker would get a meal. However, it was found that sometimes, when the Oxpeckers are feeding on the parasites, they are also opening wounds on the animals and drinking the blood. This changes their relationship from one of mutualism to one of parasitism, which is like the example that was given at the beginning of class between a parasite and its host.

Integrated Listening & Speaking

A

1. A glial cell is a non-neuron cell of the central nervous system that provides nourishment and support to the neurons.

2. Low-grade describes the glioma as less aggressive in nature and provides a better prognosis for the patient.

3. Radiation therapy, chemotherapy, surgery, and experimental treatments.

Last week, we discussed tumors of the central nervous system called gliomas. These tumors are called gliomas because they are particular to glial cells, which are cells in the central nervous system that are not neurons but provide nourishment and support to the neurons. When a patient is diagnosed with a glioma, the doctor must first identify the type. For example, an ependymoma is a glioma that affects the ependymal cells. Once the doctor identifies the type, he or she must also list the glioma as low-grade or high-grade. A low-grade glioma is less aggressive and has a better prognosis for the patient. A high-grade glioma is more aggressive and has a poorer prognosis. One particular type of glioma, astrocytomas, is such an aggressive high grade glioma that upon diagnosis the disease is also numbered. The numbers range from 1-4, with 1 indicating the least aggressive and 4 indicating the most aggressive. The symptoms of a glioma include, but are not limited to, headaches, vomiting, seizures, and weakness. There are new treatments being developed everyday for gliomas, but the most common forms are surgery, chemotherapy, and radiation.

B

1. Parasitism – the virus is benefiting from the relationship, but you are not.
2. The Egyptian Plover is getting an easy meal.
3. If the Oxpecker starts to draw and drink the buffalo's blood, then the relationship is parasitic.

3-21

Yesterday, we explored the idea of mutualism. Mutualism is a form of symbiosis where two dissimilar organisms benefit from a close relationship or even an invasive relationship. An example of mutualism is the relationship between the Egyptian Plover bird and a crocodile. The Egyptian Plover eats parasites that live on the crocodile's body. The Egyptian Plover benefits from the relationship by getting an easy meal, and the crocodile benefits from the relationship by having the parasites removed from its body. Mutualism sometimes merges into parasitism if one of the organisms begins harming the other. The Oxpecker bird, for example, usually eats bugs and other parasites off the backs of certain African land mammals, but, once in a while, the Oxpecker will draw blood from the mammals to drink and so therefore benefits when the mammal does not.

TOEFL iBT Practice Test

A   1. ⑩   2. ⑧   3. ④   4. ⑧, ©   5. ⑧

4-01

M: Good afternoon, Erika. It's nice seeing you outside of class. What can I help you with?

W: Hi, Professor Phillips. Well, I thought I would come to you for some help and advice because I am having such trouble deciding which graduate school to apply to!

M: Well, let me try to help you. The last thing you need is to be stressed by such a process. Applying to graduate schools should be fun and exciting. Let's

start off with you telling me what kind of subject you hope to pursue.

W: My Bachelor's degree is going to be in education with a minor in psychology. I've enjoyed both of them so much and was hoping I could combine the two subjects by getting a Master's degree in education so that I could either teach or be a school counselor.

M: This certainly sounds like a great career choice. There is such a great need for teachers right now, especially teachers who have a background in psychology. Would you like to teach elementary students, high school kids, or even college students?

W: Oh, I much prefer working with younger students. I enjoy teaching little children so much and love the way their faces light up when they discover a new concept. I have been student teaching six and seven-year-old children the last two semesters and have really enjoyed it.

M: Okay, so now you know what kind of thing you would like to pursue in graduate school. The next big consideration is to ask yourself where you would like to live. My philosophy about graduate school, or even undergraduate school, is to try and take advantage of a new place. That way you not only learn at the school of your choosing but you also learn so much in the way of meeting new people, seeing new places, and perhaps experiencing a different culture.

W: Where did you go to graduate school?

M: I did my undergraduate work in the United States, but when it came to applying to graduate schools, I decided I would like to be in a new country. I settled on a very good program in Britain and got to live in the exciting city of London.

W: London! Wow! I am from a small town, so I cannot imagine the size and pace of a city like London.

M: Well, now's your chance to experience something new. I am not advocating London in particular, but perhaps a big city experience would be good for you. The best thing to do is to pick two or three top education graduation school programs in two or three different settings. For example, I'd say you should pick a graduate school to apply to that is located in a rural location, one that is located in a large city, and one that is located in a foreign country. This way you spread your options, and, if accepted to all three, then you can really sit down and think about what new things you want to experience.

W: That sounds like a great idea. Do you have any

pamphlets specific to graduate schools that specialize in education?

M: I sure do. Here are half a dozen or so education programs in different parts of the world. Review these, and when you have narrowed your choices to three or four, come back to my office, and I will help you fill out the applications.

W: Thank you so much! Is there anything else I need to do before I come back in?

M: Yes, if you could find three people to write recommendations for you, that is one of the things required to be submitted with each application. I would suggest getting two letters of recommendation from professors and one from an employer.

W: Okay, I can do that. Would you be willing to write one of my letters of recommendation?

M: Of course, Erika! I was hoping you would ask. You have always been one of my best students.

W: Thank you so much. I will see you soon!

B 1. Ⓒ 2. Ⓒ 3. Ⓐ 4. Ⓒ 5. Ⓐ
     6. Ⓒ

🔘 4-02

W1: Good morning, class. Today we are going to continue our life sciences lectures with a discussion on the introduction of new species within the plant world. More specifically, we are going to be looking at the effects of introducing exotic plants, also known as naturalized plants, into an area containing established native plants, also known as endemic plants. Someone start off our discussion by telling us what I mean when I say introduced. How does a plant become introduced?

W2: Introduced simply means that the plant has been brought into an area that it has not previously been before.

W1: Good. Who is bringing it and how?

W2: Well, the plant can be brought into an area either deliberately, with the intention of planting it, or accidentally, by a human being.

W1: Very good.

M: But sometimes introducing a plant species could be a bad thing, right? For instance, what if a scientist introduced a new plant to an area it had never previously been before, and the introduced plant killed off an endemic plant?

W1: Sadly, this can happen, and oftentimes it does. Before we develop this idea, however, let us think about why people would want to introduce exotic plants into other areas in the first place. Ideas?

W2: Well, I guess maybe when people immigrate to other countries. They want to be able to take the plants they are familiar with to make it feel like home.

W1: An excellent example and one that has happened quite often. Can someone list another reason?

M: Maybe someone would introduce a new plant just for aesthetic reasons? For example, a new park is being built and the landscape artist wants certain colored flowers.

W1: Again, this answer is also correct, and I can give an even more specific answer. The Norway maple is a very beloved tree in Scandinavia, and, when Scandinavians began migrating to Canada, they brought their Norway maple with them. Fortunately, the Norway maple has thrived well in Canada, eventually spreading to all of North America with little harm to other native species; however sometimes a well-intentioned introduction has led either to an overpopulation of the introduced species or a curbing or even completely killing off of other native species.

M: Can you give us an example of this?

W1: Certainly. The purple loosestrife is an herbaceous perennial plant that grows in colonies and produces a lovely, reddish-purple flower. The purple loosestrife has been introduced into non-native habitat because of its beautiful flower; however, what people did not know was that it can easily escape horticultural control because of its rapid and widespread growth, and, when it does, the purple loosestrife chokes off all other plant life in the area. When a plant escapes control like this, it is termed invasive.

W2: Can another reason for introducing new species also be because certain plants help maintain a particular habitat?

W1: Absolutely. The flowering plant known as the Garlic Mustard is a plant that helps combat erosion control. It is native to Europe, parts of Africa, and Asia, but was introduced to North America in the mid-nineteenth century after people found that when Garlic Mustard was planted, it helped combat soil washouts and wind erosion.

M: What about national parks? Sometimes plants are protected there, correct? Are they native plants or introduced plants?

W1: Both. National parks are great places to foster the life of both native and non-native plants, as the areas can be tightly controlled and monitored.

Oftentimes the introduction of exotic plants into these areas is for means of protection since there are very specific rules governing land and growth in national parks. Whether an endemic plant or introduced plant, what is most important is that all plants be protected in their best possible environment to prevent absolute and irreversible outcomes such as extinction.

Vocabulary Review

A

1. clause
2. merge
3. momentum
4. terrestrial
5. diagnosis
6. aggressive
7. cadence
8. extraneous
9. urgent
10. lament
11. apply
12. minor
13. responsible
14. harmless
15. model

B
🔊 4-03

1. This is a form of symbiosis in which two organisms both benefit from a close relationship. (mutualism)
2. This is the term used for a plant that is being introduced into a new habitat. (exotic species)
3. This is found in the central nervous system and provides nourishment and support to neurons. (glial cell)
4. This is created when very hot air spirals upward from the ground and forms a swirling column. (dust devil)
5. This was something created during the Industrial Revolution to protect men, women, and children working in factories. (trade union)

Unit 6 Understanding Organization

Practice with Conversations

A 1. Ⓐ 2. Ⓑ, Ⓓ 3. Ⓒ
4. 2) letter of recommendation, A) student's advisor
   4) letter of recommendation, B) student's personal information - Resume
   5) information
   6) graduate studies
5. [1]inquires [2]recommendation [3]out of the country [4]resume [5]e-mail [6]mentions

🔊 4-05

M1: Dr. Drexler, may I speak with you for a moment, please? You're not too busy right now, are you?

M2: No, not at all, Adrian. Come into my office, and have a seat... So, tell me... What's on your mind right now?

M1: Well, you may or may not know this, but I'm applying to several different graduate schools, so I was hoping that you would be able to write a few letters of recommendation that I could send out along with my applications.

M2: I'm honored that you've asked me, Adrian, and I'm more than happy to help you out, but don't you think you ought to ask Professor Smith instead? After all, he is your advisor, and he's the professor that you've worked with the longest in all of your years here. I would think that he would be able to write the best, most comprehensive letter of recommendation for you.

M1: Yes, sir. You're absolutely right. The only problem is that I can't get in touch with Professor Smith at this moment. Apparently, he is still at that conference somewhere in Europe, and I don't know when he's coming back. I left him a couple of voice messages, and I've e-mailed him several times, but he hasn't responded to any of them.

M2: Ah, yes, I can see how that would be a problem. I had forgotten that he was going to that conference. As far as I know, he won't be back until sometime next week. Are these letters urgent? If they can't wait until he gets back, I'd be more than happy to write them up for you.

M1: Actually, all of my applications need to be submitted within the next couple of days... Friday to be exact. So if you don't mind, I'd love for you to be able to write my recommendation letters for me.

M2: Sure, sure. I don't mind at all. But since you're not my advisee, I'm going to need to see your records. Do you think you could give me a copy of your resume as well as a comprehensive list of all the classes that you've taken in the Physics Department? That would be extremely helpful and enable me to write the best possible letter for you.

M1: Oh, sure. I've got my resume on my computer, so I'll send that to you by e-mail just as soon as I get back to my dorm room. And I'll provide a class list with the names of the professors I've taken and all the grades that I've received in them. Oh, and I'll send you the abstract for my senior research project so that you'll know exactly what I'm doing in the lab all the time.

M2: Excellent, excellent. You know, I had no idea that you were planning to attend graduate school. What made you decide to do so?

M1: Well, there are just so many fascinating things to study in the world of physics. I am just not ready to give up on the academic side of things and get a job in industry.

M2: Yes, that makes perfect sense. Are you going to be applying to our program?

M1: Yes, sir. Actually, this school is first on my list. If I get accepted, I will definitely come here. I already know most of the teachers, and I'm really comfortable.

M2: I'm glad to hear that. Well, I'd say your chances of getting in are pretty good. But I don't want to guarantee anything.

M1: I understand completely. Well, I'm going to run back home and send you the files you need. Thanks a lot for your help.

M2: Don't mention it. I'm just glad to help.

B   **1.** Ⓒ   **2.** Ⓑ   **3.** Ⓓ

     4. 1) a reserved article
        2) a library fine
        3) ten
        4) A) disabled
        5) pays money
        6) article

     5. ¹an outstanding fine ²she would be allowed to sign ³The student asked the librarian ⁴gave her several reasons ⁵hearing disability ⁶insisted

◉ 4-06

W1: Have you been taken care of?

W2: No, I want to sign out a reserved article for Psych 420.

W1: Sure, could you give me the title of the article please?

W2: *Modern Personality Theories*. The professor is Jennifer Putman.

W1: May I see your library card, please?

W2: Here you are.

W1: Hmm… The computer's showing that you have a late fee.

W2: That can't be right.

W1: You can't sign out books or reserve articles if you still have a late fee pending… just a minute… Okay, it says you signed out *Every Woman's Guide to Weight Training*. You signed it out on September 9.

W2: Yes, that's probably true, but I've already returned the book.

W1: When?

W2: I think it was a week ago.

W1: Yes, you're right. It was exactly a week ago today. But a week ago today, which was last Tuesday, it was already a week overdue.

W2: Come on! Only a week? That's all?

W1: Yes.

W2: I don't have any money right now. How much is the fine?

W1: Ten dollars

W2: Ten dollars! I don't have ten dollars. I shouldn't have to pay ten dollars!

W1: Why not?

W2: It's too much. And I'm a disabled student.

W1: What do you mean disabled?

W2: I have a hearing impairment. The university has to accommodate my disability.

W1: Well, you're not making much sense. Ten dollars is nothing. If you really need the use the article, you may sign it out for an hour, but you'll have to pay five dollars first.

W2: What about my disability?

W1: What about it?

W2: I mean, maybe you can just let the fine slide this time. I promise I won't do this again.

W1: Why did you return the book so late?

W2: I was busy and didn't have time to come the library.

W1: I'm sorry, but I can't help you. Your disability has nothing to do with the reason why you returned the book late. And ten dollars is nothing.

W2: Ah! You mean you're going to make me go find a bank machine just so I can withdraw ten dollars to pay the fine.

W1: No, I'm just telling you that I can't loan you the article until you pay your fine.

W2: I only need it for a minute!

W1: That doesn't matter.

W2: The book I borrowed wasn't important! It was just a weightlifting book! And there were probably several copies of it in the library.

W1: No, that's our only copy. And all books here are treated with equal importance.

W2: This is so ridiculous!

W1: If you'd like, I can let you speak to the head librarian. She's in right now.

W2: No, that's okay. Here's the money. Now give me the article!

W1: Just a minute.

W2: What now?

W1: Your signature, please.

W2: Huh! Here it is.

W1: Thank you. Please return it within an hour.

W2: Weren't you listening to me? I just told you I only need it for a minute. I'll be right back!

C **1.** Ⓐ **2.** Ⓓ **3.** Ⓑ

4. 1) A) his grade
   3) list
   4) wrong file
   5) wrong
   6) Apologizes

5. ¹he suspected ²had made a mistake ³according to ⁴professor ⁵calculating grades ⁶he found the right list ⁷the correct grade

🔊 4-07

M2: Professor Sabharwal, I need to talk to you about something.

M1: Oh, please come into my office, young man. How might I help you?

M2: Yes, I'm in your quantum physics class and looked at my grade. I think you must have made some kind of mistake when you calculated it.

M1: Nonsense, young man. I never make mistakes with grades!

M2: Really!

M1: Ha ha ha! No, not at all. I must admit, from time to time, I do make errors. What makes you think there's an error?

M2: Well, you gave us a spreadsheet with our updated grades, right? And right now my score is 72, which should be impossible because on the midterm exam I got 85, and on the quiz I got 90. So I think my score should be about 86!

M1: Oh goodness! Let me take a look at your scores... just a minute, please... Why don't you sit down? I'll

need a minute just to locate the file... Aha! I got it... What is your student number?

M2: It's 2-0-0-6-1-1-8-7.

M1: Please say that again, more slowly, please.

M2: It's 2-0-0-6-1-1-8-7.

M1: I'm sorry. I can't seem to find it... I'm really sorry. Could you please say it one more time?

M2: Sure. It's 2-0-0-6-1-1-8-7.

M1: This is very strange... very very very strange... I can't find you! You're not on my list! It's as if you don't exist!

M2: Well, I'm in your morning class, every Tuesday and Thursday at 10:00 a.m.

M1: Oh, I believe you, and I remember you... but I just can't seem to find you... Did you say Tuesday and Thursday? At 10:00?

M2: Yes!

M1: Oops! I'm looking at the wrong file. Just a minute... It's 2-0-0-6-1-1-8-7, right?

M2: Yes!

M1: Okie-dokie. I got it. Your midterm exam was 85, and you got a 90 on your quiz. Does that sound correct?

M2: Yeah! That's what I've been trying to tell you. My midterm was 85, and I got 90 on the quiz.

M1: Well, you're doing very well! And you're right! I did make a mistake. Your score should be 86 right now. That's a good score! It's one of the highest in the class.

M2: So you'll change my grade, right?

M1: Yes, of course! I'm really sorry I caused you such an inconvenience. Next time, if you have any problems, just call me, okay? You don't have to come all the way down here. You can even talk to me about it during class time. I don't mind. And don't hesitate to ask me any questions in class.

M2: Okay. But I didn't have to go out of my way or anything.

M1: Well, I'm truly sorry. I did the grades late at night, probably well past my bedtime. I hope I didn't make many other mistakes like that. And thank you for bringing this to my attention.

M2: It's no problem. Thanks for your help.

M1: No, no, no, no! I thank you!

M2: Okay. See you next Tuesday.

M1: Okay. I'd better check with the other students in case I made more mistakes like that... In any event, have a nice weekend.

M2: Thank you.

D **1.** Ⓒ **2.** Ⓐ **3.** Ⓒ

4. 1) library, A) renew, B) bring books with him

3) A) research project, B) buy it

4) A) call number, B) book is not there

5. [1] to renew [2] his ID card [3] his research project [4] checked out [5] its availability [6] on the shelves

○ 4-08

M: Good afternoon, ma'am. I think that my books are almost due, so I'd like to renew them if that's possible. I don't have to bring them here to the library to do that, do I?

W: Oh, no, of course you don't have to do that. Just let me see your student ID card, and I can call up your record on the screen.

M: You have no idea how much of a relief it is to hear those words come out of your mouth. I've got a ton of books checked out, so lugging them up here wouldn't be too fun. Here's my card.

W: Okay, let's take a look... Your name is Jason Stevens, right? And you have... Wow... That's a lot of books you have checked out. Thirty-five in total? You must be some kind of a bookworm!

M: Not really. It's just that I have this upcoming report due in one of my classes, so I'm trying to do as much research as I can. Oh, so when are the books due now?

W: They aren't due until November 29. That's four weeks from today, so you should have plenty of time to finish everything up by then.

M: Excellent. You've been quite a lot of help... Say, I have a question for you if you don't mind. I've been trying to find this book... It's really crucial to my research, but it appears to have been checked out by someone. If it's not too much of a problem, do you think that you could check to see if it's actually been returned yet?

W: Oh, of course, I don't mind at all. That's exactly what I'm here for. Why don't you give me the title of the book so that I can call it up onto the screen?

M: Sure, I can do that. The title of the book is *Exploring New Methods in Historiography*.

W: Hmm, I didn't know that there were any new methods in history. But I guess that you're the expert, huh?

M: Yeah, it's not exactly the most fascinating topic in the world, but without it, I don't know what I'll do. I guess that I'd have to purchase it from a bookstore, but considering that it costs around fifty dollars, I'd much rather check it out instead. So, what's the verdict on the book?

W: I'd have to say that today is your lucky day. It appears that whoever had it checked out just returned it to the library. Here's the call number for the book. Let me write it down for you... Now here's something you need to keep in mind. Since it just got returned, it might not have been shelved yet. Why don't you head down to the stacks and take a look? If it's not where it should be, come back up here, and I'll go to find it in the returned books section.

M: Wow. That is some seriously awesome news. Thanks a lot.

W: You don't have to thank me. I'm just doing my job.

Practice with Lectures

A **1.** Ⓒ **2.** Ⓑ **3.** Ⓒ

4. 1) free trade, A) goods and services, C) wealth

3) A) trading, B) tariffs

4) A) manufacturing, C) economies

5. [1] absence of tariffs [2] flow of business [3] protective policies [4] One major advantage [5] at the same time [6] domestic businesses [7] goods and services

○ 4-09

M1: So what is free trade?

M2: Free trade means no tariffs and no quotas between countries that trade goods with one another.

M1: Good answer. But, it's not only a free flow of goods. It also means the free flow of services between nations. It's a system that allows people to buy and sell whatever they desire with whomever they desire. Advocates argue that total free trade will result in a net gain in wealth for both trading partners. Some of the characteristics of free trade are... uh, let me list them for you... First, the absence of tariffs, which are taxes on imported goods and services. Second is the absence of quotas and other trade barriers. Third... the free flow of labor between two trading partners. Fourth... the free flow of capital between the two trading partners. And fifth is the absence of subsidies and regulations on locally produced goods and services that give businesses in the home country an advantage over those of a foreign country. Now having said all this, keep in mind that free trade is a relatively loose term that means different things to different people. For instance, it can be any combination of these characteristics I just mentioned to you, and, typically, it's never completely 100% free. When you have a free trade agreement between two countries, there are usually some protective policies in place.

Protectionism, on the other hand, means government restraint on trade between two nations. Protective trade or protective tariffs are a nation's efforts to prevent its own people from trading. Such protective measures include tariffs on imported goods and services, restrictive quotas on imported goods and services, government regulations which discourage imports, anti-dumping laws, and subsidies for local producers.

There are a number of advantages to free trade. Perhaps the most important advantage of free trade is that it lowers the costs of goods and services. This is possible for a number of reasons. For example, production can take place in nations where labor and other operating costs are lower. Nike might manufacture in developing nations where labor costs are much cheaper. Likewise, it allows cheaper foreign manufactured goods from foreign businesses easily to be imported into a country where manufacturers cannot produce goods as cheaply. An example would be garment manufacturers in China. Also, jobs can be outsourced to other countries where labor is much cheaper. This explains why a lot of telephone call centers are located in India. So, with free trade, consumers can pay lower prices for foreign manufactured goods or foreign services rather than pay higher costs to local high-cost producers. Free trade also attracts investors to developed nations, improving the economies of those nations. It allows corporations easily to operate across borders. And it also results in social advantages such as the spread of democratic ideas to developed nations and the reduction of the likelihood of war between developed nations.

Despite its apparent advantages, there are a number of critics of free trade. Many people prefer protectionism. And, as I mentioned a moment ago, in the real word, even when we have free trade or a free trade agreement, there's still some protectionism. Protectionists feel it's better for local consumers to pay higher prices and thereby maintain quality jobs. So, protectionism protects businesses, jobs, and wages, but it also means higher prices.

B 1. Ⓓ 2. Ⓒ 3. Ⓒ

4. 1) history of camera, A) Chinese (and) Greek, B) all colors, C) darken
2) A) didn't fade
3) negative-positive
5) 1900s
5. ₁familiar with ₂exposure to light ₃at least eight hours ₄in salt ₅photographic plates ₆invented ₇made it possible ₈only required a few seconds

 4-10

Before we get into details about the art of photography and discuss the mechanics of cameras, I want to give you a brief history of some of the major events in the development of photography so that you'll have a greater appreciation for the art and technology that we have today.

You might have already read in your textbooks that in the fourth and fifth centuries B.C., philosophers in China and Greece described the basic principles of cameras. Now, this might not seem like a big deal because they were still far from inventing a camera, but what is of particular interest here is that they were already familiar with the basic principles of optics. In the 1660s, Isaac Newton discovered that white light was actually composed of different colors. By this time, darkrooms had already existed as a tool to assist in drawings. Then in 1727, we get our first important chemical discovery. Johann Heinrich Schulze discovered that exposure to light would darken silver nitrate. Finally, in 1814, a Frenchman, Joseph Nicéphore Niépce, became the first person to create a photographic image. However, his discovery wasn't a very practical one because his image needed to be exposed to light for at least eight hours! And, more importantly, the image quickly faded. However, after this, the development of photography quickly snowballed, and, within a generation, we had what very closely resembled modern day photography. Niépce died in 1833. But his business partner, Louis Daguerre, continued to experiment.

Finally, in 1837, Daguerre performed possibly the greatest or most important feat in the history of photography when he became the first successfully to capture an image that did not fade. In other words, this was the first permanent image. He accomplished this by immersing the image in salt. Also, he developed photographic plates, which significantly reduced the required exposure time to thirty minutes. As a result of this, many artists at that time felt that this would seriously jeopardize their livelihoods, and some predicted that painting would cease to exist.

In 1841, William Henry Talbot developed the first

negative-positive process, which made it possible to have multiple copies of the same image. But exposure times still took three to fifteen minutes. Modern-day photography is based on the same principles that he used. Finally, in 1851, Frederick Scott Archer invented the Collodion process, in which images only required a few seconds of light exposure. This was also cheaper and therefore made it possible for most middle class people to have their portraits done. The first mass-market camera was sold in 1900. It was called the Brownie. In 1913, the first 35mm still camera was developed, and then, in 1927, General Electric invented the first modern flashbulb. Polaroid cameras were first marketed in 1948. In 1973, instant cameras were introduced, and then, in the mid 1980s, we had the arrival of digital cameras.

C   1. Ⓑ   2. Ⓑ   3. Ⓓ
   4. 1) archeology, A) ancient cultures, human activities, B) ancient remains
      2) A) endangered areas, C) cities
      3) A) Mexico
   5. 1ancient remains 2source of knowledge 3digging or excavating 4examination of sites 5a lot of erosion 6with no deadlines 7all over the world

◉ 4-11

W1: I'm glad you've all done your reading assignment... So now, um, perhaps, someone can remind us what archelogy is about!

W2: Well, according to what we have read, it's a science which studies ancient cultures and past human activities.

W1: And how do we study these ancient activities?

W2: Well, the ancients left little or no written history, but archeologists can learn a lot by examining ancient remains such as buildings, tools, graves, artifacts, and stuff like that. They use these to reconstruct the past.

W1: Yes. And these remains are our chief source of knowledge of prehistoric and ancient cultures. Where do archeologists get their information?

W2: They get it by digging.

W1: Yes. They excavate the ground. Usually, this means digging a big hole. They expose, process and record the remains of each archeological site. One kind of archeology is rescue archeology, which is sometimes referred to in your readings as salvage archeology or preventive archeology. Rescue archeology is the survey and excavation of areas of archeological interest that have recently been revealed and are threatened by land development or construction. Usually, development is imminent, so archeologists must urgently excavate so that they don't impede the developers. In other words, they have to rescue the site before the bulldozers move in. Uh... these archeologists have to operate with tight deadlines. This means they need to record the details of the remains quickly. The actual fieldwork is conducted by an army of mobile, professional archeologists who are skilled in this type of work. Rescue archeology is more common in cities because that's normally where ancient civilizations were located and where the remains lie. It's also where development usually occurs.

The bulldozer is not the only concern for rescuers. Many sites have suffered a lot of erosion, which adds to the peril of the situation. This is another reason for the urgent need to rescue. The excavation becomes an exercise in damage control, where the team tries to limit the amount of damage that has or will inevitably occur. We call this damage control.

M: Is there always such an urgency to excavate? Don't they ever take their time?

W1: Oh, of course. What I described were the urgent cases. Often there is no emergency or deadlines so they indeed have a lot more time and can examine things more closely. We call this research excavation. During research excavation, the archeologists have a lot more resources to assist in their work. They can work at a relaxed pace, and they can excavate more fully. Time is simply not of the essence. Usually, the people working on such sites are the academics and private societies who have sufficient labor and funding.

M: So where does excavation occur?

W1: Right now, as we speak, there are thousands of digs taking place all over the world.

M: But, I mean, are there any near here?

W1: No, not around here. Not in this state.

M: So where are all of the excavations occurring?

W1: Well, surprisingly, despite their size, there are not many excavation sites in Canada and the U.S.. In fact, right now, Mexico has more digs than anywhere else in the Americas. The countries where extensive ancient civilizations were located tend to have more archeological sites. In the Americas, Mexico and Peru have the most excavations. But at any given time, you would likely find a lot of digging in places like Iran, Egypt, Greece, and Italy.

Ah, a good example would be Pompeii, the ancient Roman city that was destroyed by a volcano in 79 A.D. It was rediscovered in 1748, and ever since that time, a lot of excavations have been going on there, even as we speak.

D   **1.** Ⓒ   **2.** Ⓒ   **3.** Ⓑ
   4. 1) ceramics, A) clay, B) pottery, C) kitchenware
       2) A) potter's wheel, hands, D) firing again
   5. ¹combination ²various minerals ³it's the oldest form of art ⁴is mass produced in factories ⁵shapes it with his hands ⁶This hardens the clay

🔊 **4-12**

M: So we've discussed and looked at architecture, sculptures, and a number of paintings. Are there any other art forms?

W1: Yeah, we didn't discuss literature yet.

M: Nor have we discussed ceramic arts. A lot of art students are not interested in this art form because they don't see it as being glamorous. But I think it does deserve some of our attention. What exactly is ceramics?

W1: It's made from clay. It's things like mugs, cups, plates, pots, tiles, and I think bricks, too.

M: Yes! Generally, ceramic arts, which are sometimes referred to as pottery, are pieces made from a combination of inorganic non-metallic materials and heat. In other words, it's earthenware. And indeed, the most common ingredient is clay, but it's usually mixed with various minerals. Typically, pottery is something you've been using your entire life. I mean it's usually kitchenware and various other kinds of containers. It usually has utilitarian purposes, and sometimes it's designed purely for decorative reasons. Because of its practicality and durability, it's probably the oldest form of art. Many pieces date back several thousand years to the age of prehistoric man. Early man had little time for decorative art but developed pots primarily for practical reasons. Imagine drinking water all these centuries without cups or eating without plates!

W2: How do they make it look so refined? What you see in the stores and museums hardly looks like clay!

M: Oh, I'm glad you asked that question. First, much of the kitchenware that you see in stores is mass produced in factories. But making beautiful, refined-looking pottery is not difficult. Many pots are made in old fashioned, modest studios as they were hundreds of years ago. And they're made by hand. Potters might use a potter's wheel, but

that's all. The potter starts with a hunk of clay, shapes it with his hands, and then lays it out to dry. Later, the potter heats it up in an oven, which we call a kiln. This hardens the clay. Once it's heated, the shape becomes permanent and can no longer be modified. This is why pottery is so endurable. Pots are usually heated at an extremely high temperature, which varies with the purpose. Sometimes, the pots are heated twice, but they're always glazed before the final firing, which gives them that refined look and makes it non-porous. Also, when painters use pots or plates as a canvas and devote a lot of attention and detail to the design, that works wonders, too.

W1: So how high do the pots have to be heated?

M: Well, as I said, that depends on the purpose of the art form. If the temperature is heated to more than 1200℃, it will essentially turn the clay into manmade stone. We call this stoneware. It's hard enough to resist scratching. A lot of fancy plates are made this way, and, with the touch of a skilled painter, they can be made to look very beautiful. There are other types of pottery, such as earthenware and porcelain. Earthenware is heated below 1200 degrees.

Integrated Listening & Speaking

A

1. It is the free flow of goods and services between nations.
2. Protectionism.
3. Stronger domestic businesses, more domestic jobs, and higher domestic wages.

🔊 **4-13**

As I mentioned to you, there'll be a number of questions about free trade and protectionism on next week's exam. So keep in mind that free trade is basically the free flow of goods and services between nations. Usually, this means the absence of tariffs, quotas, subsidies, and restrictive regulations which limit the flow of business between two nations. Protectionism is the government restraining trade between two nations. It is basically the opposite of free trade and includes such protective measures as tariffs, quotas, government regulations, anti-dumping laws, and subsidies. One major advantage of free trade is that it keeps prices down, but at the same time, it can hurt domestic businesses and reduce domestic wages. Protectionism protects domestic businesses, domestic jobs, and domestic wages while keeping prices higher.

B

1. They use it for bowls and plates and other practical reasons.

2. Shape some clay, let it dry, cook it in a kiln, and let it harden.

3. It is the process that makes pots look nice.

🔊 **4-14**

Ceramic arts, or pottery, are items that are made from various natural ingredients like clay and other minerals. Most pottery has a practical use, like for bowls and plates. So, how do we make pottery? Well, if doing so by hand, first the potter uses a potter's wheel to mold a piece of clay into the shape he wants. Then he lets it dry, and, after that, he bakes it in an oven called a kiln. When the clay is heated, it hardens, thereby making its shape permanent. After that, the pot is done. Of course, sometimes the potter heats it again, but not before glazing the pot. That's a process which gives pots that nice look that most of them have. It sounds like a difficult process, but it's really not that hard at all.

TOEFL iBT Practice Test

A   1. Ⓓ   2. Ⓑ   3. Ⓒ   4. Ⓑ   5. Ⓒ

🔊 **4-15**

M: Excuse me. Do you work here?

W: Oh sure. What can I do for you?

M: I'm looking for the law books?

W: Law's in Section G... over there!

M: I was just there. I saw only a few books there.

W: I know. Most of the law books are sold directly from the law school. Which book were you looking for?

M: *Principles of European Business Law*.

W: Oh, sorry. We're not carrying that one anymore.

M: That can't be right. Are you sure?

W: Just a minute. Let me look on the computer... You said *Principles of European Business Law*, right?

M: Yup.

W: The author is Roman... Roman Picard?

M: That's it

W: Yeah, I'm afraid we don't have it.

M: I need it for one of my courses.

W: Are you a law student?

M: No, I'm in business.

W: Well the semester is half over. Why are you looking

for it now?

M: I know, but I didn't have time to read it yet, so I didn't bother buying it. The midterm exam is next week, so now I have read it.

W: Our shelf space is very limited. So, often four or five weeks into a semester, we send unsold books back to our supplier or directly to the publisher, especially if the textbook is not required for the next semester. This one's probably not required next semester.

M: Yeah, you're right. This course is offered next semester, but I think it's with a different professor, and he'll probably use a different textbook.

W: Perhaps you could find it in the library. From my understanding, the university is required to put one copy of each textbook in the library.

M: I didn't know that, but I prefer to buy a copy. This way I can mark it up. Can you order another copy?

W: No. Not for just one student.

M: Well, what should I do?

W: Why don't you ask your professor to contact us? We can order single copies for professors. Maybe he'd be willing to cooperate.

M: Okay, but he's out of town today, and I'm not sure when he's coming back. Are there any other options?

W: Well, law books are usually difficult to find. You'd never find them in a regular bookstore. You could check some other universities that have law schools, but unfortunately, they probably don't use the same textbook.

M: Hmm

W: I have a thought. The book was used last year, so you might be able to find a copy of it at one of the used bookstores.

M: Oh, good idea! I didn't think of that.

W: Yes, there are two used bookstores on campus. O'Hara's is in the Student Building, and there's also Bargain Books, which is next door to us.

M: Okay. Are there any other used bookstores on campus?

W: No, but it wouldn't hurt to check out Spider Books. It's just a block south of campus, and it carries a lot of used textbooks from this university. It's the biggest used bookshop in the city.

M: Okay, and if that doesn't work, are there any other alternatives?

W: Yeah, just do what my sister and a lot of her friends are doing.

M: What's that?

W: They're buying a lot of their textbooks online. Check the online bookstores. Check Amazon and

E-Bay. They've got just about everything, including textbooks. And they ship things very quickly.

M: Oh good idea. Thanks a lot.

W: No problem. Good luck.

B   **1.** Ⓓ   **2.** Ⓒ   **3.** Ⓑ
    4. Ⓐ Torpor Hibernators   Ⓑ Deep Hibernators
      Ⓒ Torpor Hibernators   Ⓓ Deep Hibernators
    5. Ⓑ   **6.** Ⓐ

🔊 4-16

M: So for these reasons, when you're camping, be sure you take all of the necessary precautions to avoid bear encounters.

W1: I have a question.

M: Please, go ahead.

W1: This winter, I'll be going camping. It'll be the first time I've ever tried winter camping. I was wondering, um, since bears usually hibernate during the winter, do we ah, do we still have to take the same precautions as when we go camping in the summer?

M: Yes! First of all, you don't know when bears are going to start hibernating, and you don't know when they're going to stop hibernating, and most importantly, bears don't hibernate!

W1: Oh! Really?

M: Yes, really. The stories you were told as a child about bears hibernating are not true. Bears are not true hibernators. Let me repeat that. Bears don't hibernate! True hibernation essentially means total inactivity for several days or weeks. It's a state or a phase that some animals experience when the days become very short, the temperature cools, and food quantities are limited. Furthermore, there are different kinds of hibernators. True hibernation is also referred to as deep hibernation because the animal's body is inactive for a very long period, its body temperature decreases to five degrees or less, its metabolism decreases, and its breathing slows down. True hibernation is a survival mechanism during the long, cold winter season when food is scarce. Deep hibernation allows the animal to conserve its energy. Their sleep is so deep that they cannot be awakened. This allows animals to skip over the cold, stressful winter. Bears are not true hibernators! They can awaken during the winter. Please remember that!

W1: Ah, so what happens to bears during the winter?

M: Well, bears are torpor hibernators. This means they are not true hibernators like some smaller animals.

Torpor hibernators are inactive only for a short time, perhaps during the coldest hours of the night. They don't sleep for several weeks like true hibernators, and their temperature never drops to five degrees. In fact, bears' temperatures rarely drop below thirty degrees. When an animal is in torpor, it's capable of quick arousal. Some bears will sleep for several weeks, but even if they do, they are capable of waking up very quickly. That's why bears are dangerous all year round!

W2: How do animals know when to hibernate?

M: Well, some hibernators, like reptiles, are capable of predictive dormancy, which means that as the days decrease in length, they can anticipate winter approaching, and then they begin hibernating automatically. Because they can anticipate cold weather, they can avoid the potentially lethal cold season by going into hibernation. Other animals are not capable of this anticipation. They're only capable of consequential dormancy. In other words, they don't hibernate until they've been exposed to cold weather. If the winter is mild or the animal is located in an area where the seasonal weather conditions are unpredictable, it might stay active all winter if conditions permit. If it gets too cold, it can start hibernating.

W2: So which animals are deep hibernators?

M: Some of the deep hibernators are chipmunks, woodchucks, snakes, box turtles, and toads. Torpor hibernators include bears, raccoons, and skunks. The non-hibernators are red foxes, gray squirrels, and wild turkeys.

Vocabulary Review

A

1. furor
2. subsidize
3. jeopardize
4. resemble
5. reconstruct
6. incinerator
7. dwindle
8. disabled
9. erosion
10. durable
11. upset
12. make
13. accomplish

14. snowball

15. quantum

1. This is the digging of a big hole to expose ancient remains and other findings so that we can learn more about ancient cultures. (excavation)

2. This activity saves energy and natural resources and reduces greenhouse gas emissions. (recycling)

3. This is a government policy that allows people to trade whatever they want with whomever they want, without any government interference. (free trade)

4. This art is made from clay and other materials. Usually, it requires a very hot kiln. (pottery)

5. This technology slowly developed over several hundred years but finally started to capture images in the 19th century. (photography)

6. This science is the study of ancient cultures by examining ancient remains. (archeology)

Unit 7 Connecting Content

Practice with Conversations

 1. (B) **2.** (B) **3.** (A)

    4. 1) B) to explain more

      2) high altitude sickness, A) going high up,
        B) oxygen, C) lightheadedness, nausea

      3) Hydration

    5. ¹understand a concept ²ascend into the atmosphere ³oxygen molecules ⁴40% fewer ⁵ways to acclimatize ⁶of refraining from strenuous activity

M1: Hello, Professor Cronkite. I was just wondering if I could speak to you for a few minutes.

M2: Certainly, Patrick. What can I do for you?

M1: Well, I guess I had a little trouble understanding your lecture today when we were discussing mountaineering and the dangers of high altitude sickness. Could you go over what causes high altitude sickness again if it's not too much trouble?

M2: Of course, Patrick. It's no trouble at all. Let me start at the beginning so there is no confusion. First of all, high altitude sickness refers to an illness that can occur in people when they travel above a certain number of feet, say, if they are driving a car up a steep mountain, mountain climbing, or flying in an airplane. Was that part of the lecture clear this morning?

M1: Oh yes. I only started getting confused when you began discussing the chemistry behind it and what happens inside the body.

M2: Okay, so what causes high altitude sickness is the lack of oxygen in the atmosphere the higher you ascend. The concentration of oxygen in the air that most people are used to is around 21%, and the barometric air pressure is around 760mmHG. Now, as you ascend, the concentration of oxygen in the air does not change, but what does change is that the number of oxygen molecules per breath is reduced due to a lower barometric pressure. For example, if you were to climb a mountain that peaked at 12,000 feet, you would be inhaling 40% fewer oxygen molecules per breath at the top than you would at the bottom of the mountain.

M1: I see. So a person feels ill because he cannot get as much oxygen into his bloodstream as he is used to. But how does a person know he has high altitude sickness? What kinds of symptoms does he display?

M2: Well, if you've ever ridden on an airplane, you know that there is always one or two people on board who feel lightheaded or nauseous. However, others on the plane may not show any symptoms since they are acclimatized to the conditions.

M1: I know you talked about it in class, but what does acclimatized mean again?

M2: Acclimatized means that you've allowed yourself to become used to the conditions little by little. There are some simple things each person can do to become acclimatized to altitude, especially if you are doing something like hiking. The main cause of high altitude sickness is that you ascend too quickly, so your body has no time to adjust, but here are some things you can do to help you acclimatize. Try to start your ascent under 10,000 feet, and ascend slowly. If you are flying, try not to do anything too strenuous the following day. Always try to stay well hydrated.

M1: What does hydration have to do with preventing high altitude sickness?

M2: Oftentimes, the process of acclimatization is accompanied by fluid loss, so staying properly hydrated will help replenish your body.

M1: Thank you very much for your time, Professor Cronkite. I think I understand high altitude sickness much better now.

M2: You're very welcome, Patrick. And thank you for being brave enough to come by and ask for my help. So many students are too embarrassed to admit they need help, but that is what we are here for... to make sure you understand the concepts and help you realize your full potential.

B 1. Ⓐ 2. Ⓑ 3. Ⓐ

4. 1) housing office, A) stay in dormitory longer
   2) foreign student
   4) foreign student
   5) understands

5. ¹extra semester ²complete her student teaching
   ³foreign student ⁴find new housing ⁵This angers the student ⁶help them get comfortable ⁷needs a roommate

🔊 4-20

M: Hello. How may I be of assistance?

W: Hi. My name is Sally Morgan, and I am a senior on campus. I'm here because I would like to extend my stay in my dorm room for one more semester.

M: And why is it that you need to extend your stay?

W: Well, you see, I am getting my major in education, and I thought I would be through with all of my classes by this winter, but my professor reminded me that I need to remain in the area for one more semester to do my student teaching. Student teaching is the main part of my degree.

M: Okay, can you tell me what dormitory you currently live in?

W: Carter Dormitory.

M: Okay, let me check my computer here to see what it says about the Carter Dormitory. Oh, I'm sorry, but it looks like we have allocated all of the rooms in your dorm to some incoming foreign students next semester. I am afraid you will have to make other arrangements.

W: But why can't I stay? I am a paying student, and this is my fourth year. I have to remain in the area! If I don't do my student teaching here, then I forfeit my degree!

M: I understand that, Sally, however you must remember that you signed an agreement last semester stating that you would not need your dorm room after the term. Do you remember that agreement? We have given that room to a foreign student.

W: But can't you just tell the foreign student that you made a mistake? She could live off campus or in another dorm! Surely I should have first choice since I have been here the longest.

M: All of the other dorm rooms are accounted for, and to have the foreign student try to fend for herself off campus would be very irresponsible on the part of this university. Imagine if you were only just learning Chinese and decided to study abroad in China for one semester. Do you think you could take it upon yourself to find your own housing if your student housing fell through? How would that make you feel?

W: I suppose I would feel very alone and scared. Oh... I see your point.

M: I am sorry you cannot live in your dorm room next term, but think about it this way. Those dorm rooms are due for an upgrade. You see how old they are and how desperately they need repair work done. I am sure you can find a really nice place off campus, perhaps with your friends, where your room is much nicer than the one you are in right now.

W: Yeah, I guess so. My friend did say that she needed another roommate for next semester. Sorry I was so spiteful initially. I apologize.

M: That's no problem, Sally. Thank you very much for understanding the situation.

C 1. Ⓒ 2. Ⓑ 3. Ⓓ

4. 1) noise, B) piano playing
   3) practice for concert
   4) different piano

5. ¹complains to the official ²cannot hear ³making too much noise ⁴are necessary ⁵one week ⁶six weeks ⁷compromise ⁸written permission

🔊 4-21

W: Excuse me?

M: Yes, Miss. Can I help you?

W: I certainly hope so! My name is Cherie, and I have booked a room in Lincoln Hall to practice the piano. However, when I went in the room just now, I heard a large group of men working on the building. They are making so much noise pounding and sawing that I can hardly hear myself play!

M: Oh, yes. I am so sorry for the inconvenience, Cherie, but I am afraid we are in the middle of renovating the hall, and we need to get this construction done before the big concert. I know it seems very inconvenient for you, but now was the best time for the construction crew to come in.

W: But I am also preparing for the concert, and it's only six weeks away! I have decided to play a challenging Bach piece and I need all the practice I can get. Can't the construction workers come in after hours or early in the morning?

M: Well, perhaps the construction workers coming in during the early morning or evening would be convenient for you, but I doubt it would be very convenient for all of the students trying to sleep in the dorms next door. No one wants to hear the sound of a hammer or saw at midnight! I do not want to sound rude, but you are not the only person who is involved with the concert. There are many students who seem to be making other arrangements while the men finish the work.

W: Yes, but I don't want to hear the sound of a hammer or a saw when I am practicing! And of course it may be easier for other students to practice. A flutist can take his flute wherever he wants to practice, but a piano is not very mobile!

M: Again, I understand that this is an inconvenience, but the construction workers will only be here for one week, so we decided that if they need to be here for a week, we would at least book them early enough before the big concert so that everyone would be guaranteed good, silent practice times five weeks prior to the performance.

W: But what am I supposed to do? I need a full six weeks of practice to get this Bach piece polished.

M: How about we make a compromise? There is a piano in the basement of the theater building that is utilized during stage musicals that is not being used at the moment. I could give you written permission to get into the building for one week so that you can practice your piece in silence while these construction workers are finishing up. Does that sound fair?

W: Oh, yes, that sounds wonderful! I am sorry for being so pushy about this, but it is the final performance of my senior year, and I want it to go perfectly! Thank you very much!

M: You are welcome.

D 1. Ⓑ 2. Ⓐ 3. Ⓑ
    4. 1) A) go on field trip, B) denied
       2) skipped
       3) A) popular
       4) graduate
       5) show up
    5. ₁could not understand ₂submitted an application

₃had not shown up ₄call in and inform ₅forfeited his chance ₆must be a way ₇wait at the bus stop ₈fill a vacancy

◎ 4-22

M: Excuse me, but can I ask you a question?

W: Yes, what can I do for you?

M: My name is Charlie Myers. I applied to go on the ecology field trip to Inglewood Forest next week, but for some reason my application was denied and returned to me in the mail. I can't seem to figure out why it would be denied, as I should have preferential admissions for this trip since I am in the class. I was just wondering if you knew why I was denied.

W: Ah, yes, Charlie Myers. When I look into your file, it says here that you applied to go on this same field trip last term but did not go. Is this information correct?

M: Yes, that is correct. I signed up to go on the field trip last term but came down with a bad case of the flu. I was too sick to make the trip that day. It took me one week to get over my illness, and that excluded any possibility to go to Inglewood.

W: Did you call the office to let anyone know you were sick, or did you cancel your application? Did you let your professor know so that he could delete your entry for the trip?

M: No, I'm afraid I didn't. I asked a friend to cancel my application for me, but he forgot. I was also going to call myself, but I lost my voice due to my illness.

W: That is too bad. I am so sorry you came down with the flu, but I'm afraid that, due to the popularity of this field trip, the science office has a policy that you must call and cancel your application if you cannot attend. The waiting list is always long for this trip, and, had you called, we could have filled your spot. I'm afraid that because you did not call, you've now forfeited your chance to attend the field trip. It is the office policy.

M: But this field trip is a crucial part of my major! If I don't go on it, I won't graduate! You must be able to let me go!

W: I'm sorry, Charlie, but you should have read the application more closely. The only consolation I can offer is that there are generally one or two students, like yourself, that cannot make the trip for whatever reason. On the morning of the field trip, wait at the bus stop, and, if a student does not show up, you can fill that vacancy. I would suggest that you get up early, however, as the vacancies are filled on a first-come, first-served basis, so you will want to make sure you are first in line.

M: Okay, if this is the only way, then I will do it. But I am going to make sure I am first in line!

W: That sounds like a good idea, Charlie. Sorry I cannot do more.

Practice with Lectures

A 1. Ⓐ Negative display Ⓑ Negative display
Ⓒ Positive display Ⓓ Negative display
Ⓔ Positive display

2. Ⓓ 3. Ⓒ

4. 1) inhibition, A) negative, B) – Housefly
   2) inhibitions, A) – bad, good

5. ¹ to follow through ² to get to food ³ fly's instinct
   ⁴ finding another method ⁵ viewed as negative
   ⁶ problem solving ⁷ risking the child's safety
   ⁸ make a safer choice

🔊 5-01

Good morning, class. Today we are going to be looking at a concept in psychology called inhibition. Inhibition is a mental state in which a person is unable or hesitant to complete a certain action. Oftentimes, the action in question is one that is instinctual. Inhibition can be either a positive or negative response, depending on the situation. For example, a housefly, seeing food on the other side of a window pane, will repeatedly bash itself against the window in an effort to try to reach the food. Because the fly has no higher form of intellect, it cannot exercise inhibition. In this case, it would be to stop bashing itself against the window, overriding its instinct for food. Therefore we would deem the fly's lack of inhibition in this instance to be negative. It is expending energy to no avail in an effort to retrieve food that it cannot possibly obtain. Let us take a look at another example. A young boy is so fascinated and unafraid of fire that he tries to enter a burning building. Now, most people have a healthy relationship with fire, using it responsibly for everything from warmth to preparing food, but when a fire rages out of control, our instinct tells us not to approach it since it could burn or possibly even kill us. In the case of the little boy, his lack of inhibition means that his brain does not send a signal to his body to avoid danger or possibly injury. If the little boy learns how to exert some inhibition over the situation, perhaps he would make a good firefighter in the future, but until he learns how to do this, his lack of inhibition for fire may mean that he will perish before he reaches adulthood.

Now, we all know that our natural instinct to do one thing or another is sometimes very hard to control. Just like the fly, we too, as human beings, have a strong instinct to consume food so that we do not starve to death. However, because of our higher state of thinking, we realize that if a glass door separates us from our food, bashing ourselves against the door will not help solve the problem. Our minds must inhibit ourselves long enough to delay our gratification for the food whilst we figure out how to open the door. In this way, our inhibition helps solve problems. However, just like a total lack of inhibition is not always a good thing, too much inhibition can often be detrimental to a situation. Let us take the case of little Sally, who is starting school for the very first time. Sally is so shy, or inhibited, that she is afraid to speak to her teacher or to any of her peers on the first day of school and cries until her mother comes to pick her up. Sally's inhibition means that she does not make any new friends on the first day of school. Sally also does not allow her teacher – a trustworthy and helpful adult – to comfort her or introduce her to her new classmates or ideas. In this instance, little Sally's inhibition does not help her solve the problem of meeting new people. Okay, now let's change the scenario for little Sally. Say she was on the playground bouncing a ball, and the ball rolled into the street. Sally's instinct would be immediately to race out into the street to retrieve the ball, but now her inhibition is a good thing, as her mind tells her body to pause long enough to wait and watch for passing cars. Let us take the situation one step further. Sally stopped and watched for cars, and now she is crossing the street to retrieve her ball. On the sidewalk stands an older man who asks Sally if she would like to go for a ride in his car. Sally has never seen this man before. He is a stranger. Because she is so shy, Sally runs from the man back to the playground. Sally's shyness, an inhibition that was seen negatively inside the classroom, is now viewed as something positive since it means she did not approach the stranger and get into his car with him.

B 1. Ⓐ Baleen, Migrates Ⓑ Teeth, Migrates
Ⓒ Teeth, Migrates Ⓓ Baleen, Migrates

2. Ⓒ 3. Ⓑ

4. 1) whales, B) Blue
   2) A) plankton
   3) B) Bottlenose, C) Killer
   4) B) mating
   5) C) complex sounds

5. ¹ those with baleen ² keratin ³ blue whale ⁴ sperm whale ⁵ to breed and give birth ⁶ to feed ⁷ work together in groups

🔊 5-02

W1: This afternoon, we are going to talk about one of the largest mammals on Earth, which just so happens to live in the ocean. Does anyone know what mammal I am talking about?

W2: A whale?

W1: Yes, a whale. And during today's discussion, we are going to focus not only on the different types of whales and their body structures, but we will also discuss whale migration and intelligence. Can anyone here name a type of whale and then tell us about one of its distinct features?

M: There is the humpback whale, and they are called that because, well, they have a hump on their back.

W1: Good. The distinguishing feature of a humpback whale is pretty self-evident in its name, isn't it? Another type of whale is the blue whale, which happens to be the largest living animal in the world. Blue whales can grow up to thirty meters in length and have exceeded 177 metric tons in weight! You have named two whales that also share something in common, something that is used to divide all whales into two different groups. Does anyone here know what these two whales have in common that also separates them from different whales?

W2: Is it baleen? I think a blue whale has baleen, but I am not sure about the humpback whale.

W1: Yes, it does. Can you elaborate on that? What is baleen?

W2: I'm not really sure. I think it is something that is found in a whale's mouth.

W1: You are on the right track. Baleen is a sieve-like structure in a whale's mouth that filters the water from the plankton that it eats. It is made of out of keratin. Non-baleen whales, such as the sperm whale, are known as toothed whales because they have teeth, and so they feed on larger creatures such as fish or squid.

M: Can you name some more toothed whales?

W1: There is the bottlenose whale and the killer whale. We already named blue whales and humpback whales as two types of whales that have baleen.

W2: Do whales need to travel far for food? They are so big... It must be hard for them to swim far!

W1: Oh, on the contrary, it is not hard for whales to swim far for food, and indeed they do! Whale migration is a complex and time consuming event

in the life of whales. Each type of whale varies slightly, but the two main reasons for migration are for mating and for feeding. Now, does anyone have an idea as to why a whale must migrate for these activities and why they do not just stay in one region?

M: Aren't some of the waters they live in too cold for giving birth?

W1: That is part of the reason, yes. Typically, whales travel to warmer water to give birth and colder water to feed. Whales are known to travel for thousands of miles to complete these activities. One type of whale, the southern right whale, lives along the southern coasts of Africa during its mating season and then will swim all the way to waters near Antarctica in the summer so that it can feed.

W2: But that doesn't seem to make any sense. A whale must expend so much energy to get to its food source. Wouldn't it be safer and smarter for the whale to just try to find food where it is?

W1: One would think so, but once the whale gets to where it is going, it is able to gorge itself on the plentiful food, thus gaining more energy than it ever would if it were to stay in one type of water year round. And let us not forget that whales are very intelligent mammals. First of all, they have a larger brain than any mammal, including human beings. Whales are highly social animals, able to communicate with each other through complex sounds, and, if need be, they will form into groups and swim together as a means of protecting each other. Evidence of this can be noted when whales are under threat by whaling ships. The whales will either find new migration routes or they will swim in a tight formation to try to protect each other.

C   **1.** Ⓒ   **2.** Ⓓ   **3.** Ⓐ

4. 1) Mount Rushmore, B) Sculptures C) tourism
2) A) crown, B) France D) symbols

5. ¹South Dakota ²granite hillside ³Black Hills ⁴bring more tourists ⁵holding a stone tablet ⁶gesture of friendship ⁷pure copper ⁸New York Harbor

🔊 5-03

This morning I am going to be giving a lecture on the differences in the origins of two American landmarks, Mount Rushmore and the Statue of Liberty. To start off, let's talk about Mount Rushmore. Mount Rushmore is a national memorial located in South Dakota. The monument represents the first one hundred and fifty years of the American presidency and is comprised of sixty-foot-tall sculptures of four United States presidents: George Washington, Thomas Jefferson, Theodore Roosevelt, and Abraham Lincoln. One interesting fact about Mount Rushmore is that it was originally known to the Lakota tribe of Native Americans as Six Grandfathers. At that time, the most notable point of the Black Hills was Harney Peak, the highest mountain in the range. It wasn't long, however, before American settlers eventually moved through and into the area, at that time giving Harney Peak a succession of names: Cougar Mountain, Sugarloaf Mountain, Slaughterhouse Mountain, and Keystone Cliffs. In 1885, the peak was renamed Mount Rushmore after a New York lawyer who was representing a mining company in the Black Hills area. Looking to increase tourism into the Black Hills area, in 1923, the historian Doane Robinson conceived of the idea of chiseling the visages of different United States presidents into the granite hillsides. The following year, Robinson was able to persuade the sculptor Gutzon Borglum to complete the task. It took Borglum and a group of 400 other workers over fourteen years, from October 4, 1927, to October 31, 1941, to complete the sculptures on Mount Rushmore. Mount Rushmore became part of the National Park Service in 1933, with the total cost of the project very nearly reaching one billion dollars. Remarkably, no workers died during the project despite some very precarious working situations.

The second monument I'd like to discuss is the Statue of Liberty. This monument, also known as Liberty Enlightening the World, is a statue of a woman dressed in a robe and wearing a crown while holding a stone tablet in her left hand and a flaming torch in her right hand, that was given to the United States by the Parisian-based Franco-American Union in 1885. The statue was given to the United States by the French as a gesture of friendship and goodwill between the two nations. The Statue of Liberty stands on Liberty Island in New York Harbor as a welcome to all visitors and immigrants and returning Americans. If anyone has ever seen this monument, it is a welcoming sight to behold! The statue is made of pure copper, with the exception of the torch flame, which has a coating of gold leaf. Etched on the tablet that the woman is holding is the text July IV MDCCLXXVI, which was the date of the United States' Declaration of Independence, July 4, 1776. The Statue of Liberty was constructed by two Frenchmen, the sculptor Frederic Auguste Bartholdi

and the architect Alexandre Gustave Eiffel, who was also the designer of the Eiffel Tower. During July of 1884, the Statue of Liberty was completed in France and broken down into three hundred and fifty pieces and crated so that it could be stacked onto the French frigate Isere and shipped to America. It arrived in New York Harbor on June 17, 1885. Reassembly took four months to complete, but finally, on October 28, 1886, the Statue of Liberty was dedicated by President Grover Cleveland. For the first sixteen years that it stood in New York Harbor, the Statue of Liberty served as a lighthouse. Now, the Statue of Liberty is one of the most recognizable American icons, and millions of tourists visit the monument each year.

D **1.** Ⓒ **2.** Ⓓ **3.** Ⓒ
   4. 1) tyranny, B) helping poor, C) archaic period
      2) B) monarchies
      3) A) tyrant, B) poor people, C) equal representation
   5. ¹unjust exercising ²absolute ruler ³known as populists ⁴poor people ⁵mistreated ⁶was to bribe them

🔊 5-04

W1: Good morning, class. Today, for our history lecture, we are going to be discussing the rise of tyranny that occurred in ancient Greece around the 7th century B.C. A good way for us to begin is for someone to give us the definition of tyranny. Anyone?

W2: Doesn't tyranny refer to the unjust exercising of power by one ruler?

W1: Yes, good. This is the definition that we use nowadays. Harsh, isn't it? However, the origins of this type of power were not quite this brutal. This form of government began in ancient Greece, when aristocrats found that they could gain power over others first by securing the support of the poor people either by giving them land or money or even freeing them from slavery or prison. Eventually, the aristocrat was able to gain absolute power because the people he had previously bribed for their support were now beholden to him.

M: But that is such an unfair form of gaining power! How did the poor people allow that?

W1: Well, it was unfair, but people did not have the same rights as we do now, and let's try to approach it from the point of view of a poor ancient Greek. 7th century B.C. Greece fell into what has come to be called the archaic period. New political structures were only just beginning to be formed following the previous period, which didn't have much structure. The rise of democracy was in its infancy, and the population was booming, from hundreds of thousands of people to millions. Originally, Greek cities were monarchies – a rich land owner had control over the subjects that worked his land – however the monarchies were soon to be overthrown by groups of populist aristocrats from outlying rural areas because these particular groups of populists, also known as tyrants, were promising the poor money or freedom.

M: Populists? What is a populist? I thought we were talking about tyrants?

W1: A tyrant is a type of populist leader. A populist is a person who believes in standing up for the little guy or poor man. A populist wants equal representation between the elite and the underclass. That is why the populists became so popular with the poor… They were speaking on the poor person's behalf. If you were poor or perhaps a slave, what would look more appealing to you… to be offered money or freedom if you supported the populist, or to stay and work on a piece of land for little or no money?

W2: I guess I understand why a poor person would support the populist initially, but doesn't the word tyrant conjure up negative connotations?

W1: Nowadays, yes. When we refer to a tyrant, we are referring to a leader who has ridden roughshod over his people, making empty promises along the way, and ruling with an iron fist of absolute power. Initially, however, tyrants were trying to buoy the poor people against the elite. However, as it happens in many situations, those who had lofty and moral aspirations in the beginning were gradually corrupted by power. Eventually, the ancient Greek tyrants, like the Greek monarchs before them, abused their positions over the people, and the term tyrant gained the definition that we use today.

Integrated Listening & Speaking

A

1. South Dakota.
2. The first one hundred and fifty years of the American presidency.
3. A stone tablet and a flaming torch.

Last week, we took a look at two different national monuments in the United States: Mount Rushmore in South Dakota, and the Statue of Liberty in New York Harbor. The monument at Mount Rushmore is a giant sculpture of four United States presidents that is etched into the highest peak in the Black Hills mountain range. George Washington, Thomas Jefferson, Theodore Roosevelt, and Abraham Lincoln are the featured presidents, and the monument represents the first one hundred and fifty years of the American presidency. The monument was first conceived as a way to lure tourists to the Black Hills. The monument was sculpted by a man named Gortzon Borglum and four hundred workers. It was completed in 1941. The Statue of Liberty is a monument of a woman wearing a robe and crown and holding a stone tablet and a flaming torch. It sits on a small island in New York Harbor. The Statue of Liberty was given as a gift of friendship to the Americans by the French in 1884. The designer of the Statue of Liberty was Alexandre Gustave Eiffel, the man also responsible for designing the Eiffel Tower.

B

1. The tyrants promised money, property, or freedom.
2. Eventually, power corrupted the tyrants, and they no longer made good on the promises they made to the lower class.
3. It originated in ancient Greece.

During the last class period, I gave a lecture on the rise of tyranny in Ancient Greece. We started the lecture by identifying today's definition of tyranny as the unjust exercising of power by one absolute ruler. The origin of tyranny, however, was not quite so harsh. The rise of tyranny came about in ancient Greece, when a certain group of aristocrats, known as populists, were unhappy with the way poor people were treated under monarchies. A populist is simply a person who advocates not just for the elite but also for the poor; He wants representation for all people. The tyrants gained the support of the poor, and slaves, by promising them money, freedom, or both. Initially, the tyrants ruled by the ethics they first believed in, but eventually the power they gained led to corruption and the bribery of poor people without fulfilling the early promises became commonplace.

TOEFL iBT Practice Test

A   1. Ⓑ   2. Ⓐ   3. Ⓒ   4. Ⓓ   5. Ⓐ

W: Hi there, Mark. How are you! What are you doing here in the library?

M: Hey, Nancy! Good to see you! I'm doing fine. Just in the library to pick up a few books for my English class. How are you?

W: Oh, I'm good. I'm just here checking out some books for my art history project.

M: Sounds like you have just as much work as I do!

W: No kidding! It's been a very busy semester, and, speaking of a busy semester, I don't think I've seen you in our communications class lately. Did you switch sections so that you could take it at a different time?

M: Oh, no! Actually, I dropped that class in favor of this new class that was being offered. It's called Interviewing: Preparing For Your Career. It's the best class I've ever taken!

W: Really? It sounds so dull! What kinds of things do you do in class?

M: Oh, it's not dull at all. In fact, it's been very exciting. It's a class that focuses purely on practicing for job interviews. We do a lot of role playing. For instance, just last week I got to pretend I was the CEO of a major company and interviewed two of my classmates. One of them got so nervous he had to leave the room, and we were only role playing!

W: Wow! Was he okay? I'll bet it's helping him get over his fear of being interviewed though.

M: Yes, he was fine, but, as the professor pointed out, it just goes to show you how much practice you really need to feel comfortable and prepared for an interview. The guy who got nervous and had to leave was being very cocky beforehand and going on and on about how well he was going to do. He did no preparation whatsoever, and it showed. I asked him a question about how much he thought he deserved as a starting salary and he started sputtering and got red in the face!

W: Oh my goodness! I could use a class like that since I tend to get very nervous before any kind of interview or public speaking engagement. What other kinds of things do you work on in class?

M: Well, we also talk a lot about how to write a good resume, how to dress for an interview, and how to write follow-up letters. The professor also explained to us that, despite how wonderful you may appear on your resume, an interviewer will make his overall impression of you in the first few seconds of an interview based upon things such as how smartly you dress, how firmly you shake his hand, and how articulate and polite you are.

W: Gosh, I wish I could take this class. I never knew it was being offered. Is there any chance I could get in?

M: I am pretty sure there are a few more spots open, and you probably didn't hear about it because it's a class being offered through the College Community Center. Just stop by there sometime this afternoon, and they should have an application. If you have any problems, find Professor Smith, and tell her that Mark recommended you for the class. She loves new students and believes everyone could use these skills.

W: Thanks, Mark! I will be sure to stop in this afternoon right after lunch. Thanks for the tip, and, if I get in, I shall be seeing a lot more of you again!

M: No problem, Nancy. Good luck! And I hope to see you in class soon!

M1: Today, class, we are going to be learning about John Dewey, an American educational reformer who was also a psychologist and philosopher. Has anyone here heard of John Dewey?

W: I think I have. Wasn't he one of the men who supported the idea of progressive education?

M1: Yes, very good. We will get to that in today's lecture. But let's start with a little background. John Dewey was born in the state of Vermont. He received his bachelor's degree from the University of Vermont and then went on to get his PhD from the Krieger School of Arts and Sciences at Johns Hopkins University in Baltimore, Maryland. Starting in 1904, John Dewey taught philosophy at Columbia University. It was during these years that Dewey began forming his ideas about psychology and education. In his book *Democracy and Education*, John Dewey formulized his educational philosophy. Dewey believed that the development of the human mind was a communal process and that a person only became truly meaningful when they fully engaged within his or her society. John Dewey strongly believed that children should not be taught by rote, nor should they learn simply by having a teacher regurgitate facts. Dewey believed in the process we know as learning by doing. Can someone tell me what this means?

M2: Well, let's say you were teaching us a concept in chemistry. Learning by rote would mean that you would stand in front of us and perhaps read us something or write something about the concept on the board. John Dewey's way of teaching us the concept would be to have us actually do something in the laboratory, correct?

M1: That is a very good way of putting it. Yes, John Dewey believed in more of a hands-on approach to learning and also in having the students be involved with the society they lived in, so the idea of field trips or talking to professionals outside of school would be something that he would also support.

W: When was John Dewey spreading his ideas? Did many people accept his new approach to education?

M1: Excellent question. Dewey was continuously formulating his ideas in the early part of the twentieth century, and initially, his idea of progressive education was popular and widely accepted. During the 1950s, however, during the Cold War years, there was a slight reaction against progressive education, as many Americans felt that students in other parts of the world, namely the Soviet Union, were accelerating faster in the classroom than Americans. In the post-Cold War period, Dewey's ideas reemerged, and they have thrived in classrooms ever since.

M2: Can you elaborate on the concept of progressive education? What does that mean?

M1: Of course. Educational progressivism is the idea that because humans are social animals, we learn better if we are involved in real-life activities with other people. John Dewey had a five step approach to learning. First, become aware of the problem. Second, define the problem. Third, propose a hypothesis or set of propositions to solve the problem. Fourth, evaluate the consequences of the problem from one's past experience, and fifth, test the most likely solution.

W: Hey! That sounds just like the step-by-step process we use in laboratory experiments!

M1: And well it should as this model of evaluating a problem is the one that is most widely used in classrooms.

M2: So, if you could summarize John Dewey's philosophy on education, what would it be?

M1: The main concept behind John Dewey's educational philosophy is that the most important part of learning is the broadening of the intellect and the strengthening of critical thinking and problem solving skills as opposed simply to memorizing facts from a book. For instance, if John Dewey were alive today, he might put it to us this way... Would you learn more about swimming if you were to read about some man's exploits of swimming in a book, or would you learn more about swimming if you actually got into the water yourself?

Vocabulary Review

1. encompass
2. peers
3. obtain
4. persuade
5. inconvenience
6. upgrade
7. perish
8. conjure
9. visage
10. distinguish
11. tourist
12. connotation
13. gorge
14. tedious
15. pushy

5-09

1. This is a philosophy of teaching and learning that emphasizes a hands-on approach and integration into society. (progressive education)
2. This is a monument in South Dakota that features the sculpted faces of four American presidents. (Mount Rushmore)
3. This concept defines what happens when the brain stops the body from reacting instinctively. (inhibition)
4. This was a type of ruler that gained support from the poor by promising them money. (tyrant)
5. This is a field of science that looks at the effect people have on large weather patterns. (bioclimatology)

Unit 8 Making Inferences

Practice with Conversations

A 1. Ⓓ 2. Ⓑ 3. Ⓒ

4. 1) bookstore, A) textbooks
   2) high price, A) 25, B) 50
   5) 25

5. ¹box of textbooks ²original purchase prices ³The student asked ⁴unwilling ⁵25%

5-11

M1: Hi. I want to get rid of these books.

M2: Wow! That's a lot of books. You want to get rid of the whole box?

M1: Yeah, the whole thing.

M2: They look brand new! Didn't you use them?

M1: No, I never went to any classes, so I never read them.

M2: Well… Why don't you return them to Campus Books?

M1: It's too late. I bought them about fourteen months ago.

M2: Oh, so they're already a year old… That's a real shame. These textbooks must have cost you about four hundred bucks. And they are in mint condition!

M1: Yeah, I think if you add it up, they cost 430 dollars, but I'll sell them for 300.

M2: 300! We can't afford to pay 300.

M1: Well how about 250? That's almost a 50% discount.

M2: No, I'm sorry. I can't do that.

M1: But that's a great price! How much did you pay for all of these other books?

M2: We paid 25% of their original prices.

M1: Well what about for the newer looking books?

M2: No, that's what we pay for all used books. We pay 25% for each one. That's 25% of the original purchase prices.

M1: You mean it doesn't matter what condition the books are in?

M2: That's right.

M1: Well, why's that?

M2: That's our policy.

M1: Can't you pay more than 25%? That's only about a hundred and five bucks. So little!

M2: I'm sorry. Most of the books here are in good condition. And from our experience, twenty-five percent is generally considered to be a fair price.

M1: What makes you think 25% is a fair price?

M2: Well, we used to negotiate a price with every individual that brought books in, but 25% is what we usually ended up agreeing on, so after a while, we decided to stop wasting time negotiating, and we made 25% our across-the-board policy.

M1: What if the book is falling apart?

M2: If a book is falling apart, we won't accept it. If it's in good condition, we pay 25%.

M1: But still… 25% doesn't seem fair.

M2: Well, I'm not trying to rip you off. If you worked here, you'd understand what I'm talking about. People are simply not interested in paying a lot for used books. It's the same at every used bookstore. They're looking for bargains and very few of them will pay more than 50%. So we usually sell our books for 50% of the original price. Basically, we sell them all for half price. If we paid more than 25% to get them, we'd go out of business.

M1: I see.

M2: The fact that your books are almost brand new doesn't help us. Even if they're in mint condition, our customers still want a big discount. And remember, textbooks quickly become obsolete.

M1: Okay, okay. I'll take 25% then.

M2: Are you sure?

M1: Yes, I'm not going to find another buyer. And I don't want to carry this box everywhere.

M2: Okay, I'll give you $110 for them. Go to the register, and our cashier will pay you.

M1: Thank you.

B 1. Ⓐ 2. Ⓑ 3. Ⓓ

4. 1) drop off CD
   2) B) library
   4) student's information
   5) CD

5. ¹a week earlier ²she borrowed from the library ³he had not seen it ⁴nobody ⁵her name ⁶he wasn't going to charge her

5-12

W: Excuse me. I want to return this CD.

M: Oh, next time, you can just deposit it in the drop-off box as you come in.

W: I know, but there's a problem.

M: A problem?

W: I had intended to drop this CD off last week. It was due then. So I came here and I dropped it off and went about my business. Then yesterday, my brother asked me where his CD was. I looked all over the house, but I couldn't find it. Then this morning, when

I was getting ready for school, I decided to take my backpack. As soon as I opened it up, I saw this CD in it. Suddenly, I realized what must have happened. Last week, I returned my brother's CD! You might still have it.

M: Oh. I hope your brother wasn't too angry.

W: Oh… Well, I haven't told him yet. So now I want to return this CD and possibly get my brother's CD back.

M: What's your brother's CD?

W: It's MLB06, a baseball game. It looks almost the same as this CD. It has a lot of red and blue print on the cover. There's no photo or drawing, but it says something like MLB06 on it. I think you might be able to find it because you don't have many computer games here.

M: No, we don't. When did you return it?

W: I think it was last Monday.

M: Okay, well, nothing has been brought to my attention. But sometimes miscellaneous books, cassettes, CDs, and DVDs get tossed in with our library materials. Yours is not the first one. Eventually, someone will notice it and toss it into our miscellaneous basket. In fact, let me take a look… No, it's not in there.

W: Ah, too bad.

M: But that doesn't mean it's not in here somewhere. This is a big library, and it's possible that nobody has noticed it yet.

W: Or someone kept it.

M: Yes, that's certainly possible, too. But most workers in here probably aren't interested in your computer game. If it was something more generic and useful, like a dictionary or an atlas, they'd be more likely to take it.

W: Okay.

M: Why don't you give me your name and number, and, if I see it, I'll call you?

W: Okay. My name is Maria… My phone number is 4-6-8… 7-9-7-9.

M: 4-6-8… seventy-nine, seventy-nine?

W: Yes, that's it. What about my library fine?

M: What fine?

W: The fine for returning this CD so late.

M: Don't worry about it. I'm not going to charge you. I understand your problem, and you've already lost a CD.

W: Oh great! Thank you very much. I appreciate it.

M: No problem. If I have a chance, I'll mention your brother's CD to the other workers. If someone comes across it, I'll call you at 4 6 8, seventy-nine, seventy nine.

W: Thanks again.

C 1. Ⓒ 2. Ⓑ 3. Ⓐ
4. 1) upcoming interview, A) interviews, B) McDonald's 3) orphanage, B) work experience
5. ¹asked his professor ²he was nervous ³he didn't have any experience ⁴he worked at KFC ⁵smiling person

🔊 **5-13**

M1: Brian! What's up?

M2: I have an interview tomorrow with Social Services. I'm very nervous.

M1: Why?

M2: Well, I have no experience doing social work, and I'm not used to doing job interviews. I think the last time I had an interview was about six years ago when I applied for a job at McDonald's.

M1: Oh, how did that go?

M2: Well, probably not well. I wasn't hired.

M1: Ha ha ha! You mean McDonald's rejected you?

M2: Yes.

M1: Wow! You never had a job before?

M2: Sure. I was a cook at KFC, but I didn't do an interview there because my sister got me that job.

M1: How was it?

M2: Well… ah… actually… ah… to tell you the truth, it was, ah… it was great! I had a lot of fun. I really enjoyed cooking chicken, and I made some nice friends there. I met my first girlfriend there! Everyone got along well with one another.

M1: How long did you work there?

M2: Two years.

M1: Okay, that's great. That's the kind of thing your interviewers want to hear, and those are the kind of questions they'll ask you. You don't have to tell them about McDonalds… Don't volunteer any negative information about yourself. Just tell them what you did. Don't tell them what you didn't do.

M2: But should I mention KFC? It has nothing to do with social work.

M1: Yes! They're going to ask you about that. They know you're young. They know you've got no experience as a social worker. But they'll understand. Because you have no experience, they're mostly interested in knowing about you! They want to see what your attitude is like. They're going to ask you what it was like to be a cook at KFC. If you smile and speak positively about your job at KFC and you tell them that you got along well with your co-workers, they'll be happy to hear that.

M2: Really?

M1: Yes. Often when employers interview university students or people just graduating from university, they realize the interviewee has little experience. But many of them are looking for bright, positive, easygoing people who are good team players. Tell them you're a good team player. Smile a lot. Have they seen your resume?

M2: Yes.

M1: May I see it?

M2: Sure. Here you are.

M1: Hmm... You also worked at an orphanage for two summers?

M2: Well, ah... actually, that, ah... that was a volunteer job. My mother works there. She made me do that.

M1: Well, thank God for your mother! When you go home tonight, give her a big hug. And then tomorrow tell the interviewers you worked at an orphanage. What did you do there?

M2: Well, I helped them take the children on field trips and special outings. Also, I help organize special events at the orphanage. For example, baseball games, soccer games, and birthday parties. Some of the kids were disabled, so I taught them to play wheelchair basketball. Sometimes, I took the blind children for a walk.

M1: Fantastic! You've barely mentioned this in your resume. Make sure you tell them tomorrow! Tell them about all of your work experience! Tell them you enjoyed your work! Tell them you're a great team player! And smile a lot! You'll do fine.

M2: Oh, thank you, Professor Baker.

D   **1.** Ⓓ   **2.** Ⓓ   **3.** Ⓑ

    4. 1) A) her failing test, B) some topics
       2) exam
       3) visit before next test
    5. ¹she failed ²an essay question ³most of the topics ⁴two of the three questions ⁵she did well ⁶next time ⁷the final exam

🔘 **5-14**

W1: Andrea, may I speak to you for a moment?

W2: Sure, Dr. Jenson.

W1: I was very surprised with your exam. Why did you fail?

W2: I didn't understand some of the topics

W1: In class, you seemed to understand.

W2: Yes, I understood most of them. But there were two topics I didn't understand. The exam had three questions. Each was an essay, and by coincidence, two of the questions were on the topics I didn't understand.

W1: I see... Perhaps, you had some bad luck. It happens... And maybe your study methods need some adjustment. When you study for essay exams, you need to know at least a little about each topic. Don't just read and get to know some of the topics well. That's too risky.

W2: I know. I know. I just assumed that because I understood most of the topics, there would be at least two questions on the topics I understood. Usually I have no problem.

W1: Well, let's go over the questions.

W2: Okay.

W1: The first question was, "Explain the events that led to hostilities in the American colonies." Here you did great! You got twenty-eight out of thirty-three. You made one mistake. You included George Washington as one of the participants at Bunker Hill. In fact, Washington was nowhere near Bunker Hill. He was still in Virginia at that time.

W2: Oh! That's right! I forgot!

W1: That's okay. Let's look at number two.

W2: Yeah, I couldn't understand what you were asking here.

W1: The question was, "Explain Benjamin Franklin's mission to Paris." Here, I only gave you five points. You just wrote that he sought the help of the Marquis de Lafayette. Didn't you come to class when we spoke about Franklin's work in France?

W2: No, I was absent that day.

W1: Ah! Well, Franklin, on behalf of the Continental Congress, sought the support of the French. The Americans wanted to be recognized as a nation, and they desperately needed money, supplies, and military assistance from the French.

W2: Oh, I see.

W1: And the last question..."Give your opinion about the British tactics in New York." Don't you know what that was about?

W2: Well, we studied that the British occupied New York for a few years. But I wasn't sure what tactics you were referring to.

W1: Well, I'm talking about the initial battle of New York. The British could have won the war at that time but, instead of pursuing the disorganized and fleeing rebels, they delayed. These delays might have cost them the war.

W2: Oh, I see. I vaguely remember us talking about that, but I had forgotten about the delay.

W1: Well, I gave you ten points for that question because you at least mentioned that the British overran the Americans in New York and occupied New York City for a long period.

W2: Thank you.

W1: Next time, speak to me before you take the final exam, okay? You're doing well. Your assignment was good, and your participation is good. I want to make sure you're on the right track. And try not to study topics in detail or memorize the details until you at least have a basic understanding of each issue. I'll be glad to give you more guidance before the final exam.

W2: Oh, that would be great.

Practice with Lectures

A 1. Ⓐ 2. Ⓒ 3. Ⓑ

  4. 1) Inuit art, A) Arctic areas, B) Canada, C) artwork
    2) B) miniature, C) realistic, E) many raw materials
  5. ¹Inuit carvings ²permanent settlements ³realistic
    ⁴sometimes birds ⁵unique characteristic
    ⁶available from the land ⁷green to black

◉ 5-15

Another form of indigenous art is Inuit art, which has flourished in recent years, both in quantity and commercial demand. The Inuit are the northern people who live in the Arctic areas of Canada, Alaska, Russia, and Greenland—the Eskimos, but today, that term is regarded by many Inuit as derogatory. The Inuit seem to be associated with Canada more than with any other country, possibly because the Canadian government has incorporated and promoted Inuit culture as part of Canada's cultural identity. If you have ever been a tourist in Canada and you've visited a souvenir shop there, you'll know exactly what I'm talking about because they seem to overflow with Inuit art, which may include sculptures, paintings, prints, and so on. As for architecture, you're all familiar with the igloo.

But I want to focus more specifically on Inuit sculptures, which have become very commercialized in the last few decades. Prior to the 1950s, the carvings were small enough to hold inside your fist. When a Canadian government official visiting the Artic in the 1940s was approached by an Inuit carrying a piece inside his fist, the official mistakenly believed the Inuit

individual was going to start a fistfight. The official was so impressed with the miniature carving that he bought all of the sculptures in the community. And thus began the commercialization of Inuit carvings. So today, many of the carvings are very small because historically the Inuit were a nomadic people who traveled lightly. Since the 1950s, many carvings have become bigger because the Inuit have settled into permanent settlements and because many buyers prefer larger sculptures. Today, we have miniatures and larger sculptures. Also, since the 1980s, the carvings have become more polished and realistic, again because of market demands in Canada and internationally, where they are now considered a fine art.

The subjects of these carvings are usually animals and humans. Some pieces are very realistic looking while others have less detail and are cruder or more primitive in appearance. The animals are bears, seals, whales, walruses, and sometimes birds. Some of the carvings I mentioned are now very polished while others are still very unpolished or dull. The themes may be humorous, such as the waving walrus and the dancing bear. Others are more serious, such as the hunting scenes. The characteristics of these carvings vary from region to region and with the specific artist.

A unique characteristic of Inuit carvings is that they're never made of wood. This is because there are no trees in the Arctic. So the artists use whatever raw materials are available from the land and sea. Animal bone, ivory, and, most commonly, stone are the primary ingredients. Soapstone is very soft, but most areas in the Arctic don't have soapstone. So most Arctic artists use serpentine, which is not as soft. It's available in a range of colors from green to black. Other stones used includes marble, quartz, and dolomite. Finished sculptures are sometimes imbedded with metallic minerals. In recent years, soapstone has been imported from other countries, causing the perception of being less authentic. But many successful Inuit artists use the imported stone.

We're running out of time, so next class we'll continue our discussion of Inuit carvings and also look at Inuit art prints and Inuit baskets.

B 1. Ⓑ 2. Ⓒ 3. Ⓐ

  4. 1) meteorology
    2) A) warm water, B) 5-8, C) fish (and) plant life
    3) A) cold water, B) El Nino
    4) El Nino
  5. ¹Pacific Ocean ²unusual weather phenomena

5-16

M1: You should realize that not all weather phenomena are perfectly understood by meteorologists. That's one reason why we can't always make accurate forecasts. You will read a number of explanations in your textbook as to what causes El Nino and La Nina, but, in reality, nobody knows for certain what causes these phenomena.

W: Sorry, uh, I get El Nino and La Nina confused. Which one occurs in the northern hemisphere, and which one is in the southern hemisphere?

M1: They both originate in the southern hemisphere, and both take place in the Pacific Ocean. And they both cause major temperature changes in the surface waters of the Pacific Ocean, and eventually they trigger unusual weather phenomena worldwide.

W: So what's the difference between the two?

M1: Okay, perhaps, this might help. El Nino brings warm water to the west coast of South America, and La Nina brings cold water to the west coast of South America. El Nino occurs every five to eight years. La Nina occurs about half as frequently. El Nino causes changes to the currents of the ocean by bringing uncharacteristically warm water to the coast of South America, particularly in the northern areas of South America. Warm water spreads from the Western Pacific, moves eastward, and eventually reaches the coast of South America. By the time the warm water reaches the coastal waters of Peru, it rises and replaces the cool nutrient-rich seawater at the surface. Because the warmer water has no nutrients, it drastically reduces the amount of plant life and fish in the area.

El Nino's impact can be felt worldwide, causing unusual weather in many different areas. For instance, it can cause droughts from Indonesia to Mexico and Central America. Its impact on the United States is less obvious, but it can cause or at least contribute to excessive rainfall in the Gulf states and in California. In 1982-83, much of California suffered record amounts of rainfall and consequent floods and mudslides. Some of the mudslides obliterated communities in a flash, killing many people. It also brings rain to deserts in South America, which normally don't receive rain in non-El Nino years. This causes floods, a subsequent swarm of musquitos, and then disease. Flooding occurs in Bolivia, Peru, Ecuador, Cuba, and the Gulf states.

M2: Does El Nino have any positive impact?

M1: Good question. It's my understanding that El Nino can snuff out hurricanes with its warm winds at 40,000 feet above sea level. Ah, La Nina, because of its cool water, can dramatically change upper-level air currents, contributing to storm development. La Nina can also affect winter weather in the United States. As an example, it can cause Florida, which is already dry, to become warmer and drier in the winter, which may increase the number of forest fires. In the winter, it tends to accentuate regular weather patterns, causing colder areas to become colder and warm areas to beome warmer.

C **1.** Ⓒ **2.** Ⓑ **3.** Ⓓ
   4. 1) write memoir
      2) biography, B) writer's own life
      3) A) autobiography, D) important people,
         E) narrative
   5. ¹a detailed story ²personal history ³a lot of research ⁴a part of your life ⁵a public figure ⁶military leaders

5-17

W1: Hi. I hope everyone had a nice weekend. The weather is beautiful!

M: Let's go outside!

W1: Ha ha ha! That would be nice, but unfortunately, there's nowhere to sit and write out there.

M: That's okay.

W1: But, what I can do for you is finish early so that you can all go outside and start your next writing assignment.

W2: Excellent! What's the next assignment?

W1: Your assignment is to write a memoir. I'm going to explain to you what a memoir is and then give you some suggestions as to how you can write it. It's essentially a story about one part of your life.

W2: Wait! What's the difference between a memoir and a biography?

W1: Don't write a biography! That's not your assignment. A biography is an account of another person's life rather than your own. I want you to write only about your own life. And don't write an autobiography! That's different, too. It would take too long. An autobiography is a detailed story of your life, usually from childhood to old age. It's a chronological, personal history that requires a lot of research and interviews. You're just writing a memoir. That doesn't require any research!

For your information, memoirs are a type of autobiography. An autobiography typically requires a lot of detailed research to reconstruct a detailed chronological story of your whole life. Memoirs, on the other hand, have a more narrow focus. You merely write what you recall. So you don't have to look anything up. You don't have to go to the library. You don't have to use the Internet. You can literally go outside, sit down, and start writing. But remember! Don't write about your whole life! Just write about part of it. Let me repeat. You are not writing an autobiography.

Ah, as I said, a memoir is restricted in scope, and it can be short. You focus on part of your life which you feel was important or significant to you. And don't be afraid to describe your feelings because a memoir is usually an intimate account that gets into the writer's head, describing his or her emotions, as they relate to certain periods and events in his or her life.

M: Aren't memoirs are just for famous people?

W1: Historically, they were usually written by world leaders, politicians, government officials, and military leaders to explain their thinking during critical moments in their public lives. Leon Trotsky, Albert Speer, Mahatma Gandhi, Richard Nixon, and, most recently, Bill Clinton, have all written their memoirs. Some memoirs are eyewitness reports by private citizens who participated in significant historical events. Among these are American slaves and holocaust survivors... All you need to do is tell a story based on what you can recall about an important time in your life. And keep in mind that memoirs are usually written in narrative form. So you can include a lot of the usual elements of storytelling... plot, characterization, imagery, conflict, flashback, foreshadowing, symbolism, irony, and anything else you think will make it an interesting read. While writing a memoir, a writer usually contemplates the meaning of events in retrospect. So it can be a very therapeutic experience, especially for those who focus on stories of survival and hardship. Perhaps, you'll feel the same.

Oh! And to answer your question, you don't have to be a famous person to write a memoir. Until twenty years ago, they were written mostly by famous people, but that seems to be changing. Look

at Franck McCourt! He was an ordinary person, yet he wrote *Angela's Ashes*.

D 1. Ⓒ 2. Ⓑ 3. Ⓑ
4. 1) lithosphere, A) the crust, B) ocean floor
   2) A) molten rock material, C) tectonic plates
   3) A) earthquakes, C) 7 ,12
5. ¹Earth's exterior ²the upper part ³about 5km thick ⁴slide along ⁵the extremely hot interior ⁶seven major plates ⁷a few inches

5-18

To understand earthquakes, you first need to understand the content and workings of the lithosphere and asthenosphere. So, I'll begin by describing the lithosphere.

The lithosphere is the Earth's exterior. It's the crust. It includes all of the continents, the rocks, and the ocean floor. It also includes the upper part of the asthenosphere, or mantle, located just below the crust. On the continents, the crust is about 80km deep, but below the ocean it's only about 5km thick.

The lithosphere is very much like a giant puzzle. In fact, if you were to buy one of those puzzle globes... I mean those puzzles that are shaped like a globe, it would give you a pretty good idea of what the lithosphere is like. The exterior of the Earth, therefore, is like a puzzle broken up into giant plates that fit around Earth as though it were a jigsaw puzzle. We call these giant pieces tectonic plates. The continents rest on these plates, and the plates move about two inches every year. Their movement is a sliding motion as they glide along the upper part of the asthenosphere, which is not as solid as the surface.

The asthenosphere consists of a semi-plastic molten rock material, which is like silly putty. It is more fluid, and it moves as it responds to the churning motions of the extremely hot interior of the Earth below. These movements inside the asthenosphere cause the tectonic plates to move as they glide or float on the moving asthenosphere. The plates, by the way, are made of rock, but these plates are lighter than the denser, fluid layer beneath. This allows them to flow on top of the denser material.

Over millions of years, the movement of the plates has given the surface the look that it has today. This movement of the tectonic plates is called plate tectonics, and, as we'll learn later, plays a major role in earthquakes and other Earth-shaping events. An example of how the movement shapes the surface is when two plates collide head-on with one another, followed by an upward movement of the edge of the plates. This lifting of the crust is how mountain ranges form. The Rocky Mountains formed as a result of two plates crashing head-on, and then their edges moving upwards and lifting the crust. The resulting uplift is the Rockies.

There are seven major plates and about twelve minor plates. The plates also have been given names, usually according to their geographic location. For example, there is the Pacific plate, the North American plate, the African plate, the Australian plate, the Philippine plate, and so on. Because the plates only move a few inches a year, it takes millions of years for the continents to move. But at one time, the continents and oceans were in different locations, and, about 250 million years ago, the continents were mostly connected together.

Remember that the interior of Earth is extremely hot. It is this heat that generates movement above. However, the core is expected, someday, millions of years from now, to cool off. When that happens, movement of the asthenosphere will stop, causing the tectonic plates to stop moving and thereby stabilizing the surface. In other words, the continents will stop moving. This has already happened on the moon, on Mars, and on other planets and satellites.

Integrated Listening & Speaking

A

1. They are small enough to fit in the palm of your hand.
2. They live in the Arctic areas of Canada, Alaska, Russia, and Greenland.
3. They are made of stones like serpentine, marble, quartz, dolomite, and soapstone.

⊙ 5-19

Today, we're going to continue talking about Inuit baskets and paintings. Last week, if you'll recall, I told you that the Inuit are the northern people who live in the Arctic areas of Canada, Alaska, Russia, and Greenland. I mentioned to you the different kinds of Inuit art, but we spoke mostly about Inuit carvings. Prior to the 1950s, Inuit carvings were small enough to hold inside your fist. Today, some are much bigger to satisfy market demand and because the Inuit are no longer nomadic. Also, since the 1980s, Inuit carvings have become more polished and realistic looking. The subjects of these carvings are usually animals and humans. The animals are bears, seals, whales, walruses, and sometimes birds. Some of the sculptures are humorous, such as

the dancing bear. Others are more serious. Because of a lack of trees, Inuit carvings are never made of wood. The artists use whatever raw materials are available. The most common substance is a stone called serpentine. It's available in a range of colors from green to black. Other stone used includes marble, quartz, and dolomite. Also soapstone is imported from other countries.

B

1. Autobiographies describe one's entire life while memoirs only focus on part of a person's life.
2. There's no research required to write a memoir.
3. Historically, they were written by world leaders, military leaders, politicians, and other famous people.

⊙ 5-20

There are a few more things I'd like to review with you before we have our... ah, written examination, next week... One of thing you'll need to do during the exam is distinguish autobiographies from memoirs. Remember that an autobiography is a detailed story of your own life, usually from childhood to old age. It's a chronological, detailed, personal history that requires a lot of research and interviews. It takes a lot of work. A memoir is a type of autobiography which focuses on only a part your life. The writer merely needs to recall some events that have occurred in his life. It doesn't require any research. You don't have to go to the library or use the Internet. It's usually shorter than an autobiography and focuses on events that are significant to the writer. If you're a public figure, then you will probably write your recollections and emotions regarding some of the important public events of your life. Historically, they were written by world leaders, politicians, military leaders, and other famous people, but that's now changing.

TOEFL iBT Practice Test

A   1. Ⓒ   2. Ⓓ   3. Ⓐ   4. Ⓓ   5. Ⓐ

⊙ 5-21

W: Hello, you look a little lost. Is there anything that I can help you with?

M: Er, yes. I'm new here. I just transferred from another college this semester, and I was wondering about the school's gym. Is anyone able to use it?

W: Well, that depends on what your enrollment status is. Here, let me see your ID card, and I can tell you exactly what kind of usage you're allowed.

M: Oh, yeah, sure. Let me just find it here in my wallet… Uh, why can I never find this thing when I need it…? Aha! Here it is. Take a look at it.

W: Okay, according to your ID card, you are a full-time student here at the school, so that means you are able to use just about every single one of our facilities for free. Let me tell you what that means… You can use both of the basketball courts… when there isn't a game or practice going on, of course. And you can use the squash and racquetball courts as well. They are located on the second floor. And you can also use the swimming pool on the third floor.

M: Wow, that sounds pretty cool. At my last school, we had to pay extra money just to use the facilities there. It's really nice not to have to do that here.

W: I'm glad that you're happy about our arrangements. If you don't have any more questions, then I should…

M: Wait a minute! How about using the locker rooms? Do we get our own lockers or what?

W: No, only members of the school's athletic teams get their own lockers. But don't worry about your stuff. You can get a temporary locker anytime. All you have to do is talk to the attendant outside the locker room… That's me, by the way… And I'll give you a key that you can use for a locker to store your clothes and valuables in. Once you're finished, just give the key back to me. And no, it doesn't cost a thing either.

M: That's great. You know, some of my stuff at my last school got stolen when I was working out before. Somebody just came in and took my wallet and a few CDs right from my bag. That was unbelievable!

W: I'm sorry to hear that. So… do you have any more questions for me?

M: Er, yes, I do. Sorry to be taking up all of your time. But I'm a little curious about the weight room. Can anyone use it, or do we need a membership?

W: Okay, that's a good question. We actually have two different weight rooms. The big one is called Collier Gym. That's open to the entire school. It has pretty much everything that you could possibly need to work out. And it won't cost you a single dime. The smaller one is called Peterson Gym. It's located up on the fifth floor. It's much more specialized and has some really cool equipment. But it's only open to members of the athletic teams and other members. If you want to become a member of that gym, it will run $200 a semester. Are you interested in that?

M: Oh, no, I don't think so. Not at that price at least. I just like to get in a light workout every now and then. I'm not that serious about it.

W: Yeah, most people are satisfied with Collier Gym. It's really nice. That's where I work out most of the time.

M: Great. Well, you've been a real fountain of knowledge. Thanks so much for all of your help. I'll see you around.

W: See you later.

B 1. Ⓒ 2. Ⓒ 3. Ⓓ 4. Ⓑ, Ⓓ 5. Ⓑ 6. Ⓒ

🔊 5-22

W1: There are at least 34,000 species of spiders known to scientists. This is the seventh most diverse species in the world. Scientists believe that many species of spiders have not been discovered yet, especially in the tropics. Some arachnologists believe that we've only discovered about 20% of the total existing number of spider species…Here is a question. Are spiders predators?

W2: Yes! That's why they have webs. They catch prey with their webs and then eat it.

W1: Okay, good. In fact, spiders are the world's most diverse species of predators. And their webs are made of silk. The silk is a thin but very strong protein strand. Can anyone tell me where it comes from?

M: I think the spider shoots it from his hand.

W1: Ha ha ha! I think you've been watching too many Spiderman movies! Spiders don't have hands or anything like hands! They have eight legs. And the silk… Well, the silk actually comes from their spinnerets. These are at the end of the abdomen. They're more like fingers, not like hands or limbs.

W2: You mentioned that spiders can kill prey with their silk or webs. Is the silk only used to kill prey? Also, I'm wondering, do all spiders produce silk?

W1: Oh, yes! All spiders produce silk. But not all species spin webs. And the silk has a number of functions, not just trapping and killing insects. They can use it to climb, wrap prey, build egg sacs, rear their young, make shelter, and to temporarily hold sperm.

M: Can spiders hunt without silk?

W1: Most species can hunt without silk, but some cannot. Most species can inject venom, which they use to kill prey or for self-defense. So, most species can kill without spinning webs. They simply wait and pounce on their prey.

M: Can they kill people with their venom?

W1: Only 200 species can harm humans with their bites. Most of the injuries that people sustain are very minor. Occasionally, a wound from a minor bite might become infected which could be a concern. But usually spiders are not a serious threat to humans unless their venom is very toxic. Toxicity of venom varies from spider to spider. Very few species possess enough toxicity to endanger humans. Usually, the humans most susceptible to spider venom are children and the infirm. By far the most dangerous species to mankind are the widow spiders, for example, the black widow. The female will bite if its web is tampered with or if it feels threatened. They have killed more humans than any other spider.

W2: How do spiders reproduce?

W1: Okay. For sexual reproduction, male spiders transfer sperm to the females by using a special appendage near the mouth, called pedipalps. In fact, this is how we distinguish male spiders from the females. Female pedipalps look like short legs while male pedipalps look like boxing gloves. Eventually, the female will lay a batch of eggs. Then they wrap these in silken egg sacs. Spiderlings eventually hatch within the sac and then leave to begin feeding. Spiders have to molt their external skeleton before they can grow larger. Molt means shed. Most species of spider tend to live about one or two years. And most species of spider molt about five or six times as they grow. Once they become adults, they stop growing and no longer molt.

Vocabulary Review

A

1. fluid
2. glide
3. nomads
4. tactic
5. flourish
6. derogatory
7. obsolete
8. obliterate
9. foreshadow
10. authentic
11. buck
12. orphanage

13. core
14. meteorologist
15. disposal

B

1. This is a type of autobiography which describes only a part of your life. (memoir)
2. These people live in the Arctic. They produce various forms of art including many carvings. (Inuit)
3. This weather phenomenon brings warm water to the west coast of South America and causes strange weather all over the world. (El Nino)
4. This is the seventh most diverse species in the world and it uses silk to capture and kill prey. (spiders)
5. This part of the Earth includes the crust, continents, ocean floor, tectonic plates and the upper part of the asthenosphere. (lithosphere)

Actual Test 01

Conversation 1~5

1. Ⓒ 2. Ⓐ 3. Ⓑ 4. Ⓓ 5. Ⓑ

6-03

M1: Uh, excuse me. You work for the school, right?

M2: That's right. Can I help you with something? Looking for a classroom?

M1: No, no. I need to get a lab key so I can get into the lab to finish up an assignment for my chemistry lab. Can you help me out with that?

M2: What happened? Did you, uh, lose yours?

M1: No, not exactly. I just need to get in there for fifteen minutes tops to finish this assignment.

M2: Well, I'm going to need to see both your student ID and your registration card for the chemistry lab before I can issue you a new lab key. Do you have those with you?

M1: Sure, here's my student ID.

M2: Okay, and the registration card for the lab?

M1: I don't have that one with me.

M2: Well, I am not authorized to issue you a new lab key until I have proof that you are officially enrolled in the class. Why don't you just go get your registration card, bring it back to the lab office, and then we'll be able to issue you a new lab key?

M1: Well, that's the thing. I'm not officially enrolled in the class yet. Not yet, but I will be soon. The professor has already said that he's going to allow me to take the class even though it is full.

M2: Like I said, I can't issue you a lab key without proof. If I did and something happened in the lab or something was stolen, I would be responsible for it, and it could possibly cost me my job. Understand me? I need that registration card.

M1: I see. See, uh, the thing is, I'm on the waiting list for the class. I'll be officially enrolled in the class next week at the end of drop/add week. It's just that I can't attend until that happens. In the meantime, I'm trying to get a head start on the lab work. The professor gave me a syllabus already, so I'm, uh, trying to keep up with the first week's assignments, lectures, and homework. I just need to get into the lab to clarify some calculations, and then I'll be out of there.

M2: Look. I sympathize with your situation, but you aren't listening to me very well. I'll lose my job if I give you that key!

M1: I know. I know. I don't want to jeopardize your job or anything like that. I'm just trying to figure out how I can get in there for a little while.

M2: Listen, do you have any friends in the class? Do you know anyone else with a lab key?

M1: Sure, my girlfriend is in the class. Why?

M2: Newsflash! Borrow your girlfriend's key!

M1: Can I do that? I mean it sounds kind of sketchy. They wouldn't bust me for false representation or anything like that?

M2: Not at all. They rarely check anybody once they are in the lab, and plus, if anything should happen, I wouldn't be responsible for it.

M1: Hey, that's a great idea. I should have thought of that in the first place. My girlfriend is over laying out on Landis Green. I'll just run over there and get it from her and come back and take care of business.

M2: No problem. I'm glad I was able to help you out. I was in a similar situation back in my day, and, unfortunately, I was unable to get into a lab, and it really affected my lab grade. It was my fault because I waited until the last minute. Anyways, I'm rambling. Glad that I could, uh, help. Good luck!

M1: Thanks. I'll see you later! Hey, uh, wait!

M2: Yeah.

M1: What time does the lab close up? It's already 4, and it'll take me at least thirty minutes to run over and get my girlfriend's lab key. Will I have enough time?

M2: Oh, no worries about that. The lab is open from 6 a.m. until 1 a.m. 365 days a year, holidays included. If you needed to get something done on Christmas Eve, we'd be open. Until 1 that is. We're the only lab on campus that does that. Not the physics, astronomy, or biology labs. Those guys even close up on the weekends! Can you believe that?

M1: Uh, sure. Well, thanks again. I've got to run! See you!

Lecture 6~11

6. Ⓓ **7.** Ⓒ **8.** Ⓑ **9.** Ⓐ **10.** Ⓓ
11. Ⓐ No Ⓑ Yes Ⓒ No Ⓓ No Ⓔ No Ⓕ No

Ⓞ 6-04

If you could please sit down, I'd like to start today's lecture now...uh, let's see, right, on the methods of auditioning performing artists. Okay. What's an audition, you may ask? Well, an audition is a sample performance by an actor, singer, musician, dancer, or other performing artist. It is used in the casting process to demonstrate the level and range of a performer's talent and functions as a, well, let's put it this way, a job interview for the performing arts. A typical audition involves the performer displaying his talent through a, um, a previously memorized and rehearsed solo piece. One example would be a monologue used for actors.

Generally speaking, for actors, the audition piece is typically, um, not from the show being considered. For example, um, an actor wishing to be cast in, let's say, *Hamlet*, would not likely do a monologue from that play. However, most performers do have a, um, range of audition pieces and select something appropriate. For instance, an actor auditioning for *Hamlet* would have a dramatic Shakespearean monologue ready and not perform a monologue from an Oscar Wilde comedy or a contemporary playwright.

But for the most part, the most important method of auditioning an actor is through the use of the monologue. A monologue is a, um, speech made by one person speaking his or her thoughts aloud or directly addressing a reader, audience, or character. It is a common feature in drama. Monologues are also a feature of, um, opera, recital, or other sung section may carry out a function similar to that of spoken monologues in the theater. Also, comic monologues have become a standard element of entertainment routines on stage and television. Everyone got this?

Good!

Well, there's more to this than just doing a monologue. Some auditions involve cold reading or performing from a script that the actor is not familiar with. Sight-reading is a much-needed requirement in drama, where it is often used in conjunction with improvisations to gauge a performer's ability to perform new works. It is particularly useful during auditions. A good drama sight reader is able to communicate with fluency and clarity and to project speech rhythms and rhymes well. He or she should also be able to bring out the intent, mood, and characterization of a piece through appropriate articulation and body language.

Why do actors have to go through all of this anyways, you may ask? Well, in the performing arts, casting is a vital pre-production process for selecting a cast of actors, dancers, singers, models, and other talent for a live or recorded performance. It typically involves a series of auditions before a, um, casting panel, composed of individuals such as the producer, director, and choreographer.

In the early stages of the process, candidate performers often may present, um, prepared audition pieces such as monologues or songs. Later stages may involve groups of candidates, um, attempting material from the work under consideration in various combinations. The casting panel considers both the talent of the individual actors and the chemistry of their combination. Depending on the prestige of the role, casting calls may go out to the public at large, um, which is typically done for community theater. In the production of film and television, a similar process is followed.

However, especially for, um, major productions, the process of selecting candidates for sometimes hundreds of parts and possibly thousands of extras may often require specialized staff. While the last word remains with the, ah, people in artistic and production charge, a casting director may be in charge of most of the daily work involved in this recruiting process during pre-production. In addition, the casting director may also remain as a liaison between the director, actors, and their agents once the parts have been cast.

Lecture 12~17

12. (B) **13.** (B) **14.** (C) **15.** (C) **16.** (B)
17. (A) False (B) False (C) False (D) True (E) False
(F) True

6-05

M1: Well, if you are all ready, I'd like to continue our discussion on pollution, focusing in particular on water pollution for this class. We can begin by defining water pollution as a large set of negative effects upon water bodies like lakes, rivers, oceans, and groundwater, caused by human activities.

M2: Um, you mean all water pollution is caused by man? That's news to me.

M1: Well, no. Although natural phenomena such as, um, volcanoes, storms, and earthquakes also cause major changes in water quality and the ecological status of water, these are not deemed pollution. Nature has a way of taking care of its own problems, but it's much more difficult for Mother Nature to take care of man-made problems. So, let's just stick with man-made water pollution for this class.

W: Okay. Can you tell us one of the worst man-made pollutants?

M1: Well, water pollution has many causes and characteristics. Let's begin with, ah, organic wastes introduced into the water system by man. These wastes include sewage and farm wastes which put high oxygen demands on the receiving water reservoir, like a river. This leads to oxygen depletion, or... loss of oxygen within the river system, with potentially severe impacts on the whole ecosystem.

M2: What about industry? I thought they were the worst polluters of all?

M1: You bet! Industries discharge a variety of pollutants in their wastewater including heavy metals, organic toxins, oils, nutrients, and solids. Discharges can also have thermal effects, especially those from power stations, and these too reduce the available oxygen within the system.

W: So we have industry and, um, organic waste put into the water system by man. Are there any other causes of water pollution?

M1: Sure. Silt-bearing runoff, or dirt if you like, from many activities, including construction sites, forestry, and farms can stop the penetration of sunlight through water. This restricts photosynthesis and causes the, ah, blanketing of lake or riverbeds, which in turn damages the ecology. And if that isn't enough, pollutants in water include a wide spectrum of chemicals, pathogens, and physical chemistry or sensory changes. Many of the chemical substances are toxic or even carcinogenic. Pathogens can obviously produce...um, waterborne diseases in either human or animal hosts.

M2: Gee, it sounds like what you are saying is that our water systems are in pretty big trouble.

M1: Absolutely! What's worse is that water pollution is now a serious global problem. It's been suggested that it is the leading worldwide cause of death and disease and that it accounts for the deaths of more than, get this, 14,000 people daily.

W: Really? I had no idea it was that bad. I mean, that's scary!

M1: Well, it is scary. Let's look at it this way. Most water pollutants are eventually carried by the rivers into the oceans. In some areas of the world, the influence can be traced, um, hundred of miles from the mouth of a river by studies using hydrology transport models.

W: They can do that?

M1: Gee, where have you been? Sure they can! Advanced computer models have been used in many locations worldwide to examine the effect of pollutants in aquatic systems. For example, filter feeding species such as crayfish have also been used to study the effects of pollution, um, in the New York Bight. In this study, the highest toxin loads were not directly at the mouth of the Hudson River but sixty miles south since several days are required for incorporation into planktonic tissue. Further south were areas of oxygen depletion caused by chemicals using up oxygen and by algae blooms caused by excess nutrients from algal cell death and decomposition.

M2: So, what you're saying is the loss of oxygen in the water system has negative effects on all living water creatures?

M1: You've got it! It's a vicious cycle. Fish and shellfish kills were reported because toxins climb the food chain after small fish consume copepods like crayfish, then large fish eat smaller fish, and, well, you get the point. Each step up the food chain concentrates certain toxins like heavy metals and DDT by approximately a factor of, um, ten. Well, are there any questions?

Conversation 18~22

18. Ⓒ **19.** Ⓐ **20.** Ⓑ **21.** Ⓒ **22.** Ⓐ

⊙ 6-06

W1: Uh, excuse me, Professor? You said you wanted to speak to me after class?

W2: Yes, please come in. Do you have a few minutes?

W1: Sure, I'm done with classes for today. I hope there's nothing wrong.

W2: Oh no. Nothing like that.

W1: Wow, that's a huge relief. Ever since you said you wanted to see me in your office, I've been sweating over what exactly it could be!

W2: Oh, my dear, I'm so sorry. I did not mean to cause you, uh, any anxiety. I just wanted to discuss your first draft of the writing assignment with you one on one. I try to do this with each student early in the semester to give you all tips on your writing, constructive criticism I guess you could say. So don't feel singled out! Everyone will be in here with me at one point, just like you!

W1: Oh, I see. Well, I feel much better now. I almost didn't even show up! Anyways…

W2: Good, now let's see if we can find your assignment somewhere in this pigsty of mine masquerading as a lit professor's office.

W1: Well, it looks a lot like my dorm room actually. It seems we are kindred spirits of messiness!

W2: That's funny. I think I remember a similar kind of humor in your writing, which was very fresh and free. Where is that, ah, here it is. Well, uh, first of all, I want you to know that I enjoy reading your work. It has an effortless quality to it and you definitely have a way with words. The way you combine images is stunning at times.

W1: Thank you so much, Professor! That means a lot to me, especially coming from you!

W2: Now, what I like to have students do is a kind of self-criticism of their work. What would you describe is the weakest part of your short story?

W1: Hmm, let me think for a minute. I'd probably have to say that the weakest part of the story is how I characterize… how I develop the main character, Judd. I had a hard time giving him his own voice and making him a believable character.

W2: Well, I'm going to have to agree with you on that one.

W1: Really?

W2: Yes. I, uh, thought that Judd wasn't as complete as you could have made him. And I think what you do is tell the reader what kind of person he is instead of showing the reader.

W1: I think I know what you mean. I spent a lot of time describing him, and I think I overdid it a bit.

W2: Exactly. It is okay to describe a character to a certain degree, but you must leave room for the characters to develop and grow as well as allow the reader to make their own mental image of them. That's what makes literature a creative field, on both the writer and reader's side. It is a dual process.

W1: I see.

W2: Now, don't get me wrong. I like Judd. I think he is a very interesting and unique character. I just think you need to have him talk less and say more if you understand what I mean. A technique you could use is the internal monologue. Write what he is thinking, which can give the reader a different portal into his character and personality.

W1: Yeah, I think I get it, Professor. Describe his actions, and what Judd says will help make him a more fully rounded character. Is that it? Am I on the right track?

W2: You sure are. Don't try to force your characters. Try to allow them to evolve somewhat on their own. You don't need to spoon-feed the reader. They are more often very intelligent and intuitive, so allow them to be so. They like that.

W1: That's great advice, Professor. I'll definitely do that in my next draft.

W2: Great.

W1: Is there anything else, Professor? Anything else I need to be aware of?

W2: Well, along with the character development, I think you need to understand the importance of editing your own work. Don't be afraid to cut out lines, paragraphs, and even entire pages if they don't work or fit your story or are just plain bad writing.

W1: Okay.

W2: Many young writers have this idea that once a word is on a page, it is etched there for eternity. That's not the case at all. Writing is a mutable process, ever in flux, always changing and mutating.

W1: Okay. I see what you mean. Less is more, right?

W2: Well, it depends, but in general I would have to agree with that until you develop your own distinct voice. Many people consider Faulkner to be too wordy or complex and think that it undermines the quality of his work while others consider his style his genius. Just try to remember that every word should contribute to the story as a whole, and if it doesn't, you might want to consider taking it out. Okay?

W1: I've got it, Professor. Thank you so much. If there isn't anything else, I'd like to get back to my dorm and start revising this story while it is fresh in my mind.

W2: Sure. That's all I wanted to talk to you about. And keep up the good work!

W1: Okay, Professor. I'll see you in class!

Lecture 23~28

23. Ⓒ **24.** Ⓑ **25.** Ⓓ **26.** Ⓑ **27.** Ⓑ **28.** Ⓐ

🔊 6-07

Okay. For this morning's lecture, um, I have some pretty technical stuff to discuss, so I will try to give this to you as simply as possible. I will allow voice recorders for this as well, so... Well, ready or not, here we go. You probably have all seen or read news stories about fascinating ancient artifacts. For example, at an archaeological dig, a wooden tool is unearthed, and the archaeologist finds it to be 5,000 years old. A child mummy is found high in the Andes, and the archaeologist says the child lived more than 2,000 years ago. With this in mind, you may be asking yourself, how do scientists know how old an object or human remains are? First, let me go through a process which will help us understand how we can date old objects.

Well, the fact is that all plants and animals on Earth are made principally of carbon. How is this possible? Well, carbon goes through many living things because it's part of the cycle of life. Let's start at the beginning of this cycle. During the period of a plant's life, the plant is taking in carbon dioxide through photosynthesis, which is how the plant makes energy and grows. Animals eat plants, and some eat other animals in the food chain. Carbon follows this pathway through the food chain on Earth so that all living things are using carbon, which is building their bodies until they die. Does everyone follow me so far? Great!

Moving on then, a tiny part of the carbon on Earth is called carbon-14, or radiocarbon. It is called radiocarbon because it is radioactive. This means that, ah, its atomic structure is not stable and there is an uneasy relationship between the particles in the nucleus of the atom itself. Eventually, a particle is emitted from the carbon-14 atom, and the carbon-14 disappears. Most of the carbon on Earth exists in a slightly different atomic form although it is, chemically speaking, identical to all carbon. How are we doing up to this point? So far so good? Excellent!

Now that we know carbon atoms follow many living things through the food chain, I can now explain how carbon-14 dating works. In the 1940s, scientists succeeded in finding out how long it takes for radiocarbon to disappear or decay from a sample of carbon from a dead plant or animal. A scientist named Willard Libby first measured the half-life of radiocarbon. Now here's an important definition, so write this down. The half-life refers to the amount of time it takes for half the radiocarbon in a sample of bone or shell or any carbon sample to disappear.

Well, Libby found that it took 5,568 years for half the radiocarbon to decay. After twice that time, or, about 11,000 years, another half of that remaining amount will have disappeared. After another 5,568 years, again another half will have disappeared. You can work out so that after about 50,000 years of time, all the radiocarbon will have gone. Libby figured out that radiocarbon dating is not able to date anything older than 70,000 years old.

Since carbon is very common on Earth, um, there are a lot of different types of material which can be dated by scientists. For example, Libby tested the new radiocarbon method on carbon samples from prehistoric Egypt whose age was known. A sample of, um, acacia wood from the tomb of the pharaoh Zoser was dated, for example. Zoser lived during the Third Dynasty in Egypt. Libby figured that since the half-life of carbon-14 was 5,568 years, they should obtain a radiocarbon amount of about 50% of that, which was found in living wood because Zoser's death was about 5,000 years ago. The results they obtained indicated this was the case. Many other radiocarbon dates were conducted on samples of wood of known age. Again, the results were good. In 1949, Libby and his team published their results.

So as you can see, radio carbon dating is a... very important field of science. The carbon-14 method has been and continues to be applied and used in many different fields, including hydrology, atmospheric science, oceanography, geology, paleo-climatology, archaeology, and biomedicine. Whew! Now that I'm finished, are there any questions?

Lecture 29~34

29. Ⓑ **30.** Ⓐ **31.** Ⓓ **32.** Ⓑ **33.** Ⓒ **34.** Ⓐ

Ⓞ 6-08

W1: So, what are we going to learn about today, Professor?

W2: Well, today we will learn about the history of American theater.

So, if you're all ready, I'll begin. Ah, excuse me, yes, you, are you in this class? Then take a hike! Then maybe I can get this lecture started. Okay, if you're ready? Taken from a historical context, the birth of professional theater in America is usually thought to have begun with the Lewis Hallan troupe, which arrived in Williamsburg, Virginia in 1752.

M: It started that far back?

W2: Of course. How do you think the early settlers entertained themselves? Gee! Anyways, there was a drawback to this form of entertainment because throughout the 18th century there was widespread opposition to theatrical performances. For example, in the puritanical climate of the time, especially in the North, the theater was considered a "highway to hell." Laws forbidding the performing of plays were passed in Massachusetts in 1750 and in Rhode Island in 1761, and they were banned in most states during the American Revolutionary War at the urging of the Continental Congress.

W1: Certainly you are kidding.

W2: Certainly I am not. Anyways, by the early 19th century, theater became more common in the United States, and many celebrity actors from Europe toured the United States. The Walnut Theater is the oldest, um, continuously-operating theater in America, located in Philadelphia, Pennsylvania. It was built in 1809.

M: You mean Philadelphia was the only city in America with a theater at that time?

W2: Oh no. But most cities only had a single theater. Productions were much more rudimentary then, and sometimes plays would be staged in barns or dining rooms when no theater was available. Provincial theaters frequently lacked heat and even minimal props and scenery. Kind of basic really. Anyways, as the Westward Expansion of the country progressed, some entrepreneurs staged, um, floating theaters on boats which would travel from town to town. Eventually, towns grew to the size that they could afford long runs of a production, and, in 1841, a single play was shown in New York City for an unprecedented three weeks.

W1: What kind of plays did they perform?

W2: Well, ah, Shakespeare was the most commonly performed playwright, along with other European authors. American plays of the period were mostly melodramas, often weaving in local themes or characters such as the heroic but ill-fated Indian.

The most enduring melodrama of this period was, um, you guessed it, *Uncle Tom's Cabin*.

M: Other than the kinds of plays you already mentioned, did they do anything else?

W2: Sure. A popular form of theater during this time was the minstrel show, arguably the first uniquely American style of performance. These shows featured white actors dressed in blackface and playing up racial stereotypes. Ah, another type of performance was the burlesque show. Burlesque became a popular form of entertainment in the middle of the 19th century. Originally a form of farce in which females in male roles mocked the politics and culture of the day, burlesque was condemned by opinion makers for its sexuality and outspokenness. The form was hounded off the legitimate stage and found itself relegated to saloons and barrooms.

W1: Well, how did the modern theater come about in America?

W2: By the 1880s theaters on Broadway in New York City and along 42nd Street took on a flavor of their own, giving rise to new stage forms such as the Broadway musical. These were strongly influenced by the feelings of immigrants coming to New York with great hopes and ambition, many of whom went into the theater. New York became the organizing center for theater throughout the U.S.

M: So, we can say Broadway was the most influential part of what we call modern American theater?

W2: Well, that's partly correct, but there are other important factors that have influenced the modern theater in America. For example, vaudeville was common in the late 19th and early 20th centuries and is notable for heavily influencing early film, radio, and television productions. This was born from an earlier American practice of having singers and novelty acts perform between acts in a standard play. Anyways, that about covers it.

Actual Test 02

Conversation 1~5

1. Ⓒ **2.** Ⓓ **3.** Ⓓ **4.** Ⓑ **5.** Ⓑ

🔊 **6-09**

W: Hi, there. How can I help you today?

M: Uh… hi. I came to talk to you about a problem I'm having. Is this visit confidential… It's sort of embarrassing.

W: Of course it's confidential. That is university policy concerning all counselors. Nothing you say to me here will leave this office.

M: Oh, good. Well, my problem is… I don't have any money. I don't even have enough to buy a packet of instant noodles. I'm dead broke.

W: Oh, I see. Well, that is a problem. But it's not so bad. Let's talk about the source of your problem. First of all, when you do get money? Where does it come from?

M: Oh yeah… Uh… My parents send me an allowance. They send me $400 each month. But it's never enough. I always manage to spend it in the first week or two.

W: Sure, I hear this problem all the time. You know, there are a lot of students here whose parents give them no money! Some of them have to work two jobs plus attend classes just to get by.

M: Yeah, well, I… uh… I'm a microbiology major, so I study too much to have even one part-time job. There's just no way I can balance the two.

W: Okay, I understand that you need your time to study. Microbiology is not easy. So let's go back to your $400 allowance and see if we can figure out some creative budgeting solutions. Four hundred bucks. That equals a hundred bucks a week. So, in a given week, what are you spending your money on?

M: Well, I stop and have a coffee at Starbucks every morning, and then…

W: Wait a minute! You have a coffee at Starbucks every morning? Seven days a week?

M: No, I don't usually make it on weekends.

W: Okay, even five days a week… A coffee at Starbucks costs at least three dollars.

M: Try four… The prices went up recently.

W: Okay, four dollars a day, five days a week… that means that twenty percent of your overall weekly budget is going to coffee in the morning.

M: Okay… I hadn't really thought about that… It's just coffee after all.

W: Yeah, but it really adds up. Try going over to McDonald's, where a cup of coffee is only one dollar… or, better yet, buy some coffee at the grocery store… or just drink water. How about your other expenses?

M: Well, then there's lunch, which I usually have at a pub or get some fast food.

W: There you go again with eating out. Do you have a card for the cafeteria?

M: Yeah, but the food there is terrible! I probably spend about ten bucks a day on lunch.

W: Okay, well, why don't you start buying some cheap groceries and making your lunch at home? You could save at least eight dollars a day, which would add up to forty per week. Between your lunches and coffee, we're up to about sixty percent of your weekly budget.

M: And then there's a pack of cigarettes a day…

W: Cigarettes? Those cost at least five dollars a pack! You have to quit smoking or get a job! I would recommend quitting altogether. That's an expensive habit.

M: Yeah, I guess you're right. I could cut down at least.

W: Well, it's obvious to me that you have a consumption problem. You consume too much and much more than you need. If you want to survive on this budget, start eating at home, cut down on the smoking and other luxuries, and try to do fun activities that are free, like going to the library or campus events, and go to the park instead of a pub, where you won't be paying five or ten bucks an hour just to sit there.

M: I'm going to try all of these solutions. Thanks.

W: No problem. Good luck, and I'll see you next time.

Lecture 6~11

6. Ⓑ **7.** Ⓓ **8.** Ⓐ **9.** Ⓑ **10.** Ⓑ
11. Ⓐ Yes Ⓑ No Ⓒ Yes Ⓓ Yes Ⓔ No Ⓕ Yes

⊙ 6-10

M1: Okay, class. Today we are going to talk all about badgers. We're going to discuss their natural habitats, their feeding habits, their families, and, most interestingly, their coloration. So, to get started, what can you tell me about badgers' habits and habitats?

W: They are nocturnal creatures that hunt at night, usually by digging. They are also carnivores and feed on several species of insects and small mammals. They live in marshlands across North America and the U.K. They're great tunnel diggers and they hibernate through the winter.

M1: Very good, uh, except, contrary to popular belief, it has been proven that badgers do not hibernate. But they do have adaptations that allow them to survive on less food during the hard winter months when their regular diet of earthworms and grubs is in shorter supply

W: Aha, I see. They're adapted for leaner winter months.

M1: That's correct. Badgers live in underground tunnel networks called setts. Setts are usually found on sloping ground where there is some cover. They dig these with their incredibly strong front claws. They live in groups of about fifteen and are led by a dominant male and female. These setts usually have one or two main entrances and several lesser used entryways. Now, who else can tell me something about the badger?

M2: Uh… males are called… I think… boars?

M1: That's right, and what about the females?

M2: They're called… uh… sows?

M1: Yes, boars and sows. Now, the males are tough. They are also very territorial and are known to patrol their setts constantly, especially during the mating season. Let's talk about badger mating.

W: Uh, isn't their method a little different than that of most animals?

M1: Yes, they reproduce through delayed implantation. They can mate at any time of year, but the embryo does not implant into the womb and start growing until winter. This means that all cubs are born around the same time of year, between January to March. Litter sizes range from one to five cubs but usually average about three.

M2: Ha! They are so cute when they're born!

M1: Sure, they're blind and pink with white, silky fur. They suckle for about eight weeks, and once they have sufficient fat reserves, begin to achieve independence from their mother, which doesn't usually fully occur until their fifteenth week. Now, let's talk about the badger's coloration. What can you tell me about that?

W: Well they've got those black and white stripes on their heads and faces. I'm not sure why though.

M1: That's a good point… Why do they have those strange, sharp lines of color on their heads? Is it just the randomness of nature that they have those markings?

M2: Wouldn't it have something to do with an adaptation to disguise them?

M1: Close, but not exactly. You could definitely say that those markings are an adaptation but not to disguise them from predators. Instead, they are a warning to any animal that might want to mess with a badger. Those sharp black and white stripes are one of nature's ways of saying, "Stay back! Don't mess with me!" And you can see similar color markings on other animals that have them as a warning, such as certain snakes, the skunk, and even some insects.

M2: Aha, so those markings are like a danger sign.

M1: Exactly. Danger! Do not touch me! But remember, not all badgers are lucky enough to have this built-in defense system. It all depends on the amount of melanin pigmentation in the badger's skin and fur. That is the genetic chemical which decides whether the badger has the warning stripes on its head or if its an albino or black or even ginger colored. So that's all for today. Don't forget to study your notes for next week's quiz.

Lecture 12~17

12. Ⓑ **13.** Ⓐ **14.** Ⓒ **15.** Ⓓ **16.** Ⓓ
17. Ⓐ Yes Ⓑ No Ⓒ No Ⓓ Yes Ⓔ No Ⓕ No

🎧 6-11

All right, everybody. I suggest you turn on your voice recorders now. I'm going to give you an overview on the topic of attachment theory, which covers the way we establish bonds with our caregivers when we're babies and how that continues into our adolescent and adult life. This theory is especially important when exploring psychology since it affects each and every one of us at such a core level of our personalities. Now, the basis of attachment theory hinges on what psychologists call an affectional bond. This is a type of attachment behavior an individual has for another individual. This bond is most typically held between a mother and her child. In this type of bond, the mother and child are partners, and they tend to remain within proximity of one another. The term was developed by psychologist John Bowlby, who published an important paper in 1958 entitled "The Nature of the Child's Tie to His Mother." According to Bowlby, there are five main criteria that must be present for an affectional bond to be established and a sixth for it to last.

The first of the main criteria is that an affectional bond is persistent rather than transitory. This means that it lasts. It doesn't come and go like less meaningful relationships. The second criterion is an affectional bond involves one particular person. The person cannot be interchanged or replaced with anybody else. The third is that the affectional bond involves a relationship that is emotionally significant. And, uh... the fourth criterion is that the individual who has established the bond wants to remain physically close or within proximity of the person with whom he is bonded. Fifth, and last of the main criteria is that the individual will become saddened or distressed if he is involuntarily separated from the person to whom he is bonded. Does this remind you of being a kid with your mom?

Okay… moving along… after the five main criteria, it's important to tack on this extra sixth one, which is a characteristic of a true attachment bond. This is that the person who's formed the bond will always seek security and comfort in the relationship.

Now, the other important paper that was published in 1958 was by Harry Harlow. It was entitled "The Nature of Love." This seminal work was based on a series of groundbreaking experiments with infant rhesus monkeys.

These experiments showed that the baby monkeys preferred an emotional attachment with the object of their affectional bond rather than life sustaining food. In short, the experiment worked like this: the baby monkeys were separated from their mothers at birth. Then they were introduced to two surrogate mothers. The first mother was made of cold metal wire mesh. The second mother was the same mesh frame, but it was covered in soft cloth and foam. The cold metal mother also contained a bottle with milk, and the soft mother had nothing. What Harlow found was that the young monkeys would quickly drink the milk from the cold metal mother and then quickly seek contact with the soft mother, with whom they'd already formed affectional bonds.

This study showed that babies ultimately desire their mother's warmth rather than their physical survival needs. But even the soft doll did not totally satisfy the baby monkey's needs. Later on, the baby monkeys that were raised apart from their natural mothers proved to be maladjusted to social situations with the other monkeys. They… uh… acted abnormally when placed in these situations. In most cases, they were either very fearful of the other monkeys or responded with unprovoked aggression.

Also, the female monkeys who were raised in isolation often abused and neglected their own infants when they too became mothers. These experiments were very important, especially since such long-running and deep-seeded tests such as these could never be ethically performed on human beings. And, as researchers have found in so many cases, these rhesus monkeys serve as excellent analogues to human beings, especially in the infantile stages.

So, uh… now that we've discussed Bowlby and Harlow's scientific contributions to establishing the field of attachment theory, let's call it a day. Tomorrow we'll cover the positives and negative aspects of affectional bonding.

Conversation 18~22

18. (A) **19.** (D) **20.** (C) **21.** (C) **22.** (B)

🔊 6-12

W: Hello, Mr. Adams. May I speak with you for a moment?

M: Mary, sure. Come into my office, and have a seat. How can I help you today?

W: Well, I'm here to talk to you about our group project in your intro class…

M: Okay, yes…The group projects that are due next week…How is your group faring?

W: Well, uh, not so well. That's what I was hoping to discuss with you. We met last night and failed to make any progress. We just kind of sat there, with nobody saying much.

M: So, the first thing I want to know is, who did the group elect as a leader? I'm assuming it was you since you're the one who is here representing them now.

W: No, we just kind of avoided selecting a leader. It was like nobody wanted to step up and take the responsibility.

M: Aha, I see. Nobody wanted to assume the leadership role, and therefore no productive decisions were made.

W: That's right. We couldn't really decide on what topic to choose for our research project or even how we should go about choosing a subject.

M: Well, Mary, I think the correct decision is sitting there right under your nose. It's you! You should elect yourself leader of this quiet little group and start making decisions to get something accomplished.

W: Yes, but being the leader takes so much effort. With my other studies, I just don't know if I have the time and energy to invest in this.

M: Do you want a good grade?

W: Of course.

M: Well, if you're willing to invest the time and effort into coming to see me here and you really want a good grade, I think it's in your best interest to assume

leadership of this group and to start making some strong decisions.

W: Uh… Okay…Tell me more.

M: Well, the benefits are trifold. First of all, you'll steer your group towards success. This will give you the respect and admiration of your fellow students. Secondly, by asserting yourself, there will be some long-term benefits in the boost of confidence and ability you'll receive.

W: Sure… I'll feel stronger, sharper… more capable.

M: That's right! You've got it. By stepping up into the leader's role, you'll play a role that is required in any human endeavor. And thirdly, you'll impress me… your teacher… which means you'll get a better grade than the other students, who were too meek to do anything for themselves.

W: Okay, I think you've talked me into it. I'm going to call another group meeting and nominate myself as group leader.

M: Sure, that's right. But don't assume all of the burden yourself. As soon as you're the leader, you need to allocate the responsibilities. Make one of the group members in charge of researching the various topics and another member in charge of assembling information. Before you know it, your group will be working towards its goal like a well-oiled machine!

W: Oh, Professor, thanks so much for your valuable guidance!

M: No problem, that's what I'm here for!

Lecture 23~28

23. (D) **24.** (D) **25.** (B) **26.** (B) **27.** (C)
28. (A) Yes (B) Yes (C) Yes (D) Yes (E) No (F) No

🔊 6-13

M1: Okay, class, today we're going to chat about the timber crisis that began in ancient Sumeria during the Bronze Age. Once copper smelting developed from pottery-making, the use of wood fuel accelerated. By the time the Bronze Age was well underway, wood was being consumed around the Eastern Mediterranean on a scale that could not possibly be sustained on a long-term basis. So, who can tell me why these guys needed so much wood?

W: They would have needed it for mining, smelting, metal-working, ship-building, pottery-making, and construction industries. They all had massive appetites for fuel, and almost all domestic fuel was also wood.

M1: Very good! That's exactly right. As cities developed around the seasonally dry eastern Mediterranean, they had to build large cisterns for water supply. Most often their construction demanded large quantities of cement and plaster. Mediterranean private and public buildings all contained large quantities of cement, plaster, brick, and terracotta, all of which required far more wood for production than the equivalent amount used directly for construction. The effects on local fuel supplies would have been increasingly severe.

M2: What about Egypt? It has almost no trees.

M1: That's a good question. Egypt was trading with Byblos on the Lebanese coast for cedar for shipbuilding, temple construction, and furniture-making as early as 3000 B.C. But perhaps the most famous documentation of the shortage of wood around the ancient Mediterranean is the Epic of Gilgamesh, the earliest epic poem that has survived. Gilgamesh was a Sumerian, the king of Uruk around 2700-2500 B.C. He conquered Kish, Uruk's great rival city, thus gaining power over all of southern Mesopotamia. Apparently, the first epics about him were written in Sumerian around 2000 B.C. We do not have the originals, but we have copies made by scribes in old Babylonian times for their libraries. They were separate stories, and the welding of these separate pieces into an epic was an Akkadian literary innovation, not a Sumerian one. This means that the central theme of the Gilgamesh epic may date to 1500 B.C. rather than Sumerian times, but it is still illuminating. I'm curious. Has anybody here read the Epic of Gilgamesh?

W: I have! The Gilgamesh epic is totally about deforestation. Gilgamesh and his companion go off to cut down a cedar forest, braving the wrath of the forest god Humbaba, who has been entrusted with forest conservation.

M1: Wow, I'm really impressed with all of you. You've really done your homework this time. It's interesting that Gilgamesh is cast as the hero even though he has the typical logger mentality: cut it down, and don't mind the consequences. The repercussions for Gilgamesh are severe: he loses his chance of immortality, for example. But the consequences for Sumeria were even worse. It's clear that the geography and climate of southern Mesopotamia would not provide the wood fuel to support a Bronze Age civilization that worked metal, built large cities, and constructed canals and ceremonial centers that used wood, plaster, and bricks. Most timber would have to be imported from the surrounding mountains, and deforestation there, in a climate that receives occasional torrential storms, would have led to severe erosion and run-off. The loss of Gilgamesh's immortality may be a literary reflection of the realization that Sumeria could not be sustained. Now, who can tell me what Theodore Wertime, the foremost scholar of this period, said about the timber crisis?

M2: Theodore Wertime suggested that massive deforestation of the Eastern Mediterranean began about 1200 B.C. It was for construction, lime kilning, and ore smelting.

M1: Right again. But it probably began earlier in the drier regions further east. King Hammurabi's laws, from around 1750 B.C, carried the death penalty for the unauthorized felling of trees in Mesopotamia. The problem may have been even worse in intensive metal-working regions like Anatolia. Metal smelting and forging had been going on in Anatolia for at least 3,000 years by 1200 B.C. So, I hope you got all of this in your notes. Now, let's look at how the timber crisis extended into ancient Greece and how it affected the Peloponnesian War.

Lecture 29~34

29. (A) **30.** (A) **31.** (D)
32. (A) Yes (B) No (C) Yes (D) Yes (E) Yes (F) No
33. (D) **34.** (A)

○ 6-14

Now let's talk a little more in depth about the lens. The crystalline lens is a transparent, biconvex structure in the eye that, along with the cornes, helps to refract light to focus on the retina. Its function is thus similar to a man-made optical lens. Are you following me?

So, uh... during the fetal stage, the development of the lens is aided by the hyaloid artery. In adults, the lens depends entirely upon the aqueous and vitreous humors for nourishment. Some of the most important characteristics of the lens are that it is non-renewable and transparent and has no blood vessel and no organelles.

In humans, the refractive power of the lens in its natural environment is approximately fifteen dioptres, roughly one-fourth of the eye's total power.

The lens is... uh... made of transparent proteins called crystallins. The average concentration of lens proteins is about twice that of other intracellular proteins and is thought to play a structural role in the lens. It is about 5mm thick and has a diameter of about 9mm for an adult human. But these figures can vary. The proteins are arranged in approximately 20,000 thin concentric layers, with a refractive index varying from approximately 1.406 in the central layers down to 1.386 in the less dense cortex of the lens. This index gradient enhances the optical power of the lens. The lens is included in the capsular bag, maintained by the zonules of Zinn.

It is composed of fibers that come from hormone-producing cells. In fact, the cytoplasm of these cells makes up the transparent substance of the lens. The crystalline lens is composed of four layers from the surface to the center. They are the capsule, the sub capsular epithelium, the cortex, and the nucleus.

The lens capsule is a clear, membrane-like structure that is quite elastic, a quality that keeps it under constant tension. As a result, the lens naturally tends towards a rounder or more globular configuration, a shape it must assume for the eye to focus at a near distance. Slender but very strong suspensor ligaments, also known as zonules, which attach at one end to the lens capsule and at the other end to the ciliary processes of the circular ciliary body around the inside of the eye, hold the lens in place.

When the eye is viewing an object at a far distance so that parallel rays of light are entering the eye, the ciliary muscle within the ciliary body relaxes. The ciliary processes pull on the zonules, which in turn pull on the lens capsule around its equator. This causes the entire lens to flatten or to become less convex, enabling the lens to attempt to focus light from the faraway object. Conversely, when the ciliary muscle works or contracts, tension is released on the suspensor ligaments and subsequently on the lens capsule, causing both lens surfaces to become more convex and the eye to be able to focus on near objects.

Okay, so the lens is flexible and its curvature is controlled by ciliary muscles through the zonules. By changing the curvature of the lens, one can focus the eye on objects at different distances from it. This process is called accommodation. You need to pay close attention here because it is most important to understand how the lens ages. The lens continually grows throughout life, laying new cells over the old cells, resulting in a stiffer lens. The lens gradually loses its accommodation ability as the individual ages.

The loss of the individual's focusing ability is termed presbyopia. It's really important that you become very familiar with the principals of the accommodative process since much of your future work in the field of optics will consist of helping your patients adapt to changes in their own accommodative process over time... Okay?

Normally, the accommodative process of the crystalline lens is smooth and effortless. When one changes one's focus from far to near, the ciliary muscle quickly contracts, causing the crystalline lens to accommodate become thicker and the object at a near distance to become clear. Then, when looking back again at a far distance, the ciliary muscle immediately relaxes, causing the crystalline lens to revert to a thin shape and one's far-distance vision to become clear again.

Now, I know I just hit you with a mouthful. But I hope you've got it covered in your notes because your final exam is coming up next week. Don't be afraid to come to my office in case you want to ask any questions. Or feel free to drop me an email.

《托福考试官方指南》

（第4版）（含光盘1张）

ETS（美国教育考试服务中心）编著

◎ ETS中国唯一授权版本
◎ 托福考试的必备权威辅导书
◎ 数百道托福考试题目及写作题库

定价：118元　开本：16开　页码：664页

《托福考试全真试题集》

（含光盘1张）

ETS（美国教育考试服务中心）编著

◎ ETS官方独家版本，托福考生必备辅导用书
◎ 5套托福全真考试试题，体验真实考试情境
◎ 提供考题答案详解及全部音频内容，深入、透彻分析托福题目
◎ 提供托福考试备考计划，帮助考生高效科学备考

定价：108元　开本：16开　页码：560页

《新托福考试综合教程》（第2版）

（含互动模考光盘1张 + 9张CD）

Deborah　Phillips　著

◎ 8套专项训练题目，全方位强化应试技能
◎ 2套完整的全真模拟试题，帮助考生熟悉真实考试形式

定价：148元　开本：16开　页码：704页

《托福考试备考策略与模拟试题》

（含光盘1张）　Nancy Gallagher　著

◎ 35个包含阅读、听力、口语及写作的语言技能训练单元
◎ 4套完整的全真强化试题
◎ 为考生设置了15周的学习计划，提供大量练习资料

定价：108元　开本：16开　页码：720页

《新托福考试全真模考题与精解》

（含MP3和模考盘各1张）

Pamela J. Sharpe　著

◎ 详细说明听说读写四部分的特点及有效的应试策略
◎ 含650分钟录音光盘1张，包含书中所有音频内容
◎ 含模考光盘1张，模拟真实考试情景

定价：118元　开本：16开　页码：832页

《新托福考试冲刺试题》

（含光盘1张）　Nancy Gallagher　著

◎ 6套完整全真冲刺试题，600道经典测试题目，体现托福考试的最新特色
◎ 文章题材、出题角度、考题类型以及话题内容等与实际考试一致
◎ 随书配有360分钟录音光盘1张，语境逼真，契合真实考场情景

定价：58元　开本：16开　页码：396页

《TOEFL官方题库范文精讲》

（附MP3）　Lin Lougheed　编著

◎ 提供TOEFL写作三步法，详解写作技巧和策略
◎ 精编大量练习题目，针对性极强
◎ 10篇综合写作参考例文 + 185篇独立写作题库范文

定价：58元　开本：16开　页码：432页

《托福考试口语胜经》

翟少成　编著

◎ 深入剖析各个口语题型，点拨回答技巧
◎ 3份真题详解 + 4套模拟试题 + 5个核心章节 + 6大实用模板 = 实现托福口语高分

定价：49元　开本：16开　页码：320页

《托福主题词汇与阅读》

（附CD-ROM）　赖水信　编著

◎ 以历年真题为蓝本，精编48个Advanced Test
◎ 每个Advanced Test包含50道词汇题目，全书共计2400道
◎ 全书涉及的主题广泛而多样，充满知识性与趣味性

定价：55元　开本：16开　页码：524页

《新托福考试写作高分速成》

陈向东　著

◎ 详细阐述托福综合写作解答的7大步骤及5大写作原则，给出独立写作3大写作策略和5大解题原则
◎ 深刻剖析写作思路，并提供解题策略及思维训练，解读真题
◎ 精心打造托福写作题型、解答原则与黄金模板

定价：35元　开本：16开　页码：280页

《TOEFL 写作/口语论证论据素材大全》
韦晓亮 编著

◎ 全面性：全面补充TOEFL写作和口语论证论据素材
◎ 权威性：汇集世界优秀外文期刊、报纸、书籍、检索数据库和权威新闻网站的英文内容
◎ 指导性：汇集新东方TOEFL考试培训项目数年教学经验和写作、口语教学成果

定价：25元　开本：32开　页码：248页

《新托福考试核心语法》
（含光盘1张）Nancy Gallagher 编著

◎ 全书涵盖20个重要的英语语法点，紧扣托福考试语法要点
◎ 结合经典的例子，对各个语法点进行精辟深入的讲解
◎ 提供大量模考练习，设有计时测验

定价：50元　开本：16开　页码：308页

《新托福考试阅读特训》（第2版）
Ji-Yeon Lee 著

◎ 62篇精选文章，题材广泛，全面满足备考需求
◎ 特设仿真阅读试题，体验真实考试情境
◎ 全书结构编排科学合理，实用性强

定价：55元　开本：16开　页码：472页

《托福考试口语特训》（第2版）
（附MP3）Ji-Yeon Lee 著

◎ 68个单元精练详解，6大题型逐个突破
◎ 提供多种练习方式，逐步掌握答题技巧
◎ 特设口语模拟试题，体验真实考试情景

定价：65元　开本：16开　页码：520页

《新托福考试听力特训》（第2版）
（含光盘1张）
Ji-Yeon Lee 著

◎ 59篇精选听力练习语料，题材广泛，全面满足备考需求
◎ 提供多种练习方式，逐步掌握答题技巧
◎ 特设听力模拟试题，体验真实考试情景

定价：58元　开本：16开　页码：452页

《新托福考试写作特训》（第2版）
（含光盘1张）
Ji-Yeon Lee 著

◎ 三个章节精练详解，两种题型各个击破
◎ 提供多种练习方式，逐步掌握写作技巧
◎ 特设仿真写作测试，体验真实考试情境

定价：46元　开本：16开　页码：304页

《TOEFL 巴朗词表》（附MP3）
Steven J. Matthiesen 编著

◎ 系统研究真题，提炼高频词汇
◎ 收录双语释义，遴选同义派生
◎ 提供经典例句，加深理解记忆

定价：35元　开本：16开　页码：256页

《托福词组必备》
俞敏洪 编著

◎ 紧扣真题，选词科学
◎ 例句经典，原汁原味
◎ 收录同义词组，扩充词汇量
◎ 幽默插图，巧妙助记

定价：22元　开本：32开　页码：256页